7202

INSIDE THE COUNCIL

JOHN XXIII
From a drawing by Pietro Annigoni

[*Frontispiece*

INSIDE THE COUNCIL

The Story of Vatican II

by

ROBERT KAISER

LONDON
BURNS & OATES

TO
UNCLE B., PUSHKIN AND EAGLE
WHOM POLLY LOVES

Published in America under the title Pope, Council and World:
The Story of Vatican II *by The Macmillan Company,*
New York.

The Frontispiece is taken from the Cover portrait for Time
by Pietro Annigoni.   Reprinted by permission ;   Copyright
Time Inc. 1962.

© Robert Kaiser 1963

Catalogue No. : 5/4448

MADE AND PRINTED IN ENGLAND BY
HAZELL WATSON AND VINEY LTD
AYLESBURY, BUCKS, FOR
BURNS & OATES LIMITED,
25 ASHLEY PLACE, LONDON, S.W. I

Contents

Chap.		Page
1.	New Dimensions	1
2.	Sailing Orders	12
3.	The Walls Come Down	30
4.	Dry Dock	51
5.	Down the Slips	75
6.	A New Crew	103
7.	Charting New Waters	120
8.	The Winds of Change	144
9.	The Smoke Screen	179
10.	The Barque of Peter	200
11.	Under Way	228
	Epilogue	244
	Index of Persons	247

Chapter One

NEW DIMENSIONS

I

ON October 11, 1962, 2,381 scattered successors of the Apostles, came together in the Second Vatican Ecumenical Council to remind millions of Christians and one or two billion other members of the human race that Jesus Christ is still with us—which was, on the whole, a refreshingly simple idea to propose. Of course, those original Twelve had been simple fellows, many of them fishermen. At first, they worked out of an old boat that belonged to Peter, and later, when their Master made them fishers of men to carry on his redemptive work on the sea of the world, their *ekklesia*, their community, was called the barque of Peter. That *ekklesia* (the Greek word means *church*) grew, by the normal laws of any growth, into a complex organization. Sometimes the successors, sometimes even the Peters, forgot their apostolic origin. Sometimes they forgot all about their barque, or the fact that they were supposed to be, before all else, fishers of men, sailing out to all nations, bringing them Christ. They became instead, many of them, rulers and kings, or the puppets of kings, and went out to all nations, not to bring light, but to fatten on sacred trust.

Inevitably, the community split; other Christians, not willing to pay so high a tribute for a place on the barque which to them had become a vessel of tyranny, sequestered themselves, first to the East, then to the North. Those left on the barque, their hearts contracted over the divorce (for which they had to bear more than a share of the blame), pulled back within themselves and erected walls of defence, not only around their *ekklesia*, but also around their minds, so that even when they followed the Master's injunctions to go out to all nations, they went with narrowed minds and shrivelled hearts, not to minister, not to serve, but to conquer and reign with a rule-book mentality that did not commend Christ as a light to the nations in darkness but rather a scandal to millions.

The whole sorry picture was actually done in oils by a young Florentine painter who brought his masterpiece, "The Barque of Peter," to Pope Adrian VI in 1523. His barque was carried by angels blowing eschatological trumpets. The waters beneath the ship were calm, but all around the waves were whipped up in fury and full of drowning sinners, heretics, and schismatics. The Pope sat on the deck of this barque, eyes closed, hands clasped in prayer, surrounded by his Curia, his household, and his guards, while the faces of the faithful peeped out of square portholes below. The sails were limp and white and the papal yellow stood straight out from the masts. The rudder was raised out of the water, and around it three figures read a Bible open to the illuminated words "Thou art Peter; and upon this rock. . . ."

Adrian (who was a Dutchman, the last non-Italian pope in history) cried out at this monstrosity, "No, no, this is not my ship, this is not my ship." The startled painter hastened to explain. "This is the barque of Peter," he said, "high above the stormy seas of heresy, preserved from contamination by the angels of light." "No, my son," replied Adrian, "you do not understand. Perhaps we ourselves have understood only lately. The dimensions are wrong." The painter's patron, a rich Florentine merchant, broke in and told Adrian respectfully that the Master, Giacomo, had trained the lad and he really ought to know what the dimensions should be. Adrian answered sadly: "No. No. Put my ship upon these troubled waters. Fill the sails and dip the rudder in the sea and let me steer my bishops and their flocks. We must calm the waters and be saved with these." He knocked his fisherman's ring against the writhing figures in the water. "And these, and these, and these."

Some days later, Pope Adrian died (some say he was poisoned), and the barque did not set out on the sea of the world. It remained, safe and secure and superby well ordered, in an insular haven.

Then, at a peculiar turning in time, came another simple fellow sent from God whose name was John, the 262nd successor of

Peter, who would be, according to the ancient prophecy of Malachy, *pastor et nauta*, shepherd and sailor, which can, of course, be translated "fisher of men."

John came to the poop of the barque after a lifelong odyssey of his own, with little more than an oar on his shoulder and a spark of intuition in his heart, and decided it was time to move out of port, to move that barque as it had never been moved before.

This is a story of how he moved it. And why.

II

To say that John moved the barque as it had never been moved before does not mean that the great modern popes had not helped the Church survive. They did. Each of them—Leo XIII, Pius X, Benedict XV, Pius XI, Pius XII—had a tremendous influence on the Church; but it was an intramural influence. They hardly commended Christ to the so-called Christian world: Communism took hold in Russia in reaction to that world bereft of Christ, Fascism and Nazism were born in Christian countries, and it was a Christian country that dropped the Bomb on the innocents of Hiroshima and Nagasaki. The gates of hell did not prevail. But no more than that could be said.

John XXIII came to the papacy attuned to the world outside. Was the Church at all relevant to this world? Patently no. Could it be? Paradoxically yes. The world, full of the strangest wonders of science and yet sick in its self-sufficiency, had need of Christ. In his intuitive way, John felt that the time had come to break the isolation of centuries—now.

In this sense of quiet realism and quiet faith, John was unique.

Other popes may have wanted to move the barque; but the tides were against them.

Adrian, for one, had excellent intentions.

At a time when a new and challenging interpretation of Christianity was being hammered out by a Saxon monk at Wittenberg, when protest was hardening in the North—protest against the papacy and all its pomps and works, its silver trumpets and ostrich plumes, its traffic in indulgences and ecclesiastical offices—Adrian

sent these instructions to Francesco Chieregati, his Nuncio at the
Diet of Nuremberg in 1522:

> You are also to say [he wrote] that we frankly acknowledge
> that . . . for many years things deserving of abhorrence have
> gathered around the Holy See. Sacred things have been mis-
> used, ordinances transgressed, so that in everything there has
> been a change for the worse. Thus it is not surprising that the
> malady has crept down from the head to the members, from
> the popes to the hierarchy. We all, prelates and clergy, have
> gone astray from the right way. . . . Therefore in our name give
> promises that we shall use all diligence to reform before all
> things the Roman Curia.

Within months of penning these lines, Adrian was dead, his
reform plan scrapped, and Rome breathed a sigh of relief. Popes
with their visions may come and go. The Curia holds on forever.

Inscribed on the tomb of Pope Adrian in Rome's Santa Maria
dell'Anima is a judgement he once pronounced on himself:

> How decisive it is for the work
> Of even the finest man
> That it be attuned to the times.

The response of Catholic bishops and non-Catholic observers,
of Christians in general and of the world at large would seem to
testify that in John the right man with the right manner had
appeared with the right idea at the right time.

There was little in Angelo Giuseppe Roncalli's career to suggest
that he, out of all likely candidates gathered in elective conclave in
October 1958, had the capacity or the will to attempt things few
popes had dared before. His past career, certainly, had given few
clues.

He was a peasant, reared on a farm in the foothills of Piedmont.
As a ruddy-faced, round-eyed lad, he had laboured through an
academic course without notably impressing his mentors as a
soaring intellectual. After ordination he took on a succession of
jobs. He became secretary to a bishop who was a capable and

dedicated man bent on grappling in a new way with the transition-
al world of the turn of the century. He served as a handlebar-
mustachioed sergeant in the army. He took a travelling job to
help the Church's missionary office revamp its outworn methods of
money raising. He taught a course on the Fathers of the Church
in Rome's Lateran Seminary for a year. He was removed for not
seeming quite "safe." The Romans had heard of Roncalli's tendency to ramble in his lectures and to toss out revolutionary pastoral ideas. ("It may be quite all right to allow mixed marriages
in certain cases," he was supposed to have told one of his classes.)
He was shunted off to the central office for the Eastern Churches as
a *bracciante*—a copier of letters—until named by the Holy See
Apostolic Visitor to a glamourless post in Bulgaria. Roncalli
was there for ten years. Another ten years in Istanbul, and at
sixty-three, his best days were apparently over.

As it happened, however, post-war Paris considered the Holy
See's Nuncio in France *persona non grata*. Few of Rome's profes-
sional careerists were anxious to plunge into the French farrago
of 1945, and as a result Roncalli was sent to Paris. If he were
gobbled up, what difference would it make?

Roncalli with his total unpretentiousness fitted into the French
scene curiously well. A keen observer, he avoided direct involvement in France's internal affairs. He had the knack of calming
angry protests against a list of supposedly "collaborationist"
French bishops by the age-old Italian tactic of agreement and
delay. He was imperturbable, affable, a good raconteur, *une bonne
fourchette*. At length he was given a red hat for a job well done,
and, at the age of seventy-one, a sinecure as Patriarch of Venice.

But a lifetime's varied experience had taken hold in Roncalli,
a rich synthesis made in terms of people: the farm folk of Bergamo;
earthy army types; petty fund-raisers for a curial congregation;
Romanists at the Lateran; beleaguered Orthodox Christians in
Bulgaria; Moselms in Turkey; Communists; collaborationists;
the Resistance; priest-workers. We can only guess what effect
these persons had on him. Poets and pragmatists do not catalogue
men.

On the day when the iron of the Holy Spirit struck the rock

which was the poet and pragmatist Roncalli, originality sparked out and new fire was kindled in the Church.

III

When the dean of the cardinal-deacons came to Angelo Giuseppe Roncalli on a day in October, 1958, and told him, in a quavering voice, that it was he who would sit on the Chair of Peter, Roncalli replied, very calmly and very directly, *"Horrefactus sum."* The phrase was from the Book of Job and it meant quite literally that Roncalli was aghast. His reaction was not unlike the natural fright of a Jesus who had just learned He will be crucified for the sins of the world. The spiritual writers say that Christ's was a vision of all time and all the world that night He sweated blood in the Garden of Gethsemani. Roncalli's *horrefactus sum* was similarly global. He saw in his election as Christ's vicar on earth the commission to love the world in a special way, to minister to it, and to serve it. His *horrefactus sum* came from the terrible realization that no modern pope was equipped to serve the world, to respond to such need and to such anguish.

To Catholics, the Pope was the chief lawmaker and someone you "saw" when you came to Rome. To those "outside the fold," he was a relic of the past or the Antichrist. To hundreds of millions of other human beings around the world, the Pope simply did not exist.

And so, on that drab October afternoon when the doubtful wisps of white smoke wafted up from the narrow pipe announcing "we have a pope," the barque of Peter might, for all its positive impact on the world, have been a tiny sampan in a Yellow sea of sampans.

What was this world to Roncalli? It was a complex of contradictions. In much of the Northern Hemisphere, it was millions of Pyotyrs and Natashas and Georges and Bettys caught up in varying forms of materialism, wondering *why* they were. In wide areas of the Southern Hemisphere, it was millions of Juans and Marias caught up in a flash evolution, no longer knowing *who* they were. It was the poverty of Luluabourg and the idleness of

Rangoon and the disease of Kuala Lumpur multiplying like tadpoles after a rainstorm. It was intellectual Europe rebelling against a rigid system now somehow irrelevant and smarting under military economic occupation now somehow unnecessary. But most of all, it was a world of tensions: thermonuclear tension, economic tension, sociopolitical tension, racial and religious tension.

And it was all of these things because it was not lit by the one finally effective light of the world testifying to the love of the Father or the freedom of the Spirit.

In the thirteenth century, the Church's greatest philosopher-theologian, St Thomas Aquinas, philosophizing on the facts at his disposal, never even considered the possibility that the greater portion of the human race then living had not so much as heard of Christ. St Thomas thought that the Gospel of Christ was truly *ubique praedicatum*—preached everywhere—and that the only one untouched by it was the hypothetical *homo in silva*, the unfortunate born and reared in the deepest woods of Dalmatia or the hinterland of Corsica. Such a view fostered the presumption that non-Christians were simply in bad faith. But when the age of discovery turned this idea inside out and demonstrated its absurdity, the Church never faced the facts and never reacted creatively. It merely considered the new peoples "pagans" and converted them, sometimes forcibly, to the "true faith," and imposed European thought and culture patterns on them or damned them to hell.

When the Jesuits following Matteo Ricci did attempt to make Christ the light of the peoples of China, by adaptation of the rites to Chinese civilization, Rome clanged down with an iron *non expedit* and changed the history of the world. It was the classic example of the unconscious distortion imposed on the Message which Christ had ordered preached to all peoples.

Did Christ's command "Going therefore, teach ye all nations" imply an acceptability of the Message? If not, it was narrow, absurd and impossible and, therefore, no command that could commend execution. But if the Message was acceptable, why was it not accepted?

In the apostolic and post-apostolic ages, when the tidings of Christian salvation were passed from mouth to mouth and the great mass conversions took place, we have to presuppose that these tidings answered the needs of the day. The Message touched the hearts of the Roman matron, the Greek slave, and the Gallic chieftain differently but with equal force. Thereafter, the Message developed within a sociopolitico-ecclesiastico-juridical framework that denied certain human elements. It affronted the East because it was tied to the political imperialism of Rome; it ignored the little man because it was tied to the feudal system which could not exist and still recognize him as a person; it failed to fertilize the flowering of the natural sciences and the Industrial Revolution because they were "worldly"; it struck thinking men as an instrument of willed ignorance, of religious serfdom. To Karl Marx, it was "the opium of the people."

Throughout Christendom, the idea grew that the Church was a huge cloister. Withdrawn from the world: no compromise, no contact, no approaches; opposition, separation, enmity. Let the world develop and grow. Let new structures and new governments be born. Let the heretics and schismatics unite. Let the Jews reap the fruits of their deicide. Let men somersault and gyrate with new sins and new sciences. They would pass. Only the Church, the barque of Peter held high above the waves by trumpeting angels, would remain. Ruin might come to the world but the Church was above it all, clinging to ancient formulations, to the old worlds, whether they made sense to moderns or not, content finally to rest in the phrase "Heaven and earth will pass away."

To Roncalli, to the practical, intuitive Roncalli, as to Adrian, these dimensions were all wrong. This negation of the unified Christian presence in the world had not worked and would not work. And for this reason, as Christ himself predicted in the Last Supper, men did not believe, did not receive the Message.

The essence of Roncalli's vision was positive. The world had need of Christ. He knew this view was shared by many in the Church, but knew also that Rome's exclusive spirit prevented it from becoming the official vision. Intuitively, then, and at the first possible instant, Roncalli signalled a change in direction for the Church. When Cardinal Canali approached the Pope-elect on that day in October 1958 and asked him what his name would be, Roncalli answered that he would not take his place in line behind the succession of Piuses. The choice was, significantly, a biblical one. "His name is John."

IV

Only in this context, then, can anyone understand the Second Vatican Ecumenical Council. It was not to be an end in itself, not an ecclesiastical event (in the latter-day sense of the word). John's dimensions were much grander: he wanted a world event, an event that would signalize the service of Christ in the world. So instead of attempting the impossible, instead of sitting down and writing a letter to reveal to his bishops the mind of the Church, he brought them, black and brown and yellow and white, from every corner of the globe, to come *in persona gregis*, in the name of their flock, and bring the vast charismatic insight of Christians to Rome. Only they, he knew, could make the Message acceptable. Only they could help him move the barque out onto the sea of the world.

Theoretically, a pope enjoys absolute power, but that is only theory. He is constricted by the silken strings of the curial congregations running this way and the invisible threads of protocol running that way, wrapped with the ribbon of monarchism and forced to sit on his throne while around him sycophants chant the Eleventh Commandment in unison, "Thou shalt not rock the boat." One can hardly be surprised then at the manner in which John XXIII described his condition to the no-nonsense American Cardinal Richard Cushing, "*Sono nel sacco qui.*" "I'm in a bag here."

It was a measure of John's peasant cunning that he did not make his calling of the Council an obvious attempt to cut himself or his successors out of the time-encrusted bag. If he had, the Council would have been blocked by the concatenation of influences in the Vatican.

Indeed, the Curialists tried to dampen John's early enthusiasm, but he was more clever than they. He let them think his Council would be their Council: make all the preparations, draft the official letters, squelch the rambunctious theologians, write all the rules. But then, when everything was set, he stayed up one whole night preparing the final pre-conciliar message and delivered it by Vatican Radio on September 11, 1962. It was not a churchy document, and it was filled with love and concern for the world. "The world indeed has need of Christ," said John, "and it is the Church which must bring Christ to the world." No human care went unmentioned: the love of the family, their daily bread, peace, education, progress, liberty. He spoke of social justice, the underdeveloped nations, a new political world, science, the economic welfare of all nations. And all of it was to be furthered by the unity of Christians, "one in thought, in word, in work."

If the Curialists were stupefied by this turn of ideas, they were equally shocked by John's words to the 2,381 conciliar Fathers on October 11, and, on the next day, to the representatives of seventy-nine governments and seventeen separated Christian Churches. Here was an innovation the like of which they had never known, a man who actually talked as if the ancient formulations of the faith could be changed in a burst of irenic good will.

The shock increased when they found that the Church as represented by bishops they had always known to be so docile, was really, incontrovertibly, bewilderingly Catholic, diverse, argumentative, unsatisfied with curial proposals, groping for a consensus, first on picayune, intramural matters, then on increasingly important issues: and that the Church outside, the large agglomeration of Christians and would-be Christians, would actually be able to sense something of the revolution that was taking place in the Church—despite every curial precaution to cover it all up.

By the end of the first session, on December 8, 1962, despite all obstructive efforts, despite the serious illness of the Pope, despite the difficulties of achieving a common purpose in the world's largest parliamentary body, the Council had finally found its way, had finally realized that it was the Council, Pope and bishops together, which would move the barque of Peter onto the sea of the world.

John's faith and optimism won out. In February, 1963, as the interim work proceeded, he told a friend that the barque was still not out of port. But he could not help feeling that it had finally unfurled its sails, and was pointing in the right direction. Soon, Christians, united after a fashion (but not in the sense of "returned to Rome"), would bring Christ and His Message to the world. That world, John felt, and therefore the Church, would never be the same again.

And who knows? he mused. Maybe a christified world would be ready to meet the unpredictable challenges of a journey on the seas of space.

Chapter Two

SAILING ORDERS

I

THE world's first impression of Pope John XXIII reflected nothing of the intrepid captain who would pilot Peter's barque. He was just the *Papa di passaggio*, just a genuinely likable fellow. Among the first available photographs that turned up in the Associated Press Wirephoto networks was a grainy shot of the new Pope in his old Paris days, standing with a group of diners, an empty champagne glass forgotten in his hand. He was the first pontiff on record to admit smoking an occasional cigarette. At one of his first audiences, he was quoted as saying, "Well, here I am, at the end of the road and the top of the heap." When his farmer family came to visit Rome, he shocked his chamberlains by abandoning the rule that the Pope eats absolutely alone. The story went around Rome that the General of the Society of Jesus formally presented himself to place some 37,000 Jesuits at the Pope's disposal: John smilingly offered to place some 500,000,000 Catholics at the General's disposal. He was a great stroller, and the press lost no time in dubbing him "Johnny Walker." He visited the sick. He told the inmates of Rome's Regina Coeli prison not to feel so bad; a couple of his own cousins had been in jail and they had survived.

That initial image of the Pope as a good-humoured, informal, winning, harmless old gentleman was, as events proved, very incomplete. After scarcely a month in office, John had an inspiration that was to astonish, to stir, and to challenge the Church and the world.

Significantly, the inspiration came in a global context.

Cardinal Domenico Tardini, in his capacity as pro-Secretary of State, had come to John's apartment high on the fourth floor of the Vatican Palace and began to riffle through his daily reports to the Pope. The Vatican diplomatic corps is nothing if not diligent, and its communiqués about matters ecclesiastical and political pour into Rome every day. In that second week of January in 1959, France had just given the mantle of presidential power to General Charles de Gaulle. The people of Soviet Russia were cheering over the government's successful launching of a 3,245-pound rocket into orbit around the moon. And in Cuba a bearded leftist named Fidel Castro smashed the dictatorship of Fulgencio Batista. In Italy the Catholic Demochristian Party wanted to make an alliance with the Socialists. From Rio came a disturbing study of the peoples pouring into that city and the anonymity and squalor of the *favelas* they lived in.

What to do? Tardini, raised to the purple by John, but a Vatican figure for decades, droned on. What to do? John rose and walked slowly over to his window overlooking Rome. A light rain slanted down across St Peter's Square, dimming the view beyond the Tiber.

To John, the geopolitical world of 1959 was a world in transit, a world passing through the treacherous shallows of a time-lag between two worlds: between the ancient order originated by Richelieu, perfected by Bismarck, flowering in the colonial empires of England, France and Germany, and the shadowy world of the near future in which he foresaw the unity of mankind as a whole. That unity, he thought, could come about in several possible ways; through a refined internationalism; through the centripetal instincts of men face to face with the expanding universe of outer space; or through a cataclysmic disintegration. In each possibility, he saw that the critical factor was the same: the confrontation of East and West.

But John viewed this confrontation uniquely. He did not see it as a facing off of Christ with Antichrist, nor of religion with anti-religion. Looking beyond the obvious externals, he saw that in East and West, and in the new nations of Africa and Asia, men were building a self-contained, man-dominated, self-satisfied ethos of human behaviour—which could only lead to an aseptic hell on earth. With many another modern thinker, John saw the modern dilemma as one of moral dimensions. His pain came from the fact that Christianity was taking such a small part in solving this dilemma.

Tardini was finishing his report .... On Africa now, where new nations were springing up like mushrooms. The Congo missions. The Algerian revolt. A bishop's report on vast possibilities, on a new set of problems. Possibilities and problems. Progress. Agitation. Dissension.

John could plainly see that the whole world "was plunged in serious distress and agitation, deepened in dissension and threats." The Church, he thought, should come to a confrontation with the world. But how? In Rome, the Curia had learned to keep the world apart, to play the politics of preservation. The faith was a pearl, meant to be guarded from outside contamination. John thought of it as a seed, meant to grow and have influence on Bologna and Bombay, Chicago and Cambrai, Montreal and Warsaw and Mwanza. All of a sudden, the thought came to him (he said later it was an inspiration of the Holy Spirit): get help from Bologna and Bombay, Chicago and Cambrai, Montreal and Warsaw and Mwanza and all the other bishops of every land.

"A Council!"

Tardini's assent to this proposal was "immediate and exultant," according to John's first recorded report of that meeting, and, according to another, later report given by John, "restrained but nevertheless positive." Tardini told persons in the Curia that John would soon forget he had even mentioned a Council.

John didn't forget. Some days later, on the second day of the Church Unity Octave, a week dedicated by many Christian bodies to prayer for world religious unity, John's feeling became a certitude. He said Mass in his private chapel of the Holy Family, with his *coppiere*, Monsignor Loris Capovilla, attending, and afterwards he knelt in thanksgiving and meditated on the 17th chapter of St John's Gospel—"that they all may be one, as thou, Father, in me, and I in thee, that they also may be one in us; that the world may believe that thou hast sent me. . . ."

Thus, right from the start it would be a Council with a triple finality. First, for human unity and peace. Second, for Christian unity, a necessary step to that goal. Third, internal renewal of the Church, a necessary step to Christian unity. There would be three obstacles to such a Council. The Curia. The Curia. And the Curia. The cabinet of the Church. The defenders of the fortress. The guardians of the faith. The early drama of the Council would revolve around the obstinacy of the Curial view and the bankruptcy of its ideas.

A week later, John announced his idea to eighteen curial cardinals, and he chose to do it in the Roman shrine to the Apostle of the Gentiles. At St Paul's Outside the Walls, John celebrated Mass—the Mass of the Conversion of St Paul—and then crowded the cardinals around him there in the Benedictine monastery. He announced his intention to call a Council of the universal Church "to proclaim the truth, bring Christians closer to the faith and contribute at the same time to peace and prosperity on earth." The cardinals were speechless. "We were too moved and too happy to utter a word," one of them later explained rather lamely. The official Vatican daily, *Osservatore Romano*, hardly ever at a loss for words, made no mention of the Council that evening, and on the next day sandwiched announcement of the Council—only the 21st in the Church's long history—between two other items of far less importance. "The Supreme Pontiff," puffed *Osservatore*, "has announced three events of greatest importance: a Diocesan Synod for the city, the celebration of an Ecumenical Council for the universal Church, and a bringing up to date of the Code of Canon law which will be preceded by the promulgation of a Code of Canon Law for Eastern Churches. In the thought of the Holy Father, the Council does not have for its goal only the spiritual good of the Christian people but he also wants it to be an invitation to separated communities to seek unity."

II

The world's press duly reported this news, and people reacted according to their own preconceptions of what an Ecumenical Council was. Very few came close to an accurate estimate of what this Council would be. Some Catholics (and non-Catholics) could not believe the news because of the common conception that councils went out with the definition of papal infallibility in 1870. Some Catholic newspapers, reacting loyally to the Pope, began to tot up statistics on past councils, counting the number of bishops who would attend, rather giving the impression that this Council would be a kind of glorified Eucharistic Congress which, since there was really nothing much that needed changing, would demonstrate the glories of Rome. One United States diocesan weekly newspaper plastered a series of "fashion photographs" across its front page, depicting the Ordinary himself as he would look in Rome, at the Council opening, at the President's reception, at the embassy dinner. Others, lacking information (an early symptom visible even then of what would become a chronic Council disease), made wildly unrealistic speculations about a reunion Council like the Council of Florence—as if a mere request by Pope John would immediately bring all Christians on their knees to Rome (or to Venice, where, one French review predicted, the Council would be held). When Catholic intellectuals in France heard about the Council, they merely yawned.

An editor of a French magazine explained to me, "The French didn't take the Council seriously at first because they didn't take the Pope seriously. And they didn't take the Pope seriously because they hadn't taken Roncalli seriously. 'Pas serieux,' is all the French could say of the proposed Council."

Some commentators speculated over what heresies the Council —like many another before it—would condemn. Others said the Council was not being called because the Church was afflicted with a crisis or threat to its faith or discipline. "Here and there in the world press," Archbishop Joseph Cordeiro of Karachi, Pakistan, noted, "statements crop up that previous councils dealt with crises (heresy or schism, for example) but the Second Vatican Council was not occasioned by a crisis." Oxford-trained Cordeiro insisted there was a crisis precisely because most men had come to look on the faith as irrelevant. Archbishop Lorenz Jaeger came closest of all to the thought of John: "Councils always take place at the great turning points of history. Today is such a turning point. The Church must adapt to the thoroughly changed conditions of the world in order to be able to fulfil her mission."

Reaction from the Eastern Churches was predictably various. Renowned theologian Hamilcar Alivisatos of the University of Athens penned a piece almost immediately in the Athens newspaper *Vima* to the effect that the Pope could never renounce his primacy and the Greeks could never recognize it. "A Papist ecumenical council facing the problem of the union of Churches," said Alivisatos, "would be impossible and unthinkable." But an official organ of the Greek Orthodox Church in Aleppo said, "We hope God crowns the efforts of His Holiness. With the help of God, as long as Christian love is the motive force, a solution will be found." And when newsmen approached the Patriarch Athenagoras of Constantinople to get his reaction, he quoted Scripture: "There was a man sent from God," said he, "whose name was John." And a little later: "The Pope of Rome is the first leader of Roman Catholicism for centuries who has grasped the mystery of Christ's seamless robe and fingered intuitively its warp and woof and its seamless wondrousness."

From Protestants, who could not help but be puzzled by John's use of "ecumenical" (a word they had adopted and charged with their own special connotation) came guarded reactions. Willem Visser't Hooft, general secretary of the World Council of Churches, commented that much would depend on "how ecumenical the council will be, in composition and spirit." A spokesman for the Presbyterian Church of Scotland said, "We are very keen on the ecumenical movement but not under Roman Catholic sponsorship." Marc Boegner, president of the Federation of Protestant Churches of France, pointed out, "There are barriers humanly insurmountable." Edwin T. Dahlberg, president of the United States National Council of Churches, said, "Anything that would bring together all the churches of Christ would be blessed of God." But, he added, "it would have to be recognized as a mutual coming together, not under conditions laid down by one church for all the others." Calvinist Roger Schutz of the French monastery of Taizé welcomed the announcement because "it

reawakened in Protestants an ecumenical consciousness that was
slumbering."

III

Around the Roman curial offices, John's idea did not exactly
galvanize the ecclesiastical bureaucrats. They went about their
business as usual—from nine in the morning to one in the afternoon (barring holidays). Ninety years ago, announcement of the
Council had caused at least some excitement. Curial Cardinal
Jean-Baptiste Pitra had cried, "What? A council? Why, the
French and German theologians will come and upset all our congregations!" But in 1959, John XXIII's announcement had all
the resonance of a drift of rose petals falling on crushed velvet.
La Civiltà Cattolica, a Jesuit bimonthly which enjoys semi-official
Vatican status, did not mention John's Council until some five
months later, on May 2. A cardinal, looking back on the whole
situation, told me, "The Curia dragged its feet. They couldn't
see any need for a Council. They thought everything was all
right with the Church. They had a sort of closed corporation here
and they were satisfied with it."

For the Church, this was not new. Though popes spoke of
reform before Martin Luther launched his own, the Council of
Trent was disastrously delayed by a conspiracy between the Vatican court and the College of Cardinals who had been dividing
exorbitant taxes on their traffic in bishoprics. The Curialists
actually played a little game arranging that every time the Pope
talked "Council" or "reform," the value of bishoprics would
drop sharply on what amounted to the Rome stock market.
According to the famous Catholic historians, Hefele and Leclercq,
it was the Roman bear market that kept the Pope from calling the
Council of Trent until it was too late, until Luther had already
posted his famous theses and fathered the Protestant Reformation.

John, for his part, not only remained firm about calling a Council (and, as some of his later remarks prove, he was aware of the
history of councils and the internal trouble they could cause),
but continued to insist on a Council turned outwards, a Council for

unity, for Christian unity, for the unity of mankind. At a general audience a few days after his announcement at St Paul's Outside the Walls, he made it clear that he was already taking the first steps towards unity: he was praying for it and asking others to do the same, suggesting that the people pray *Gloria Patri's* after the Angelus each day for the unity of those "who are separated but carry in their heart the sign of the Cross or search in their solitude for the sense of the words of God in Sacred Scripture."

As a Scandinavian prelate visiting Geoffrey Fisher of Canterbury put it: "He [John] may—like Archimedes—find the fulcrum big enough within the Romanist system whereby to lever the whole affair out of its isolation and set it down in the middle of the world." A few weeks later, John asked students from Africa and Asia for "intense prayers for the great union of Christian people, the Ecumenical Council," and repeated these two themes in many audiences that followed.

In March, *Herder Korrespondenz*, a highly respected German Catholic monthly, quoted John as saying in a public audience, "We do not intend to conduct a trial of the past. We do not want to prove who was right and who was wrong. All we want to say is 'let us come together. Let us make an end of our divisions.'" *Osservatore Romano* never reported the remark, but it did make bold to revise John's whole approach to Christian unity. For example, on April 12, when John petitioned two newly canonized saints "to ask the divine clemency for all the graces necessary to happily finish what was announced to the Catholic world, that all Christians joined in fraternal love would come together in one fold under one shepherd," *Osservatore Romano* editorialized about the prospects of "return."

This became more or less the official curial line: John could insist all he wanted on Christian unity, but it would have to be a special kind of unity—a clear "return" of the "heretics and schismatics" to Holy Church.

Osservatore Romano insisted strongly, whenever it spoke of Christian unity, on that word "return." Clearly, the *ritorno* would have to be made by the prodigals (Protestants and Orthodox) back to the father's house (the Holy See). In this picture, the Holy See possessed the truth, and merely had to wait for the heretics to come seeking it.

Pope John held no such simplist view: if he had, he could hardly have invited "the separated brethren" to "join in seeking the unity which Christ is preparing for us." John considered, rather, that the truth possessed his Church, that it gave his Church life, but that it also transcended his Church. Only with such a mentality could he ever hope to begin an ecumenical dialogue with the humility and charity that would make it possible.

But the Curialists seemed to be succeeding in their effort to narrow the Pope's first overall view. His first encyclical on the coming Council, *Ad Petri Cathedram*, said the Council would deal with "the development of the Catholic faith, the revival of Christian standards of living and the bringing of ecclesiastical discipline into closer accord with the needs and conditions of our times."

These words made the plan seem like an internal ecclesiastical affair. At the time, a highly regarded biographer of the Pope could see what was happening. "The Pope intended the Council to be far more concerned with unity than it seems to be right now. He has been deterred by the entrenched conservatives within the Curia who keep saying the Council is an internal matter. Well, the Pope's emphasis is still on Christian unity." A close friend of the Pope predicted that John would get the Council he wanted. "John keeps going around the walls of Jericho," he told me, "until they come tumbling down."

Whatever the underlying thought, the final impression was that Pope John's original inspiration was given quite a bit of toning down during those first few months. To one American editor it seemed that "fences were being erected to limit the horizon, as if the Pope needed a course in prudence from the members of the Holy Office." It became apparent that if John insisted on a Council, well, then, Rome would have a Council—a curial kind of Council run by curial people. On May 17—five long months after John's first inspiration—Cardinal Tardini (with the help of a monsignor named Pericle Felici) took over a "preprepara-tory commission" composed of the secretaries of the ten principal congregations of the Roman Curia. No slower-moving, more reactionary dozen ever sat on the board of a New England bank. It took them a month to make their first decision: to ask the world's bishops, apostolic nuncios, superiors of religious orders and the Roman Curia to suggest what the Council should consider. A month later, in July of 1959, as an afterthought, Tardini asked the faculties of the Church's major seminaries to do the same and to please submit their suggestions by April of 1960. The Curia, it was all too clear, was moving slowly—in its usual "prudent" (or was it obstructive?) fashion.

IV

Why was the Curia so obstructive? What is it about the Curial mind that is so eager to condemn anything new? Why is it so uncreative, so isolated? Because the Church had triumphed over its enemies for all these many centuries? Yes, partly. The spirit of the post-Tridentine age still lives on in many a Roman monument. The age of triumph: the triumph of Christ; the triumph of Mary; the triumph of the saints; the triumph of the Church; the triumph of the Counter Reformation. Educated in this atmosphere, the modern Curialist saw little point in coming to terms with a world so persuasively vanquished in fresco and in marble.

So long as they were carried along by this illusion of triumph, the Curialists could say to a wicked and faithless age, "I have no need of you."

Cardinal Alfredo Ottaviani, Secretary of the Sacred Congregation of the Holy Office, may have typified the spirit. The motto on his coat of arms reads *Semper Idem*—Always the same. He was, in fact, no new phenomenon. His roots went deeper into history than the Counter Reformation. He was one of a long line of *defensores fidei*, of men who down through history have identified themselves with the walled City of God. This has been an acceptable view of the Church ever since St. Augustine and it has helped fashion a theology of history that many still share today.

The Church, according to this image, was a battered caravan

of the Good, of the Divine, prepared and foretold in the Old
Testament, proximately ushered in during the great *Pax Romana*,
running from its Semitic cradle through Greek culture to settle
at the geopolitical center of Greco-Roman power and culture—
Rome. Here, once Providence had swept away the ancient cor-
ruption and power by means of the barbarian invasion, the Church
grew and taught men. The popes controlled Europe, banished the
Jews to their ghettos, divided the world into *fideles* and *infideles* and
left the bleaching bones of heretics, unrepentant sinners and rebels
along the wayside. Its glories were early monasticism and medieval
Scholasticism, and they shone until the Renaissance and the Reformation added a third dimension to the picture, that of the individual human person and his "emancipation." But churchmen stuck
to their guns, only attempting to beat the devil by "baptizing"
the other dimension, the State, that is, by attempting to assert
their rights over the State, as Pope Innocent III did at the peak of
the Church's medieval influence. The Church's authority was attacked by the Reformation, and so in the Counter Reformation
churchmen stressed that authority. They necessarily rejected the
Anglicans in England, the Lutherans in Germany, the Huguenots
in France as belonging essentially to the City of Mammon.

The churchmen of the City of God, reacting to the challenge
of that other City, restated the old ideas in a juridical application
of Trent's decrees with an emphasis on the authoritative, directive,
bureaucratic, administrative centre. They reduced the charismatic,
individual, lay element, never very dominant in the Church from
the fourth to the fifteenth century, to a nonfunctional, receptive
role, in a persisting effort to assert authority that had been attacked
and to shoal up the defences of the two-dimensional world—
which, in reality, had ceased to exist.

In this new context, the Church in France restated and con-
cretized the old Augustinian ideas. In the pre-revolutionary period
from 1600 to 1789, it formed a narrow and rigid conception of the
Church, widened the gulf between the hierarchy and the clergy,
and between the clergy and the people, condemned and constrained every movement of the individual as such. Bossuet
(whose *Discourse on Universal History* is a seventeenth-century

version of Augustine's City of God) helped concretize and impose these ideas, even proposed the idea of tradition that has come down to our day and is lodged with the Curialists and very many Catholics. It read something like this: The Church possesses a store of immutable truths. She has only to look at these ancient heirlooms to know what she believes. She carries this bag along through the ages on her pilgrimage *in via*, surrounded by the City of Mammon. She has no need to consult the surrounding landscape. She must in fact keep herself separate from this landscape because it is evil, the City of Mammon. Nothing can be added or elucidated by means of the *saeculum presens*; the world must be saved by her. Christ (who need not have been crucified) is the new Adam (the old one could have remained sinless) whom the world seeks to crucify and whose work the world wants again to nullify just as it did in the garden when God found himself up against a malice that brought his entire scheme of providence tumbling down. For originally Adam and all his descendants were destined by a gratuitous gift of God to be transplanted from a preternatural state (where fire did not burn, water did not drown, a lion's teeth did not bite and crush, ice did not freeze human blood, lightning did not strike dead, passion did not violate free will, stones did not bruise the careless foot, thorns did not pierce the flesh, poison did not poison) to a state of supernatural felicity as God's own children in his presence. In God's second and substitute plan, his Church would live through the ages dogged by enemies, by the world, by the City of Mammon, ever on guard, crucified to the world and the world crucified to her.

The French Revolution, all the revolutions of the nineteenth century, the Church regarded as an attack on authority and consequently on order as such. The revolution did not necessarily aim at the destruction of religion. In fact, there is no rational basis of incompatibility between democratic forms and the Church; but the Revolution in the mind of many churchmen was a satanic thing, a child of the City of Mammon. For the most part, the Roman pontiffs and their Curia thought in two dimensions and two dimensions only, Church and State. They never came within an ass's roar of the new third dimension, the value of the human person as an individual, conceived in the Renaissance, emergent in the reform and triumphant in the Revolution.

As a fatal result, the Church and her allies, the secular traditionalists, found themselves pitted against freedom and on the side of those who proclaimed "authority." Emancipation was just a nice word for rebellion against authority. Ridiculously enough, this view led to an alliance between the Catholic Pope of Rome and the Protestant King of England, with the anti-clerical King of France, with the Protestant German Emperor, with an anti-clerical Austrian Emperor—precisely and anomalously because the princes stood for "authority" and against the Revolution.

(Many years later, of course, but in the same spirit, both Pope Pius XII and the General of the Jesuits, Vladimir Ledochowski, accepted the Rome-Berlin Axis of Benito Mussolini and Adolf Hitler, seeing in it the providential bulwark against the Soviet colossus and the ultimate answer to Communism. When the Jesuits Pierre Charles in Belgium and Friedrich Muckermann in Germany wrote against the Axis, they were both told by Ledochowski to stop attempting to undo the work of God who was introducing, through Signor Mussolini and Herr Hitler, a new order. And during the Abyssinian War, when Britain considered sanctions against Italy, the word was passed through the Vatican diplomatic service that a vote for sanctions against Mussolini policy was in reality a vote for the Masonic lodges against Catholic Italy.)

From 1800 onwards, then, the Church attempted to think and act in a two-dimensional world that had ceased to exist. Napoleon conjured up a mirage that flattered this view, and Metternich and Ercole Consalvi, Pius VII's papal envoy to the Congress of Vienna, worked to re-establish a canon lawyer's world bounded by politics and religion. Consalvi threw a net of concordats over Europe, but it held nothing. What few if any churchmen realized was that the changes sweeping the Western world at that time were neither political nor religious as much as cultural. But cultural revolution had no place in their system because their concept of the Church was of a vast, bureaucratic, Byzantine structure immune from change.

In an effort to preserve this structure, the churchmen tightened their authoritative grip over what they thought was a revolt of the individual against the Church. In reality it was a common acceptance of a new world picture that almost necessarily arose out of the Industrial Revolution and was idealized in the Socialist movements of the nineteenth century.

To be integrated into this new world picture, to become incarnate in this new world, the churchmen of the time would have had to understand that the emancipation of the individual did not imply his rejection of Christ. Instead, having no real philosophy or theology (both sciences were in a moribund condition), they buttressed themselves against all real change. They did however set up the policy of the Uniate Churches of the East (again an expression of the Two Cities idea) and created a new series of historical tensions, taking into the system elements which of themselves excluded any practical idea of unity with the separated Churches. The Jesuits, too, returned to the scene, but their pristine spirit was badly broken by the suppression and perverted by Jansenism in the restoration. Instead of thinking philosophically and existentially in the world they lived in, they turned back the clock to revise Scholasticism, and when Pius IX fought for the definition of infallibility, the Jesuits worked loyally and diligently at his side.

The First Vatican Ecumenical Council accomplished little outside the pattern. It reasserted authority over all else, centred it in the Pope, extended it to the Roman Curia, and re-established the *ens juridicum* in a world that did not need it or want it. Only with this could the real iniquities of the modern Inquisition begin. Only then could it act with the delegated authority of the one who was infallible. Finally, when the Church signed the Lateran Treaty with Mussolini and emerged "free and untrammelled" into the world on an internationally accepted juridical basis, it continued to assert its central authority with little realization of the facts of life.

But how could it ignore those facts? The balance of political power was shifting inevitably to the United States where the rise of the individual had become the very basis of organized human existence. The true bearers of this culture in Europe, in reaction to a clericalism that was alien in the United States, were anti-clerical, and excluded religion from science, politics and social organizations. Russia arose as the first organized anti-religious State. Anciently created but still vivid historical tensions were highlighted in the Jewish holocaust of Nazi Germany and by the politicization of the Moslem ideal in newly-formed Arab States. New nations arose in Africa and Asia. Hinduism and Buddhism reawakened within a new, religiously flavoured, political framework. Tensions arose on both sides of the hostile polarization of two big world blocs. Populations exploded. The ecumenical movement grew and grew outside the Church. Teilhard de Chardin and Lagrange began Catholic explorations into the complicated world of modern science and research.

And then, all of a sudden, men of science began to advance their knowledge at an exponential pace, computer-quick. The jet age brought Rome closer to Cairo than Calabria. Men explored the mysteries of space and the mysteries of life. They met at the crossroads of knowledge and discovered their individualism, their gregariousness, their thirst for knowledge, their desire for beauty, their desire to penetrate even further into the mysteries that have enshrouded their existence since time began.

But the curialist mind, still reacting within the two-dimensional framework, continued to put all the distance it could between the City of God and the City of Mammon, took greater refuge in authority, attempted further centralization, used every trick in its ancient bag—decree and condemnation, surveillance and censorship and secrecy.

V

The logical consequence of such a spirit could mean death for any organization into which it is fused. And logically, with the Curialists running the Roman Church in their dictatorial fashion, the Church itself might turn into a petrified forest, justifying that prediction made in the London *Times* at the time of the definition of papal infallibility: "A great institution in its day . . .

Actually, Catholicism on the eve of the Second Vatican Council, though it lived in a post-Christian world, presented signs of life everywhere. The Curia might try to throttle the spirit of life, but it could not kill it.

Closest to Rome, perhaps, Catholicism was in its most moribund state. Toothless hags in Naples would cry, "Jesus Christ, pray for us to San Gennaro," until that saint's blood liquefied. The churches might be empty but few churchmen were deeply concerned because "the people vote Catholic, don't they? Twelve million votes?" But many Catholics, priests and laity alike, unable to ignore the practical unacceptability of the Message as it had been transmitted to the people, were alive and searching for new approaches.

France, in the depths of de-christianization, was re-appraising everything it had once taken for granted. Its worker-priest movement had been halted, its greatest theologians hampered by the Holy Office, but it was bounding back nevertheless.

In Spain, the Cardinal of Seville spoke out against the "scandalous" starvation wages paid labourers in the agricultural south, and other bishops were giving nudges to social reforms long overdue. In the Netherlands and Belgium, highly educated, informed Catholics were spearheading ecumenical movements at home, and continuing their tremendous missionary activities abroad. Germany was sharing Catholic manpower and Catholic technology with underdeveloped nations. Young people of both England and Ireland asserted their vitality. African Catholics, the most literate members of almost every community, were busy creating a new and adapted Catholicism. In North America, the Church and the middle class were one, and their educational efforts made them the wonder of Catholics everywhere else. The Church in the United States was breaking out of its strictly ecclesiastical mould, and, with its Canadian cousins, was achieving an intellectual involvement with the community that would be a sign to many.

Everywhere Catholics, somehow, some way (and some said it was the influence of the Holy Spirit) were attempting to make Christ relevant in the world they lived in. They were done with looking at the Church in terms of its institutional self. They were ready to look at it in terms of the world.

In seminaries, a new breed of professor was attempting to make the training of priests more than a perfunctory, formalistic thing. Creative thinkers, like the Jesuit Karl Rahner, the soft-spoken German who is regarded by many as the greatest Catholic theologian today, were laying the groundwork. "During the last 200 years," said Rahner, "changes have occurred on the plane of intellectual history which in width, depth, and power to mould men are at least comparable with those that appeared between St Augustine and the period of high Scholasticism. If this be the case, then we should expect that the dogmatic theology of the present day will differ as much from that of 1750 as the *Summa* differs from St Augustine. But the average dogma manuals do not differ from their forebears of 200 years ago."

And so, young men in the seminaries were reacting against their dusty, systematic theology, which they saw now as a reaction against a Reformation world that no longer existed. They were less inclined to feel that everything had been solved, or that the Church's solutions were real solutions.

They began to see, as Rahner pointed out, that "a calling for sound theological clarification and solution will crowd in on the man who attempts to develop theology out of the spirit of his time, his own vital religious life, and the consciousness of a living message for his own days." These would not be mere literary adaptations of dogmatic theology to our times, of new applications, new viewpoints and practical corollaries, but an application of theological insight to the world around us. "We need a theology of the mysteries of Christ," said Rahner. "Of the physical world. Of time and temporal relations. Of history. Of sin. Of man. Of birth. Of eating and drinking. Of work, Of seeing, hearing, talking, weeping, laughing. Of music. Of dance. Of culture. Of television. Of marriage and the family. Of ethnic groups and the state. Of humanity."

"Developing out of the spirit of his time," Pope John saw the problem in the same terms. His senses were alive to the world as it is, and he saw the waters of time against the hoary immovable ramparts of a bygone age. There were two conflicting tides, of course, and rough seas ahead, but no matter; he would go on repeating his simple peasant prayers and weigh anchor with a bemused smile at himself cast in such an improbable role.

Chapter Three

THE WALLS COME DOWN

I

THE story goes that Archbishop Roncalli once asked a Protestant in Paris, "Why can't we come together?" Said the Protestant: "There are different ideas . . . ." "Ideas, ideas," answered Roncalli with a shrug. "Ideas are such little things among friends."

Conservatives in the Church shivered when they heard this story, and progressives, too, rather wished it had not been quoted. Taken for what it was, however, an imprecise, unscientific statement by a man who was less a theologian than an intuitive thinker, it helped tick off exactly what Pope John's Council was aiming at: a general theology of encounter, a movement of the Church into the world as it is. Was this the result of a lukewarm attitude towards truth? Emphatically not, said the French Dominican theologian M. D. Chenu. "It represents rather an inclination to work out this truth in the concrete order and [to show] that, at the present moment, the love of truth is more efficacious, more 'true,' in the intrepid witness of dialogue than in the protectionism of interdicts and defensive bulwarks."

To the curial mind, however, which operated with a siege mentality evolved in centuries of reaction to the City of Mammon, this was precisely the objection (though perhaps an unspoken one) to the very idea of holding a Council, especially a Council "for unity" and a Council to move the Church "into the world."

To overcome this objection of many of those who should have been his closest collaborators, John needed a specific plan. He had begun with little more than a pious intuition about the unity of mankind—not merely Christian unity, but the unity of all mankind—"because Christ wants it." What John needed now was dynamite to knock down the walls separating Catholics, in their insular haven, from other Christians, walls separating the Church from the world as it is, a world in a social and scientific revolution. He would discover one form of dynamite in his own creative action, another form of it in a scholar's creative thought. Both would open up the Church, one to other Christians and even other religions, the other to a half of humanity considered up to then "completely in the camp of Satan."

II

Pope John knew that the present stance of Rome towards "the other Christians" was terribly unrealistic. Since 1910 the Protestant Churches, largely under the influence of the missionaries among them, had been watering the seeds of goodwill and common purpose that existed among their various bodies. They understood, far sooner than most Catholics, that the rips and tears in the seamless robe of Christ were a shock and a scandal to people everywhere. ("See those Christians, how they hate one another.")

But the Holy See reacted violently to such early ecumenical stirrings, called the ideas "utopian," and ordered Catholics to keep away. In 1922, '23, and '24, Cardinal Mercier and Lord Halifax had their famous "Malines Conversations," exploring the possibilities of co-operative Christian endeavour. Pope Pius XI set up a Benedictine monastery to study possibilities of union with the Eastern Churches, and Halifax hoped Rome could turn its attention to the West as well. He said to Cardinal Mercier: "If only the Archbishop of Canterbury and the Holy Father could meet some day, face to face and alone." (Halifax died twenty-five years too soon to see that day.) But if those conversations helped ease the fears of Rome towards the ecumenical movement, the first two conferences of Protestants and Orthodox from around the world, held in Stockholm in 1925 and in Lausanne in 1927, certainly did not—judging from the tone of Pius XI's encyclical *Mortalium Animos*, which stigmatized these conferences as part of a new kind of heresy called "panchristianism." Pius forbade Catholics from participating in any of them. (But in Bulgaria, at about that time, a stubby Vatican diplomat told the friends he had made there: "Some day we will end up with one flock and one shepherd because Christ wants it.")

The movement continued, progressing little by little into theological exchange. The Orthodox had great influence on the Protestants. In 1937 there was a Faith and Action Conference at Oxford and a Faith and Order Conference at Edinburgh. Four priests who attended sent a detailed report to headquarters on the positive influences at work. They got no answer from Rome.

Then came the guns of war, and those guns, together with the action of the Chancellor of the Third Reich, Adolf Hitler, gave the ecumenical movement the force it needed. In Germany, Catholics and Protestants (and Jews) learned to help one another, to live and pray and die together. In that experience many got a preliminary ride on the vehicle that would carry Christians down the road to unity.

In 1945 the Faith and Action and the Faith and Order Movements fused into something tentatively called the World Council of Churches (150 of them at first), and it planned its first meeting for Amsterdam in 1948. Moscow and Rome vied with each other to see who could disapprove more strongly. The Holy Office cracked down with a *monitum* severe enough to hand Rome the prize. But the bishops of the Netherlands reacted quite differently: they ordered all their churches to offer prayers for the ecumenical movement. The prayers took effect one year later when the Holy Office issued an instruction setting up the conditions for certain limited interconfessional contacts, and praising movements towards Christian unity.

At the next World Council of Churches meeting in Chicago in 1953, official Rome still forbade Catholic participation, but the flow of events had its own logic. Contacts between Churches multiplied. The Dutch bishops set up an Ecumenical Conference of their own (headed by Monsignor Jan Willebrands). Books were written, ideas began to expand. Biblical scholars, both Catholic and Protestant, began to find, in their historical and sociological research, a common understanding.

This ecumenical flowering had not been wasted on John, but

how was he to incorporate it into the approaching Council—a Council he had called to contribute to world peace, or to Christian unity, its necessary prelude? He might have written an encyclical letter, but somehow his healthy scepticism told him these letters just were not read, much less would they spark effective action. But if not a letter or a speech, then what? What else could be done by a man who was tied to the Chair of Peter? Finally, on March 21, 1960, the break came, and a second phase of the Council preparations began when a stoop-shouldered old scholar named Augustin Bea asked Pope John if he would be willing to start a small revolution in the Vatican.

III

Bea had been a cardinal just five months when he sent John a simple memo. "Why not a commission to study Christian unity?" asked Bea. To John, Bea's idea came as breath of fresh air in the suffocating atmosphere of the curial citadel.

Four days later John sent for Bea, and, on March 25, 1960, the two of them blueprinted a simple new device. The scholar Bea would have his study commission. But more important, John would have a window on the world. The result was, not a conciliar commission, but a Secretariat for Promoting Christian Unity endowed with a double duty: (1) to draft conciliar proposals impinging on unity, and (2) to move into the world and establish cordial relations with all Christians and all faiths. The Secretariat would become, in fact, the first effective Catholic recognition of "the others" since the abortive Council of Florence in 1438. John added an important stipulation: "You will be more free," he said, "and less bound by traditions, if we keep your Secretariat out of the normal curial channels." Bea agreed.

Deliberately, they refused to call the new creation a Secretariat for Promoting the Reunion of Christians. This would have been a stumbling-block to outsiders, a call "to be sensible and believe as Catholics believe." Neither John nor Bea could see any justification for this: they knew that born Lutherans and born Buddhists, for instance, could be in as good faith as they; and, since they had never left "the father's house," could hardly be considered as modern types of the prodigal son.

Much has been said concerning the friendship and understanding that grew up between Bea and John. The physical contrast between the two was a glaring one, between the Great Fisherman from the edge of the Lombardy plain and the red-robed Jesuit cardinal from the edge of the Black Forest. One, the hardy peasant, the war chaplain, the Papal Nuncio, the Patriarch of Venice, the *Papa di passaggio*: the other, the intellectual, the Jesuit superior, the papal confessor, the consultor of the Holy Office, the needling research worker, the biblical scholar.

John, with his square, full-blooded face, the large brown eyes, the prominent broad-nostrilled, slightly aquiline nose, the heavy cheeks, the equally substantial lips ever suggestive of a smile, the solid protrusion of the chin, the columnar neck and physical girth, the large spatular hands, the artless ease and spontaneous freedom of his movements, the weight of his physical presence, the resonance of his voice, bespoke the simplicity and external directness of the tiller. His was a physical assertion of the solid race from which he sprang, at the mercy of elemental factors, the sun, the rain, the wind, the earth, and in it all, a gentle resourcefulness based on intuition and the experience that it is good for man to be alive, that life is a profound and rich wine to be drunk beneath God's heavens and as his child.

Bea's appearance, the tiered, tranquil architecture of his head, the powerful, domelike skull-casing with its smooth straight temples, balanced impressively, subtly, on the arches of the curving eyebrows that frame the almost triangular face; beneath them the rounded blue eyes, observant, penetrating, flickering with sudden, deep intelligence; the etched lines of the mouth, the contrasting lips, the flat, chiselled upper lip, the overhanging lower lip, the strong, almost delicately fashioned chin, the narrow palms and long pointed fingers of his hands, the modulated voice; a thin, slight, stoop-shouldered frame, bowed but not weighted beneath the burden of thought, and giving the impression of a mind encased in a tenement of clay, bespoke the fire ready to be kindled, the suppleness of restraint, the measured discretion to accept the real, the reserved power to attempt the possible, the air of intellectual dominion and practical conviction that the draught of life's potion given him was to be tasted to its sublest fineness, distilled and distinguished as a fine oblation to the Father of all good things.

In one there seemed to be no reserve, no reserve at all. In the other all was reserve. One would laugh heartily and broadly, would smile paternally, would inspire affection, would inspire trust. The other would smile pointedly, would command attention, would inspire respect. One was a solid monument to God's goodness. The other was a lighthouse of God's light. The Pyramid and the Tower. The Lion and the Halcyon. The Spirit and the Mind.

Yet, between those two men, despite their physical contrast, there was a perfect meeting of minds, or rather a perfect coincidence of a broad intuitive spirit finding concrete expression in the intellectual elaboration of a mind. For Bea, John was the man sent from God, a voice crying insistently across a waste of isolation, backwardness and unconsciousness, that the rough hillocks be smoothed, that the crooked ways be straightened, so that all men might meet as brothers and march to their common Father. For John, Bea was the incarnation of the ideal curial yet non-curialist cardinal, a suitable servant and finely polished instrument, fashioned by years of intellectual activity and political awareness, shot through with a worldly wisdom that was all-important at this juncture of events.

In his years as a Jesuit and a Jesuit superior, Bea was known as a mine of information, a quick finder of solutions to personal and community problems, and, above all, an untiring listener: head bowed, eyes flickering, accompanying *ja's* or *si's* or *oui's* or yes's (he had a ready command of German, Italian, French, and English), then the shoulders would straighten, the head come up, the eyes would gleam with the light of the approaching solution or remark and he would speak. As a lecturer and director of studies and research, he was known to have a smooth hand: faced with the dilemma of doctrinal prohibitions and scientific dictates, he could point to the clear subtle path that respected the divine exigencies of the one and the intellectual honesty of the other. Engaged in biblical research, he grasped accurately the burden of modern studies, while still listening to the inner, deeper resonances of the age-old truths. He saw the need for an intellectual breakthrough on the biblical front as far back as 1938 and was known to have fathered the charter of modern Catholic biblical studies, the encyclical letter, *Divino Afflante Spiritu*, of 1943. Yet any book that could claim his approval was considered absolutely safe from the carping blind-sight of more traditionalist views. His versatility enabled him to enter the Holy Office as consultor on more than biblical matters. His discretion endeared him to Pius XII who remarked to (the then) Archbishop Roncalli: "Without this Father's counsel my ideas would be all head and no body." No one could point the finger of reproach to his orthodoxy, yet he never could be identified with the integralist view.

When he declined the red hat offered by Pius XII (a fact not known until later), he certainly had strong motives based on personal humility and self-knowledge, yet perhaps it was a calculated demur: he knew Pius XII better than any man alive, had plumbed his sanctity and seen the constricting limits of his authoritarian isolation. The moment had not come for such a step.

As cardinal he was more or less expected by some Curialists to be occupied with harmless things like indulgences and the patronage of religious foundations. And when Bea took up his residence in the Collegio Brasiliano as cardinal, not one of them foresaw that the figure which now occupied the first floor would formulate thoughts and propositions that would mould the lives and thoughts of millions of Catholics and extend their influence far beyond the limits of the Catholic Church.

No one, not even his friends, would have foreseen the instinct for public relations, the quiet insistence on principle, the heedlessness for the unessential or the banal, the adaptability to encounter Lutherans, Protestants, Moslems, Jews. They were astonished at his capacity to converse with an American Ritter, a Maronite Meouchi, a Melchite Maximos, a Lutheran Dibelius, a Jewish Heschel; to welcome Anglican Geoffrey Fisher and American Episcopalian Lichtenberger in Vatican City; to travel tirelessly to East Berlin, to Munich, to Paris, to Basle, to Copenhagen, to the United States; to establish a dialogue with Athenagoras of Constantinople and be invited by a Muscovite Nicolai; to pour out a stream of personal correspondence (he sends out more than 2,000 letters yearly); and to compose endless lectures, conferences, books and articles. One does not expect a man of 80 to undertake so successfully and so easily a task of such gargantuan proportions.

Even Bea's antecedents bear no real proportion to his present position and function on the world stage. Almost from his birth on May 28, 1881, until his appointment as Jesuit Provincial of the Upper German Province in 1921, his occupations were academic: early schooling in Sasbach, Kostanz, and Rastatt; theological studies in Freiburg im Breisgau from 1898 to 1902; his Jesuit formation from 1904 onwards at Maastricht, and at Innsbruck and Valkenburg, from 1917 to 1921. His career in Rome began as lecturer at the Gregorian University in 1924, and continued as Prefect of studies in the Gesù in 1928 and Rector at the Pontifical Biblical Institute from 1930 to 1949. In the same year he became Consultor of the Holy Office; he had already been confessor of Pius XII for four years and was to remain that until the Pontiff's death in 1958, thirteen years in close contact with that hieratic figure. In Bea's words to me, "I was preformed for this job."

Perhaps that experience had enabled him to observe from the best possible viewpoint the disadvantages of Pius' authoritarian approach to reform which was inevitably tragic in its conclusion. Pius' ideas were similar in some respects to John's—he too, had thought the Church needed changing—but his solution was a godlike one of changing it himself, while John's idea was human and, therefore (since he was, after all, a man), more realistic: to let it change itself, to let the spirit breathe, to give Christians that long-lost Pauline freedom of the sons of God. Pius XII had "reformed" the long-outdated Roman Curia, for instance, by merely ignoring it. He became his own Secretary of State, his own cabinet, his own legislature, his own supreme court, and, with the assistance of a sort of high command of German Jesuits, he brought the papacy, if not the Church, into what passed for modern times, There were flaws in this plan, however. First, Pius XII was himself a Roman aristocrat possessing the inevitable limitations that restrict any small town aristocrat. Second, his serious illness during the last three years of his pontificate prevented him from exercising his powers (illustrating the shortcomings of one-man rule, even in the Church). And third, he was simply not listened to with understanding by a Church composed of intelligent beings who, by that very fact, must take part in the judgments and not be dictated to like children. From high on the Chair of Peter, Pius XII wrote rivers of words, forty-one encyclical letters whose baroque phrases were certainly not read by the majority of the faithful nor even by all the bishops to whom they were specifically addressed.

Thus, Bea, from his own viewpoint, could appreciate all the problems of a pope.

IV

Pope John announced the founding of the Secretariat in June, 1960, while Bea was in New York City receiving an honorary doctorate from Fordham University. When the New York newspapers and wire services demanded to know "who what when where and why," Bea called a press conference, his first, with the confidence of a Roosevelt, and announced what amounted to a declaration of independence—from the mustiness of old defensive mentalities, at least.

Back in Rome, Bea began to organize his staff. He retained the services of an alter ego named Stefan Schmidt, a Jesuit biblical scholar exiled from Yugoslavia, and the two of them discovered what a store of Catholic ecumenists were available to help. Among them were three archbishops: Lorenz Jaeger of Paderborn, Germany; Joseph Marie Martin of Rouen, France; and John Carmel Heenan of Liverpool, England; and five bishops: François Charrière of Lausanne, Geneva and Fribourg, Switzerland; Emile Josef Marie De Smedt of Bruges, Belgium; Pieter Anton Nierman of Groningen, the Netherlands; Thomas Holland,

Coadjutor Bishop of Portsmouth, England; and Gerard van Velsen of Kroonstad, South Africa—not an Italian in the lot. Monsignor Jan Willebrands, also of the Netherlands, became secretary or chief executive officer. (The Dutch, plainly enough, were going to loom very large in the Catholic ecumenical movement, as they had among the Protestants. Willem Visser 't Hooft, general secretary of the World Council of Churches, is from the Netherlands.)

Bea had little difficulty finding an auxiliary team of fifteen theologian-consultors. Among them: Jesuit Gustave Weigel, Jewish convert John Oesterreicher, Dominicans Jerome Hamer and Christopher Dumont, Augustinian Gregory Baum of Toronto, and Assumptionist George Tavard. None of these men needed training in John's new approach, because they had been using it for years (although without Rome's enthusiastic approval). The approach, as Bea described it, "was intended to favour mutual understanding, dissipate misunderstanding and false interpretations, create a favourable atmosphere." The Secretariat got to work immediately, providing "the separated brethren" with information on Council activities, getting Protestant and Orthodox and Jewish suggestions for the Council, preparing reports on the current condition of Protestantism, processing proposals for conciliar discussion on matters affecting Christian unity. Said Bea: "Little by little, we are trying to create a better atmosphere between the confessions, to help along gradual and progressive approaches between Christians, and to prepare the doctrinal and practical supports for those approaches."

One of the biggest tasks was to educate the faithful. Bea's first conferences were held in Italy for Catholics: they needed to learn the new way more than anyone. Thus, Bea could write a long, carefully reasoned article in La Civiltà Cattolica on January 14, 1961, in which he painstakingly laid doctrinal groundwork for the Catholic ecumenical movement, steering a middle course between two extremes, one of "extreme reserve, of self-defence, of severity" towards a heretical system or schismatic Church, and another "placing the Catholic Church and other confessions almost on an equal level." Then in the best Roman juridical manner, Bea went on to underline the difference between abstract error on the one hand, and on the other the actual "brothers in Christ" who are not even technically heretics or schismatics.

He who knows the language of the Church, of the Holy Fathers and Canon Law, knows very well that the Church, in using the terms "heretic" and "schismatic," means those who are formally and knowingly, therefore, with full consciousness of what they do and full freedom of decision that they are such or that they may be supposed to be such (cf. CIC, Canon 1325, paragraph 2; cf. texts of the Holy Fathers cited in S. Tromp, S.J., *Corpus Christi quod est Ecclesia*, III; *De Spiritu Christi anima*, Rome, 1960, pp. 185–190). Now who would dare affirm at once that all separated brothers find themselves in these conditions? Certainly it better corresponds to justice and Christian charity, and moreover, to the reality of facts, to admit, as we have seen earlier, their good faith, leaving, in particular cases, the judgment to God alone.

But when Bea later travelled to France, or to Switzerland, to speak to the students and faculties of the University of Paris, or the University of Fribourg, he did not concern himself with anything more than a practical outline of the intellectual work that must be done by scholars, Catholic and non-Catholic alike, "to create an atmosphere of understanding and mutual confidence and authentic Christian charity." To Bea, truth was not an exclusive possession of the Catholic Church: "Our theological propositions do not always express the full depth of revealed doctrine," he said more than once.

In Germany, Bea geared his approach to another mentality. In Munich, for instance, he took evident delight in being able to point out that some historical splits were largely the fault of Rome and, to back it up, he quoted that famous instruction of Pope Adrian VI to his Apostolic Nuncio Francesco Chieregati at the Diet of Nuremberg in 1522, three years before the city of Nuremberg embraced Protestantism. "... give promises that we shall use all diligence to reform before all things the Roman Curia."

Measuring every word, having special regard for each audience, weighing every consequence, Bea got things done. And not the least of his labours, certainly the most sensational, was his contact with "the separated brethren," something which, more than any conferences of his or of John, would be a symbol to the world that the Church was leaving the bastions of the City of God and attempting to sail on the sea of the world. It was Bea who arranged the visit of Dr Geoffrey Fisher, Archbishop of Canterbury, to Pope John in November, 1960, and Bea who explained the significance of that visit in an article in the December 17 issue of La Civiltà Cattolica. It was Bea who sent Monsignor Willebrands on trips to Istanbul, to Geneva and Athens and Alexandria "to expedite the Holy Father's wishes that non-Catholic observers be invited to the Council by finding out who wants to be invited and in what manner they want to be invited."

It was Bea's idea (shared by John) that the presence of observers at a council of all the world's bishops would be far more effective proof of the Church's latent vitality than any abstract assertion to the same effect. Much of Rome's latter-day teaching (yes, even some things signed by Pius himself) was unnecessarily repellent to the separated brethren of the East and the West. If the calculations of Bea and John were correct, the bishops themselves, given the proper encouragement, would speak out from the heart, not from the inspiration of the official, juridical Roman textbooks, but out of their experience as pastors and teachers in the midst of their Christian people. Bea and the Pope felt, in effect, that the charismatic influence of the Church had lain dormant for too long, locked in the hold of the barque of Peter, as it were, not by the "keeper of the keys" but rather by the officers—or deckhands.

The Curialists, for the most part, flatly opposed the presence of any observers, but could hardly do much to quash or slow down John's wishes when he put the job of getting observers to the Council in the hands of Bea and his Secretariat, free as they were from the protocol that stifles the Roman congregations. In July, 1961, however, Ottaviani saw his chance to blunt this thrust.

He opposed the sending of any official Roman Catholic delegates to the World Council of Churches meeting in New Delhi.

For Bea this was a major crisis. If the Church did not send men to New Delhi, how could it possibly ask the Christian bodies represented there to send observers to Rome? Such a request would have been impossible and would have been treated with the contempt it deserved. Up to this point, Bea had effectively avoided any encounter with the Holy Office, because he was acting directly under the Pope for the Council. But now, when he needed to send observers representing the Church, Canon Law prescribed his sending the names of these observers to the Holy Office for what amounted to a "security clearance." Ottaviani shot back a note neither approving nor disapproving the five men selected by Bea. He denied the right of the Secretariat to send any observers at all. Bea pointed out that the Holy Office was not consulted on that larger question, but merely asked to approve or disapprove the names submitted. Ottaviani disapproved the names and repeated his injunction against any observers at all.

Bea turned to the Pope. "*Io sono solamente il Papa*"—"I'm only the Pope," said John, implying he could do nothing. In normal circumstances, he would have done nothing. In these latter days, popes do not oppose their own Curia unless they want to cause themselves a great deal of grief. But here the stakes were high. John said flatly, "We are sending observers." Ottaviani stipulated that none of Bea's proposed observers to New Delhi could participate as theologians in the Vatican Council. Bea submitted another list, and this time the Holy Office approved it.

It was a victory for the Secretariat, but it didn't bode well for the progress of the Council itself—which was securely in the hands of the retrogressive Curialists all the way.

V

"LA CROCIATA NON SI FA PIU," headlined an article on Pope John in a Rome Communist weekly. "NO MORE CRUSADES."

"This new policy of Pope John," muttered the editor of Italy's slick, satirical weekly *Il Borghese*. "This policy means the end of *la chiesa cattolica romana*."

Both the extreme left and the extreme right in Italy, their supersensitive antennae waving, kenned the course of Pope John's *politique* immediately. Both tended to misinterpret what they saw, and to see more (and less) than was there. But both were right. Pope John, anxious to move his barque onto the sea of the world, could not make the mistake of Pope Innocent III, the man who had come closest in the long history of the Church to involving it with the world. Innocent III, however, and a long line of popes who followed him, entered the world in order to dominate it, not to serve it—or if not to dominate, then to serve some one political portion of it at the expense of others.

John XXIII, intuiting the fundamental finalities of a new millenary era in human history, determined to sail free. Political pundits may call this policy "non-aligned" or "neutralist." But it is not negative in the least. In the last analysis, it is the only possible policy for a pope who considers himself the father of all and the head of a Church he wants to be the mother of all.

Italians were accustomed to popes who took sides. This new turn made the Pope appear "leftist," and the Communist press, of course, would toot about it triumphantly because in Italy it had little else to toot about. The right-wing press, too, would anguish about the crypto-Communists who had been given power at the Vatican. Already in Italy, four men have been singled out publicly as the principal culprits: Cardinal Bea; Archbishop Angelo Dell'Acqua, second in command at the Secretary of State's office; Monsignor Igino Cardinale, protocol chief under Dell'Acqua; and Pope John's private secretary, Monsignor Loris Capovilla. Any one of the so-called crypto-Communists in the Vatican could tell you plainly (if it were not for his delicate position) all about John's *politique* and its dimensions:

"The Church [one of them might tell you] is not a dam against Communism. The Church cannot, should not, be against anything. It should be positively for something. This is the characteristic note of the Holy Father's attitude. Not to condemn but to affirm. When we support only one political bloc, we alienate half of humanity. The Church is for all people, for all times. It is not bound to follow the political and economic fortunes of states. It must look ahead to eventual contact with all peoples— even if it is fifty years from now. But even now it can multiply contacts and encourage other contacts on every level, political, religious, cultural, creative. A crusade against Communism is pointless."

This new *politique* of Pope John was hardly apparent from the beginning. It was only after he had secured the release of Archbishop Josyf Slipyi, the Ukrainian primate, from a Siberian prison; only after he turned his attention to the release of Archbishop Beran of Prague and Cardinal Jozsef Mindszenty of Hungary; only after he consented to receive the 1962 Balzan Prize for Peace from an international panel of judges, including Russian members; only after he went out of his way to receive Nikita Khrushchev's daughter and son-in-law, Alexei Adzhubei, in private (but unofficial) audience, that the vague nature of the Pope's *politique* dawned on the world at large. In retrospect, one can see that the pattern was begun at the very beginning of John's papacy.

In January of 1960 came the first subtle indication. Cardinal Alfredo Ottaviani, secretary of the Holy Office, and, in his own mind at least, commanding general of the garrison of the City of God, launched a virulent attack on Italian President Giovanni Gronchi's plans to visit the Soviet Union. To a small crowd in the church of Santa Maria Maggiore, Ottaviani said:

In the twentieth century it is still necessary to deplore genocide, mass deportations, slaughters like Katyn Wood and massacres like Budapest. But some still stretch out their hands to the new Antichrist and even race to see who can first shake hands with him and exchange sweet smiles. Can a Christian confronted by one who massacres Christians and insults God smile and flatter? Can a Christian opt for an alliance with those who prepare for the coming of the Antichrist in countries still free? Can we consider any relaxation of East-West tensions when the face of Christ is once more spat upon, crowned with thorns and slapped?

Osservatore Romano added a little brimstone of its own to this fire by digging up some old quotations from Pope Pius XI's *Quadragesimo Anno* (1931) to the effect that "socialism, considered either as a doctrine or as an historic fact, or as a plan for action, cannot be reconciled with the teaching of the Catholic Church. No one can be at the same time a good Catholic and a good socialist."

Gronchi postponed his trip (he said he was sick), but then, obviously under orders, Ottaviani granted a rare press interview on January 17 to make a retraction. "Cardinal Ottaviani was giving a doctrinal sermon on the Mystical Body," recounted the favoured newspaper, *Avvenire d'Italia*, by way of explanation, and added, "The thought of Cardinal Ottaviani was simply and profoundly theological . . . and omitting this presupposition, as many journals did, his words were given a wrongly political significance." On February 5, Gronchi left Rome for his Moscow visit.

During the 1960 Olympic Games in Rome, Pope John spied a Bulgarian general in a large group of athletes from various parts of the world, and recognized him as an old acquaintance during his days as Apostolic Visitor to Bulgaria. That evening the Pope sent word to the Bulgarian contingent in the Olympic Village that he would like to see the general. This embarrassed the general in front of his Bulgarian confreres, but he could hardly refuse the invitation. When he returned from the visit, he was puzzled. He had expected a sermon at the very least, but John's conversation was purely a reminiscence. "The Pope didn't ask me anything," reported the Bulgarian general. "He just said he loved Bulgaria very much." After the games, the general returned home and soon afterwards an imprisoned Catholic bishop and a dozen priests who had been clapped into jail by the Reds were quietly released.

On November 25, 1960, John received a birthday greeting from Khrushchev who called John "a man of peace" and wished him success. This was the first recognition by any Soviet official of any pope and it marked the beginning of suspicions that perhaps this Pope was not aligned, as his predecessor had been, with the "American imperialists." The Italian press was in a *furor*, of course, and many in the Vatican advised the Pope against any kind of reply. John replied. He said simply, "Thank you for the thought. And I will pray for the people of Russia."

By April of 1961, John's social encyclical *Mater et Magistra* had been drafted for his approval. John kept the document for three months, fiddled with it, fuzzed off the sharp edges, removed all mention of Communism, added some ideas of his own (against the advice of the original writers) on the values of "socialization," and released it in the summer. Editor William F. Buckley of the conservative *National Review* characterized the 25,000-word document as "an exercise in triviality." Nikita Khrushchev, according to an aide of the Pope, read the entire thing and, when he finished it, told his ministers, "We can't laugh at this."

In 1961, Pope John turned his attention, too, to throbbing, nationalistic Africa and moved the Church ahead several centuries by ordering 13 native bishops consecrated immediately. For too long, he told a confidant, the Church had betrayed its mission by its close identification with the colonializing powers. "If a man doesn't have his liberty, he's nothing."

In 1961, too, John revealed his attitude towards the oldest tension—that between Christians and Jews. Privately he gave the sacrament of Confirmation to a Jewish lad who had been secretly baptized, told him to continue being a good Jew in his own community, go to the synagogue, support the Jewish school, because "by being a Catholic, you do not become any less a Jew." He also asked Cardinal Bea to prepare a *schema* for the Council that would revise old Catholic myths about the "deicide people," a myth that has nurtured anti-Semitism for centuries.

In February, 1962, the Catholic Demochristian Party in Italy formed a new government in co-operation with Pietro Nenni's Socialist Party. Italy's bishops, who had been opposing such types of co-operation between Catholics and the infidels since the 1920's at least, were silent. They were asked by John to keep silent, not because he felt that the *apertura a sinistra* was necessarily a good thing for Italy, but because his instincts told him the world had had enough of Church interference in partisan politics, to the detriment of both the Church and the world. And more than enough polemics, interdicts and condemnations.

In the spring of 1962, workers all over Spain went on strike, urged on their course by members of the younger clergy and by laymen who found justification for their action in *Mater et Magistra*. In May, when Generalissimo Francisco Franco finally accused Catholic lay organizations and "exalted priests" of helping foment the walkouts, the Vatican's *Osservatore Romano* did not mention his speech and the Pope hinted that that was all the answer Franco would get. The Church, John told a group of newsmen, "like a wise mother, resorts to the word and to exhortation but on occasion uses discretion and silence, which have their reason and which an attentive and sensitive son knows how to interpret." Just to make sure of a correct Spanish interpretation however, the Spanish hierarchy announced on August 31 that it had formed, "with the approval of the Holy See," a bishops' commission for the social apostolate headed by Cardinal José Maria Bueno y Monreal of Seville.

In August of 1962 I learned how much the Pope favoured Cardinal Wyszynski's policy of co-existence with the Communist Gomulka régime. "In Poland before the war," I was told, "the intellectuals, the businessmen, the nobles and the priests were all on one side and the people on the other. Now, the intellectuals and the professionals are on one side and on the other are the people and the priests."

On the desk of Pope John, during the Council, there sat a reproduction of the United States Telstar satellite hovering over a silver paperweight. On the weight were the engraved words of John himself: "Oh, how we wish these undertakings would assume the significance of an homage rendered to God the creator and supreme legislator. These historic events which will be inscribed in the annals of scientific knowledge of the cosmos will thus become an expression of true, peaceful and well-founded progress towards human brotherhood." Below them are these words in large capitals: "PRESENTED TO HIS HOLINESS POPE JOHN XXIII BY THE VICE-PRESIDENT OF THE UNITED STATES OF AMERICA LYNDON B. JOHNSON 1962".

Ironically and to the shame of Johnson's aides, these words of Pope John were not those he uttered when the U.S. Telstar went into orbit. He spoke them in his radio address of August 12 when he first heard of the simultaneous orbital flight of the Soviet Union's Andrian Nikolaev and Pavel Popovich. John took great delight in praising this feat because it gave him a small opportunity to demonstrate his joy and delight in the achievement of even those men who said they couldn't find God in space. But John was not concerned about what they *said*. He knew God was with them, and what good did it do to carry on polemics about it?

To John, the world was too filled with polemics.

VI

Any future biographer of John XXIII will be faced with a very delicate task: he must leaf through a list of achievements on the part of this Pope, must scan a series of apparently isolated actions, and reach back through the visible veils that clothe them, back to their source. A superficial observer might look at his actions, and see in them merely isolated attempts to spread some of his innate goodness and fraternal feelings—to spread them even beyond curtains of iron and bamboo.

Yet such a superficial analysis would have missed the point. From the time John called the Council, it was obvious that he did not consider it an intramural affair meant to discuss ancient dogmas and formulate anathemas; for him it would be a world event, a *balzo in avanti*, a leap forward of the Roman Church, a deliberate commitment on the part of his Church to Christianity as a world force, a commitment to the great mass of humanity bound and destined for unity in the near, foreseeable future.

There was nothing in John's formal education that should have made him a political genius, any more than Chesterton's formal education should have made him a philosopher. But Etienne Gilson could read Chesterton's book on St Thomas Aquinas (which Chesterton dictated in four days) and cry: "This man has grasped the meaning of Thomism in its utter essence. This study could only issue from a mind profoundly philosophical." And so for Pope John. Behind his actions, with their political resonances, there lies an intuitive grasp of the geopolitical situations in our world and its need to choose either the Christian ethos or its own moral disintegration.

Central to John's flaring intuition of our century was his perception that our geopolitical world of today is a world in transit. And the glowing periphery of that intuition was the warning of the past: "History knows no radical solutions. Only they who ignore history are condemned to repeat it!"

When planning his televised radio message for September 11, 1962, John decided to pronounce his words against the background of a terrestrial globe. Photographs of the Pope were taken from diverse angles as he spoke. John's favourite was one taken over his left shoulder: on the globe one could see the huge mass of continental China; on the left stretched the borders of Russia; all around lay the teeming lands of the East. These elements represented the core of his subtle world analysis.

For John, this analysis was summed up in the word "confrontation." When someone made a remark to him about the stalemate between the two giants, the Eagle and the Bear, his reaction was immediate and clear: "It is not merely that arm matches arm, or that muscle matches muscle. It is that mouth does not match mouth. They speak no common language. And we? We Christians are doing nothing to break the fatal silence. Now the emergence of China has only sharpened the dilemma and forced a new world pattern."

But what sort of confrontation was this? A confrontation of religion with anti-religion, of Christ with Antichrist? What ultimately was the difference between the ethos and the morality proposed by the West as a whole and the Soviet Russian idea? As George Orwell asked at the end of *Animal Farm*, "Who is pig and who is man?"

The heart of the matter, therefore, was a dilemma of moral dimensions. And this is what pained Pope John: the isolation of Christianity in general and the Roman Church in particular from any really active participation in solving the dilemma.

But how could the Church help solve it? Hadn't it been trying for many and many a year? Hadn't every seer, sage, moralist, philosopher and theologian in all of Christianity been trying to solve the dilemma? What made Pope John's approach any different? Was it some new formula? Or could it be that it was a matter of loving? For John, putting Christ into the twentieth century would be far better than finding any formula. For John, the effective Christian action in the world of the 1960's would mean loving even a Khrushchev. This was the meaning of John's *politique*: a searching really for the one effective sign of the presence of Christ in the world.

And in a closely cognate sense, John would affirm Christ's presence by loving the little folk everywhere, in Durrës, Sofia and Prague; in Marseilles, Meissen and Milan; in Darjeeling, Samarinda and Hsinchu; in Accra, Nyundo and Cotonou; in Cienfuegos, São Paulo, and Punta Arenas; in Hudson's Bay and Los Angeles. Loving the little folk does not come without knowing them and their needs. "I know mine, and mine knows me," says the Good Shepherd, and only in this dialogue can Christ's Church preach the Message to them. This is the ultimate sign of the divinity of Christ and his Church. The deaf hear, the blind see, the lame walk and Good News is brought to the poor.

In the 1960's man was meeting himself at the crossroads of history. At no time had his lovable traits been more evident and clear. And, paradoxically, at no time had he seen such anguish in the world, such dislocation, such disintegration, such loneliness.

Could the message of Christ be relevant in such a complex world? John, in his simply faithful, hopeful, loving way, thought it could. Hence his *politique*. Hence his Council. Both of them aimed at commending Christ to the world as it was and could be.

Chapter Four

DRY DOCK

I

MOVING the barque of Peter would not be easy. It was almost as if John had come to the water's edge and tried moving it in the dark with his own broad shoulder. When it would not budge, he lit a match to see why, and discovered the monstrosity was sitting in dry dock. Someone (was it the Curia?) blew out the match, and John, cursing neither the darkness nor the man who blew out the light, lit a candle for another look. Yes, the barque certainly was high and dry, some of its timbers rotting, its lines loose, its sails gray and rotting. Somewhere below decks, John could hear the shouts of what was obviously a skeleton crew, and when he finally found them and asked if they could help him prepare the barque for a journey onto the sea of the world, they quite naturally pointed out that it was dark and would remain so for some time. "Why not wait awhile?" they yawned. The only thing to do, John realized, was call for help from elsewhere. He was not quite sure what that call would bring. But he hoped, first for some light, next a thorough overhaul of the barque and then, maybe, it would be ready to sail.

Accordingly, then, John shouted for help and his call was heard. Help came, much to the surprise of the crew, from John's episcopal colleagues. It came from priests and theologians and laymen and laywomen. It came from his separated brothers. His cry drew assistance from all quarters.

II

Actually, in asking for general help, John XXIII was tapping the hidden sources of the faith as it was lived in every corner of the globe. He looked, of course to the books—*the* Book, and the great inspiration of the Fathers and Doctors of the Church—but books alone were not enough. He was head of a body (he believed it to be the Mystical Body of Christ living on in the world through his members) that lived and breathed in the world as it was, and he felt that any real renewal would have to come through the members, since it was they who had to bear the Message and apply it wherever they might be. If they could not apply the Message, then it was a living Message no longer, and the followers of Christ could no longer claim that he is the Way or the Truth or the Life. But the application, hardly having been made for the last 400 years (because the "world" was evil and the "Church" had to defend itself against it), would not, could not, be easy. While the barque of Peter stayed in dry dock, the sea of the world had undergone more changes—political, economic, philosophic, religious, scientific, moral, and social—than in all the centuries of time that had flowed before. How could the barque sail on it?

In May and June of 1959, John sent questionnaires out to the world's 2,594 archbishops, bishops, and abbots who could be called to a Council (according to the norms of Canon Law)—to 397 of them in Italy, to 217 in the United States, to 167 in Brazil, to 130 in France; to Spain's 89, to the Congo's 40, to Tanganyika's 21, to Nigeria's 19, to China's 116, to Czechoslovakia's 19. He also sent them to religious orders: canons regular, monks, mendicants regular, religious congregations and societies of the common life (all of them varying kinds of religious orders fitting under different categories of Roman Canon Law) and to the Church's major theological faculties around the world. Altogether 2,712 questionnaires flew out and 2,150 came tumbling back. Germany's twenty-three dioceses all replied. Many Iron Curtain bishops could not. Eighty-eight per cent of Central America's bishops, prelates, nuncios, administrators and vicars apostolic replied, and Africa's hierarchy was close behind with 83 per cent.

Their replies (which amounted to a fantastic bulk of self-criticism, in effect a pinpointing of the reasons why the barque was hardly ready to sail) were compiled into 7,770 pages and twelve tomes of good, bad and indifferent Latin, then reduced to two summary volumes. The first of the summary volumes contained 806 pages, listed 4,232 suggestions (footnoted according to their source) concerning doctrinal matters, general rules of Canon Law, reorganization of the Roman Curia (an amazing number of the bishops asked for this), handling of clergy, seminarians, religious, and laity. The second volume of 733 pages listed 4,740 suggestions concerning sacraments, holy places, worship, the Church's modes of teaching (i.e., catechisms, schools, mass media, the Index of Forbidden Books), church property, legal actions (principally the Church's marriage courts), missions, movements for unity, the charitable and social work of the Church.

All of this represented a healthy spirit of self-criticism in the Church, and fortunately this was not at all confined to ecclesiastics. Cardinal Franziskus Koenig of Vienna and Cardinal Paul Emile Léger of Montreal summoned public meetings of priests and laity to ask for their suggestions. Bishop John J. Wright of Pittsburgh held private sessions in his home and attended various Catholic conventions. "It's surprising how much intelligence you can pick up at conventions nowadays," said Wright. Canadian bishops issued a pastoral letter asking for suggestions. The Catholic press, in varying degrees, got into the spirit of things and came out from time to time with frank reappraisals of the conditions of Catholicism. Such a state of affairs would have been unthinkable even ten years ago. Somehow, perhaps under the confident optimism of Pope John, the critical faculty was restored to the once meek faithful.

Some of the suggestions showed that many so-called Catholic dogmas are still open for discussion, and they asked for restatements, clarifications and reformulations of the Church's teachings on (for example) the relationship between faith and reason, between Scripture and tradition, on the infallibility of the Church, on salvation outside the Catholic Church, on original sin, on hell itself.

Some suggestions on the way the Church was being run were equally compelling: that the Roman Curia be made more international. (It is now overwhelmingly Italian, and a French Jesuit wondered in print why there should be more than five or six Italian cardinals.) That daily and ritual garb be simplified. (One parish priest from Grenoble, France, made a refreshing demand for less ecclesiastical pomp, and asked that bishops and cardinals give up their violet and red and wear the same cassock as priests, renounce their titles of "eminence" and "excellency" and be called "father" like everyone else.) That the breviary be put into the vernacular and its recitation be limited to a half hour a day. (Many believed that as it now stands "the breviary is not an act of worship but an act of penance.") That priests who have been legally laicized by the Church also be allowed to marry. ("These priests cannot be expected to live a celibate life in a non-celibate world.") That bishops be automatically retired at the age of seventy. That laymen be given consulting capacities in each diocese. That no author be condemned by the Inquisition until he has had a chance to defend himself. That Mass be said so that people can hear it all the way through and in the language of the people. That marriage cases be expedited in Rome and bishops be given power to handle cases now reserved to Rome. (Couples still wait heroic periods of time for declarations of nullity.) That laws of abstinence be simplified and laws of fasting be taken away and substituted for by other works of mortification or mercy during Lent ("No more fish on Friday?"). That it be left to the bishop to decide whether his diocese needs a minor seminary or not. (Many questioned the wisdom of locking lads in at the tender age of nine or ten or eleven.)

All this, of course, was pretty churchy. The bulk of the suggestions revealed to John that the interests of his bishops were largely self-interests, in the sense that they dealt with matters of bell, book and candle, and the institutional affairs of their diocese, but not with the single problem that troubled Pope John—the problem of making Christ relevant to millions.

The Curia set up ten preparatory commissions to process the suggestions, and the commissions, too, in their very names, highlighted the ecclesiastical nature of the whole affair. The Commission for the Discipline of the Clergy and Christian

People. The Commission for Religious. The Commission for Bishops and the Government of Dioceses. The Commission for the Discipline of the Sacraments.

The commissions met and processed the suggestions and, purportedly on the basis of those suggestions, prepared *schemata*, or proposals, for later consideration by the conciliar Fathers. The titles of the *schemata*, too, smelled of incense. Ecclesiastical garb and tonsure. Ecclesiastical offices and benefices. Obedience to ecclesiastical teachings. The boundaries of dioceses. The precepts of the Church. Pious donations.

The Secretary-General, Monsignor Pericle Felici, a man who had written his doctoral dissertation for the Lateran University on "The Use of the Ablative Absolute in Rescript Clauses," was bogged down in minutiae, made no distinction between matters large or small, never seemed to be able to issue progress reports to the press or even indicate to the bishops in the field that it might be a good idea to study, for example, such internally important matters as the episcopacy and the primacy. One missionary bishop came to the Council and told me: "I never did know what happened to my suggestions. I can't find a trace of them. I still don't know what happened."

However, there were one or two prevailing impressions that the public managed to pick up. One, that there were changes afoot in the Church. Two, that maybe the Council would solve "my special problem."

The possible changes in store disquieted some of the faithful, not because the changes were disquieting in themselves, but because the faithful misunderstood (and, given the lack of authoritative information, no wonder). One reader wrote in to Monsignor J. D. Conway's "Question Box" in the *Davenport Catholic Messenger* to express her concern over reports that "the Church will take a second look at marriage regulations and permit marriage after divorce in excusable cases . . . and startling as it seems to me [make] a re-evaluation of the 'Real Presence.'" Monsignor Conway tut-tutted over the good reader's misplaced concern. "Divine law would seem," he said, "to give the Church little room for choice in matters of divorce and remarriage. And we can be sure that any re-evaluation of the Real Presence would only make us more vividly aware of its reality and of the sanctifying love which Jesus brings to us in it." But Monsignor Conway must have shocked his wide public even more with a catalogue of things which he (quoting German theologian Hans Küng) thought needed to be reformed: "Hopeless preaching and religious instructions. Nonsense or rigidity in the liturgy. The Index. Roman centralism. Episcopal bureaucracy. All the things wrong with the training of priests. Convent and monastic education. Political conformism. Moral theology, especially on sex and the atom bomb. Latin liturgy. Scandals in the clergy. The fussing over organization and congresses in Catholic societies. Thomism. Rationalism. Marianism. And pilgrimage rackets."

When folk read through lists of *reformabilia* like these, they naturally added their own items. Martin Work, executive director of the National Council of Catholic Men, mistakenly tabbed as the man American Catholics should send their suggestions to, was inundated by a flood of mail pleading for everything from Catholic birth control to firing a grouchy pastor.

Bishop John J. Wright returned to Pittsburgh from a meeting of the Preparatory Theological Commission in Rome and paid a hospital visit to a very old, very well-read gentleman. "Those bishops working pretty hard over there?" asked the old fellow. "Yes," said Wright. The old fellow looked Wright straight in the eye and asked in a manner too serious to be serious, "They going to do anything to cure my arthritis?" Commented Wright later: "That's the way it was. Everyone thought of the Council in terms of his own interests." Sometimes, of course, those interests happened to coincide with the central interests of the Council. Sometimes they did not. Some requests were apparently contrary to Pope John's own wishes for the Council: a fossilized bishop of the old school observed, "It's time the Church put a stop to this 'dialogue' nonsense." Some bishops in South America and elsewhere asked for a ringing condemnation of Communism (as if that had not already been done years ago—with little real effect) and some bishops in Africa asked for similar condemnations of capitalism (which as practised by some great "Catholic" colonial powers added up to a big fat zero as far as the progress of the Gospel in Africa was concerned).

III

Gradually, however, as some of the Church's great bishops and theologians began to explain what the Church could do and should do, the central importance of the coming Council began to emerge.

Cardinal Josef Frings of Cologne said that the Council should "open up the Church to the multiple aspects of the human spirit, as befits her catholicity," and re-evaluate a Christianity "concentrated a little too exclusively on the spiritual salvation of the individual in the life beyond, and not enough on the salvation of the whole world as expressed in the universal hope of Christianity."

Cardinal Julius Doepfner of Munich said the Council "must offer a world that has undergone gigantic spiritual changes the revelation of God by presenting it in its scriptural simplicity and encourage all people to undertake this work of rethinking and reformulating which will allow them to better understand and better approach the mysteries revealed by God, . . . adapting our theology, our liturgy and our churchly structures to those forms which fit the mission of the Church in the world as it is."

Archbishop Emile Guerry, of Cambrai, secretary of France's conference of bishops, said the Council had to "bring about the penetration of Christian principles in the lives of all men in all circumstances: familial, civic, economic, political, and social, in relations among men and peoples within the contemporary world . . . if the Church wishes to carry out its mission of saving the modern world." Guerry characterized that world as "anxious in the face of the fearsome repercussions of the material, technical, and atomic forces that mankind has unleashed and that are capable of exterminating it" and, in underdeveloped areas, "tempted to turn to political régimes and economic systems, which . . . sacrifice the human being, his liberties, and his rights, while only one higher law of universal morals would be capable of saving these nations and of harmonizing them with the common good."

And Cardinal Paul Emile Léger of Montreal looked to the Council for "the penetration of Christian principles into the life of man . . . and all problems of contemporary mankind: world peace, co-operation among unequally developed peoples, population increases, the liberty of man in the political, economic and social context of today." In this wide context, said Léger, "the Council takes on unsuspected dimensions. It becomes the Council not only for the believer but for all men who still believe in man, in the moral values which make his greatness."

Some began to see that if the Council proceeded along these new prophetic lines it would not be the private affair suggested by the phrase "internal renewal," but something that could have implications for other Christians and the world at large. "To a world that had lost its soul and was filled with ennui and fear," said one French theologian, "the thought came that maybe the Council would restore life and hope."

The radical implications of such revolutionary desires, however, were not lost on more conservative minds, and they did their best to scotch them. Archbishop T. D. Roberts, a Jesuit who resigned his see in Bombay in favour of the Indian Valerian (now Cardinal) Gracias, launched an imaginative proposal from Spokane, Washington, for "a pre-conciliar, extra-conciliar commission composed of experts in theology, science, medicine, economics and law representing all religions which, insulated from nationalistic and economic influences, would consider the anguishing problems of peace and thermonuclear warfare." For his trouble, Roberts was accused before the Holy Office of revealing the secrets of the Council. A judgment was passed against him and sentence pronounced without a hearing. When news of the process came out of Rome, no acknowledgment was even made to his proferred defence, and Roberts still has received no satisfaction.

Others, subconsciously falling back on the eleventh Commandment, "Thou shalt not rock the boat," began a prudence campaign against any moves at all towards a Council for unity. Never mind all this dialogue, ran the refrain. "If the Lord wants one Church, he will have it, and there's nothing we can do about it. It will come in God's own good time." That was a good phrase— "God's own time"— and it was given wide coinage among the intellectually bankrupt. But ecumenists felt that Christian disunity was brought about by men, and, unless they wanted to wait for miraculous messages from on high, men would have to work for Christian unity—and the unity of mankind—in human ways.

But perhaps this tendency was inevitable in a Church that must keep trying to understand the Incarnation and all its implications for our understanding of the relationship between the human and the divine. Some (anxious perhaps to cover up the nakedness of the Church's spiritual parents and superiors) were loath to look at the human dimensions of a Church and a Church Council incarnate in time and place. Pére M. D. Chenu pointed out with regret that "in the present perspective of the Council, there is developing here and there a certain soothing and monotonously dithyrambic literature in which, under the pretence of extolling the work of the Holy Spirit, there is, sometimes deliberately, a juggling, a playing down of the human elements and the tensions whose interplay is a matter of normal development." The dithyrambic literature was produced column after column in *Osservatore Romano* and in certain statements emanating from the hierarchies of Italy, Spain and Portugal.

In the United States some bishops tried to tone down the hopes of the faithful. Archbishop Karl J. Alter of Cincinnati told one group in his diocese that the primary purpose of the Council was to renew the Church from within, and not to be disappointed "when there's not a big change all of a sudden." Cardinal Richard Cushing of Boston wrote in his official *Pilot*, "There is a tendency, nurtured by periodicals and other influences of public opinion, to expect dramatic, even miraculous results from the Council. This is not good theology." Both Alter and Cushing had good reason to throw cold water on the burning brow of the faithful. Both of them had been to Rome, both knew how the Council was proceeding in Vatican City. Badly. Very badly.

IV

Pope John did the best he could with the Roman Curia. Instead of knocking a few heads together (which would not really have been very effective), he tried to win its members with kindness. Under Pius XII, Domenico Tardini had been serving as the top man in the Secretary of State's office without the title of Secretary of State—and without the cardinal's hat that usually went with the job. One of John's first acts was to make Tardini Pro-Secretary of State; a month later, in January, 1959, he made Tardini a cardinal and gave him the simple title Secretary of State. But even that did not soften the caustic Tardini, nor prevent him from bucking John on a variety of matters—especially the Council.

On October 30, 1959, Tardini called a press conference on the progress of the Council. He made little effort to conceal his scorn for the whole affair which he characterized as "the Pope's toy." He was amused over the press's concern about the Council. He treated their questions cavalierly. "Yes," he sighed in answer to one question, "the Pope might invite non-Catholics. The Pope is free to invite anyone he wants. He might even invite journalists to give it an element of colour." When a reporter asked him what specific matters the Council would treat, Tardini summed up his amusement over the whole idea with the offhand answer: "The Council will be about everything—and a few other things besides."

Tardini kept control of the Council's movement, however. He made sure that the members of most commissions followed the curial mind-set, excluding such theologians as Karl Rahner, Yves Congar, and John Courtney Murray. At the insistence of the German bishops, Rahner was finally appointed to a preparatory commission on March 23, 1961, but even then it was not to the Theological Commission of Cardinal Alfredo Ottaviani, but to the Commission on the Discipline of the Sacraments. Congar was appointed a consultor to the Theological Commission in 1960, but discovered, when he arrived for the meetings in Rome, that Ottaviani was ruling with an iron hand. He laid down the regulation that no "consultor" could speak unless he was asked by the chair. Congar was never asked. He returned to France more annoyed after each meeting. But if he could not get his ideas across in one way, Congar would find another. He finally gathered twenty-six collaborators and produced an 831-page tome on what he thought would be a key issue in the Council: the nature of episcopal authority. Jesuit John Courtney Murray, a man whose ideas on Church-State relations were too "American" to suit the theocratic notions of an Ottaviani, was never asked to come to Rome in any capacity. He was, as a matter of fact, disinvited and warned by Ottaviani, through his Jesuit superiors, not even to write on Church-State relations.

One group that managed to get out from under curialist control was the Liturgical Commission. A member of the commission told me, "We couldn't have had proper liturgical reform in the nineteenth-century, because we didn't have the scholarship to do it intelligently. Now, more than one thousand scientific works on the liturgy are being published each year. With that kind of scholarly foundation, we can make some progress."

They made progress all right. When the Curialists discovered how much progress was evident in the Liturgical Commission's finished schema, they removed the secretary of the commission, Annibale Bugnini, from the commission.

Such high-handed tactics caused repercussions in some parts of the world. The bishops of middle Europe especially insisted on a more rounded approach to the Council preparations. Accordingly, when the Central Preparatory Commission met for the first time in June of 1961, it represented many nations and numerous schools of thought. It was composed of sixty cardinals, five patriarchs, twenty-seven archbishops, six bishops, the superiors general of the Jesuits, Dominicans, Franciscans and Benedictines, and twenty-nine consulting theologians.

This commission was supposed to scrutinize the work of the ten commissions and three secretariats and pass on their recommendations to the Pope. Altogether, fifty-seven different nations were represented on this commission, and its members came from both conservative and progressive currents in the Church—a pluralism that contrasted heavily with the central co-ordinating commission of the First Vatican Council which was composed of nine cardinals and eight consultors selected from the ranks of the Roman Curia or the Roman colleges.

In its first meeting, this commission demonstrated its ability to speak frankly, giving one of Cardinal Ottaviani's proposals a rough going-over. This did not please Ottaviani who, as secretary of "the Supreme Congregation of the Holy Office of which the Holy Father himself is the prefect," was unaccustomed to such an open forum where ideas stood or fell on their merits. He arranged the appointment of a stalwart colleague, Cardinal Ernesto Ruffini of Palermo, Sicily, to the Central Commission to help him defend the faith against these other cardinals, patriarchs and archbishops.

By the time it ended its seventh session in June, 1962, the Central Commission had been presented with seventy proposals in 119 separate pamphlets, and was expected to pass judgment on them and get them back to their respective commissions for rewriting. The weight of the work itself was enormous, and, as if this were not enough, the manner in which many proposals were prepared defied any easy amendment or correction. As a matter of fact, the Central Commission had no real power to amend or correct anything. Their observations were supposed to be advisory to the Pope. But John did not see the suggestions of the Central Commission. They went to a subcommission on amendments headed by Cardinal Carlo Confalonieri, to the secretaries of each preparatory commission, and to the Secretary-General, Pericle Felici. When the 2,381 Council Fathers finally received their copies of these proposals, members of the Central Commission looked in vain for some evidence of their own contributions. What they saw, particularly in the theological proposals prepared by Cardinal Ottaviani's commission, was the expression of a narrow theological viewpoint, condemning "progressive" Catholic theologians. "If these schemata had been passed by the Council," said one of them, "they would have brought the theological work of the past thirty years to a halt." The proposals were phrased in the same legal and scholastic language that had pained some at the

First Vatican Council. Cardinal Rauscher of Vienna said then that the *schemata* "smelled of the classroom." In other words, these 1962 *schemata* were written in a mode that Cardinal Rauscher thought was out of date in 1870.

Shot through them was the classic curialist argument for everything: that the Church is a perfect society (an old medieval concept meaning roughly that the Church has everything it needs in order to achieve its ends), and that, therefore, it could and should impose its "rights" over the "State and education" and even "television." Imagine the absurdity of such a conception applied in the United States for example, of an American bishop trying to impose the Church's "rights" over the people of the State of New York who have banded together in a unified effort to do together what they could not do separately—build roads, sewers, beaches and parks for the benefit of all. Or his trying to impose a curriculum on the schools of the city of Atlanta. Or his trying to censor the programming of NBC Television.

Some of those at the Central Commission recognized the abstractionism of the Curialist who had worked out the *schemata* for a Council that was supposed to bring the Church into the world as it was in the second half of the twentieth century. But the fact is that they just did not have enough support within the commission to throw out the *schemata* completely, nor the time and the assistance to make the necessary revisions. Others would later wake up to the fact that the future of the Church depended on their rocking the boat now.

V

In front of St Peter's Basilica two statues sum up in their stance the attitude of the Roman mind. One of them is St Peter, the other St Paul. St Peter points sternly down. St Paul points out to the horizon. St Peter (according to the Roman legend) is saying, "This is where the laws are made." And St Paul is saying, "And that's where they're applied."

According to the Code of Canon Law, every diocese in the world is supposed to have a synod—a gathering of all its priests and religious—every ten years. Since the law was made centuries ago, Rome had never had a synod. When Pope John took over as Bishop of Rome, therefore, he saw in this canon the opportunity to get a little reform going in Rome itself as a sort of example to the rest of the Church. He also thought the staging of the synod might provide valuable experience for those members of his Curia who would have to run the Council—a trial run, so to speak.

In January of 1960, then, the synod was called. *Osservatore Romano* billed it as a "foretaste of the Council" and another "manifestation of the triumph of the Church." But if this was a foretaste, many of the young men from many lands who were completing their clerical studies in Rome wondered how the universal Church would be able to force down the dinner. The synod was a three-day ecclesiastical bore. It did not really provide for the needs of the Diocese of Rome, just multiplied many of the problems it had laboured under for years—not the least of which was the extreme juridical mentality that prevailed. Holding fast to the Roman tradition, it promulgated 755 new regulations of import. Example: when a cleric does not wear an overcoat, he should wear a cincture on his cassock. Example: clerics should not smoke in the street. Example: nuns should not beg in public. Of course, no one paid much attention to these rules. A few weeks after the synod, an American cleric, Monsignor James Tucek, Rome chief of the National Catholic Welfare Conference News Service, was approached by a begging Sister and said he thought this was now outlawed. The nun told him it was, in a sense; that now she needed a special permit from the Rome vicariat—300 lire a month. Said Monsignor Tucek somewhat drily: "You see, they didn't really ban begging in public. They just arranged to get their cut out of it."

Someone suggested to Pope John that the synod was a failure. He said, "Well, at least we tried. Doing something was better than not doing anything at all."

The point was that John was waiting for the charismatic influence of the Council itself. If he could just get his bishops to Rome . . . If the commissions did anything worthwhile, so much the better. But John was not exactly counting on them. He felt that perhaps the Secretariat for Promoting Christian Unity could help other commissions find their way, or at least guide them into ecumenical channels. But even that wish would be thwarted. The principal preparatory commission, the Theological Commission, rejected Bea's help entirely. "We don't need you, we judge you," said one of Ottaviani's aides to a member of Bea's commission.

The Pope felt that the Secretariat for the Press, Radio, Television and the Mass Media would work in the practical sphere (as the Bea commission was doing) and ensure the best possible coverage of the Council by the news press. Many Europeans who did not know Archbishop Martin O'Connor, the president of this Secretariat, assumed that as an American he would naturally be suited for this job. O'Connor, however, turned out to be more Roman than the Romans (he has been rector of the North American College for seventeen years), and certainly not the man with the imagination, the enterprise, or will to play press agent for the Council.

Indeed why advertise the Council to the world? Why should anyone know what was happening in the insular haven of the barque of Peter? In fact, reasoned the Curia, why make any effort to make sure the Council Fathers themselves understood what was happening? When the Phillips Company of the Netherlands offered to install simultaneous translation facilities in St Peter's, Secretary-General Pericle Felici delayed his decision until preparations were far advanced, then vetoed the idea. If the Fathers could not understand the Latin spoken in the Council, well then, they could not engage in much of a dialogue, could they? Language is power, one thing the Curialists were not going to hand over to foreigners, to the *periferisti*.

They feared, too, all the talk they had been hearing about vernacular in the liturgy. What could they do about that? Cardinal Ottaviani had come out second best in his battle with Cardinal Bea over the sending of official observers to New Delhi. Maybe an old curial stalwart could do better. The wand was passed to Cardinal Giuseppe Pizzardo, who had somehow become head of the Sacred Congregation of Seminaries and Universities despite an undistinguished academic career. Pizzardo promptly had a paper drawn up that reaffirmed Latin as the language of the universal Church and laid down strictures against the use of any other language in seminary teaching. It also condemned anyone who "out of a desire for novelty" talked or wrote against the use of Latin in the liturgy. This last, I was told by one of Pizzardo's minions in a moment of frankness, was "an attempt to forestall any consideration at the Council of the vernacular in the Mass." Pizzardo passed this draft on to the Pope who left it on his desk for two months, then finally signed it. It went out to the world as an Apostolic Constitution under the name *Veterum Sapientia*, and seminarians, seminary faculties, liturgists, and the hierarchies of eleven Eastern Rite Churches who had never accepted Latin in *their* language were puzzled, or disillusioned, or enraged.

John had merely signed it to appease the Curialists. He was biding his time, waiting, waiting for the Council which would help him out of the *sacco* that imprisoned him. He told several bishops who asked him about it privately to "pay no attention to *Veterum Sapientia*."

The Curialists, however, promptly pressed their advantage by forcing another papal letter, this time an encyclical, that asserted papal claims over the Orthodox Churches in terms that were strangely out of keeping with the ecumenical climate that John had already established. Emboldened by their success, the Curia also succeeded in condemning Jesuit father Riccardo Lombardi's book *Il Concilio* with a mighty blast in *Osservatore Romano*. A still stronger book, *The Council and Reunion*, by German theologian Hans Küng, got no official condemnation (something Küng had thoughtfully forestalled by getting Cardinals Franziskus Koenig and Achille Liénart to write separate prefaces for it). Someone suggested Küng encountered no trouble in Rome because the book was not translated into Italian. It is a fact, however, that as soon as the book was translated into English, Ottaviani's long right arm in the U.S., Archbishop Egidio Vagnozzi, the Apostolic Delegate, tried to get the publisher to scrap his plans for doing it in the United States. (As a matter of record, Vagnozzi failed in that, but has since tried to spike the German theologian's guns by getting his speaking invitations in the United States withdrawn in some dioceses.)

The Curia went further. It ordered the Italian translation of the Dutch bishops' pastoral letter withdrawn from circulation. Ostensible reason: "errors in translation." Real reason: it stressed bishops' collegial powers, that is, powers co-ordinate with those of the Pope. This was subversive. When the news reached the Central Preparatory Commission, it was more or less the last straw. Cardinal Valerian Gracias of Bombay blew up. He informed Ottaviani that the Curia had gone too far and the Council itself would institute its own holy inquiry into the most Holy Office—as his predecessor at Bombay put it: "*sancta inquisitio sanctissimae inquisitionis.*" Gracias was vehemently supported by Cardinals Doepfner of Munich, Koenig of Vienna, and Liénart of Lille.

VI

By October 1961, when it had become apparent that Archbishop O'Connor intended to keep the world's press in the dark, Pope John, against the advice of some curial advisers, created a press bureau to disseminate information on the Council. "We have nothing to hide," John would tell the press somewhat later on. But Secretary-General Pericle Felici's attitude was clear. He set up Monsignor Fausto Vallainc as "the press office," gave him space and a typist, and put him to work issuing communiqués (in Italian) on the progress of the Central Commission meetings. By June, 1962, those communiqués, though impressive in number, shed little light on what the commissions were doing. If you took the communiqués at their face value, you would have had to conclude that the commissions were doing nothing at all. Vallainc apparently cribbed old encyclopedia articles on Catholic doctrine that came more or less close to the subject matter of each day's Central Commission meeting. When the Central Commission got into the consideration of new material, Vallainc, though out beyond his depth, attempted to swim nevertheless, and his resultant thrashing was occasionally heard round the world. On the second to last day of the last Central Commission meeting, Cardinal Ottaviani presented his proposal on Church–State relations, and Cardinal Bea presented his proposal on religious liberty. Vallainc's communiqué reported only Cardinal Ottaviani's view, and neatly neglected to mention the main point of another Catholic view that maintains the need for freedom in pluralistic societies.

On the next day, June 21, Vallainc made an attempt at reporting Cardinal Bea's proposal on ecumenism, but gave the erroneous impression that the Central Commission had taken a strong stand against the ecumenism of Bea and his Secretariat. Said the release: "The word ecumenism as used today habitually by non-Catholics and particularly Protestants indicates a form of understanding, almost a federation of all Christian Churches, each with equal rights. According to this theory, the different Churches should consider themselves equally guilty of the separation. No Church should presume to be the one true Church of Christ. The future Church resulting from the union of the present Churches would not be identified with any existing Church but would be completely new." This communiqué was picked up by the wire services and correctly interpreted, for example, by the Associated Press, which concluded from the communiqué that "The Roman Catholic Church considers 'ecumenicalism' [sic] or Christian unity as possible only by the return to the Church of the 'separated brothers.' "

The World Council's general secretary, Willem Visser 't Hooft, called his own press conference to protest against the communiqué. Those who wrote it, said he, "are not acquainted with the basic documents in which the World Council of Churches has explained itself and they are not aware of the existence of the large number of serious studies made by Roman Catholic ecumenists concerning the World Council."

In his room at the Brazilian College, Cardinal Bea read through the AP story (headlined "CHURCH BLASTS ECUMENISM") and read it through again, shaking his head. "As much confusion here as there are words," said Bea. " 'Return to the church of the "separated brothers.' " (His face showed some distaste.) "Why, when His Holiness constituted our secretariat he called it a Secretariat for the Union of Christians—not the *Reunion* of Christians." Bea paused and let that sink in. "And when he read the bull announcing the Council, he said he was aware that many are 'gripped by a desire for unity and peace—*unitatis et pacis assequenadae desiderio teneri.*' But the *Osservatore Romano* translated this passage as 'anxious for return'—*sono ansiosi di un ritorno di unita'e di pace.*' Maybe the people at *Osservatore Romano* don't understand."

Cardinal Bea's charitable judgment is no doubt the true one. The curalist approach is rarely malicious. The Curialists just do not understand.

In the judgment of Cardinal Paul Emile Léger of Montreal, "Everything that was done [in the preparatory stages of the Council] was badly done." A French theologian said he felt this happened "because the Pope was too humble." As it turned out, John was merely biding his time, practising that high art of the possible called politics, waiting for the right moment to assert himself.

But very little of this was apparent then. Only under the later fire of the Council did observers realize there was something wrong with the whole curalist approach, so much so that a journalistic veteran of Rome, Monsignor James Tucek, could write, "There were two factors in the First Vatican Council, it should be noted also, which prevented it from accomplishing more in its four sessions. One was the great length of the debates on the issue of infallibility. The other was the drastic rewriting which the Council Fathers made of the projects submitted. No such problems are expected to stall the progress of the Second Vatican Council. Though there may be debates on some issues, there is none anticipated which would involve a protracted discussion. A clear attempt has been made to forestall the wholesale rewriting of the projects submitted. This has been done by inviting comment and suggestions from all of the bishops, instead of from a select few as was done in the previous council. A more representative and international body has likewise been engaged in drawing up the projects and preparing them in their final form."

As later conciliar criticism demonstrated, this Council's preparatory commissions may have been more international than the last, but the mentality was the same. The Curia was still in charge.

Progressive circles in the Catholic world, therefore, which were privy to some of the Curialists' tenacious and successful activity in Rome during these days, despaired of any great, important conciliar action. In Belgium, it was felt, the Curia was "too strong." The Dutch, enraged by the withdrawal of their bishops' pastoral in Italy, began to express themselves with some violence over the state of affairs. A Jesuit in Haarlem said publicly that the Holy Office was "an instrument of spiritual terror." In Austria Cardinal Koenig, who had done so much to awaken interest in the Council by his contacts with the laity, became ill, and Catholics there felt there was no one who could speak for them with the same force and eloquence. People in the United States, including their bishops, seemed rather indifferent. Many English Catholics felt their bishops would only obstruct the *aggiornamento*. Bishops from South America, Africa, and Asia made their plans for Rome with misgivings; they felt woefully unprepared. Cardinal Gracias said he expected "no smooth sailing. There will," he said, "be opposition: personal, national, diabolical."

The Pope himself added to the uneasiness when he told a public audience at Castel Gandolfo that he wanted to canonize Pope Pius IX sometime during the Council. Christopher Hollis remarked that canonizing Pio Nono "could only be a joke, but a joke in the most execrable taste." Father Gregory Baum said John "seemed to be smiling in two directions." *Osservatore Romano* continued to extol the Council in the most triumphant terms. "NEW SPLENDOUR OF THE FAITH IN PROSPECT," it headlined on August 4, 1962, and gave two reasons why: (1) it would "reflect above all light of Vatican I," and (2) it had been preceded by "the most extraordinary preparation." *Osservatore* even quoted John XXIII: "Never in the history of the councils have there been such preliminary labours, never so vast, never so accurate, never so fundamental." Knowing the history of the councils, historian Roncalli knew how little this meant.

But Catholic liberals chose to interpret the statement as an expression of papal satisfaction with the Council's preparations.

Karl Rahner wrote in the German monthly *Stimmen der Zeit* that there was no reason to expect too much from the Council. He pointed out that the Council was not simply the representation of the entire Church, that the total nature of the Church is not contained in its hierarchical structnre, that the essence of the Church included the charismatic, the non-institutional, the prophetic. "God has not renounced his Church in favour of the hierarchy," said Rahner.

But then came signs that things might begin to turn. Cardinal Alfrink told his Dutch Catholics to take heart and warned against premature defeatism. Cardinal Bea discussed prospects with me in Rome and seemed quietly confident that "the *Latini*" would not take over the Council. And the United States bishops themselves (though they had not contributed notably to the preparatory stages of the Council) drafted a joint pastoral in which they affirmed they were going to Rome "not to give hasty answers . . . or mere routine approval . . . but to deliberate unhurriedly, to express their mature judgment." For them, this would not be a rubber-stamp Council. The first session proved that perfectly, and, towards the end of the session, they were to demonstrate their own particular usefulness to a council that called on the talents of many.

Finally Pope John began to make his move. In the first week of September, he had the rules of the Council published: the Council would give ample opportunity for the expression of all shades of opinion. In a separate communiqué, moreover, he announced the names of a ten-man council presidency that balanced progressives and conservatives. Tisserant, Liénart, Frings, Alfrink and Gilroy. Tappouni, Pla y Deniel, Caggiano, Ruffini and Spellman. Spellman would later emerge as an independent. John also set up a Secretariat for Extraordinary Affairs under his trusted lieutenant Cardinal Amleto Cicognani. Only one conservative —Cardinal Siri of Genoa—made that list. The others ranged from middle-roading Cardinal Confalonieri to moderate

Cardinal Montini to progressive Cardinals Meyer of Chicago, Doepfner of Munich, and Suenens of Malines-Brussels.

This done, John returned to the theme of his first inspiration—a Council that would not be merely an internal affair, but something of a much grander vision. On September 9, he sat up most of the night drafting a special radio message to the world, and two nights later revealed a breadth of view which, taken on its face, spelled the end of that old Augustinian view of the world as an evil thing to be kept apart.

Excerpts from that radio message:

The world indeed has need of Christ, and it is the Church which must bring Christ to the world. The world has its problems and it is with anguish at times that it seeks a solution. Man seeks the love of a family around the domestic hearth. He seeks daily bread for himself and for his dear ones, his wife and his children, he aspires towards peace and feels the duty to live in peace within his own nation and with the rest of the world. He is aware of the attractions of the spirit which lead him to educate and raise himself. Jealous of his liberty, he does not refuse to accept its legitimate limitations in order the better to correspond with his social duties.

These most grave problems press ever upon the heart of the Church. Hence it has made them an object of attentive study and the Ecumenical Council will be able to present, in clear language, solutions which are demanded by the dignity of man and of his vocation as a Christian. Where underdeveloped countries are concerned, the Church presents itself as it is, and wishes to be—as the Church of all and especially as the Church of the poor. The duty of every man, the impelling duty of the Christian, is to look upon what is superfluous in the light of the needs of others, and to see to it that the administration and distribution of created goods are placed at the advantage of all.

This is the social and community sense which is innate in true Christianity and all this is to be energetically put into action. We are living in the midst of a new political world.

The Ecumenical Council is about to assemble, seventeen years after the end of the Second World War. For the first time in history the Fathers of the Council belong in reality to all peoples and nations, and each of them will bring his contribution of intelligence and experience, to cure and heal the wounds of the two conflicts, which have changed profoundly the face of all countries.

The mothers and fathers of families detest war. The Church, mother of all without distinction, will raise once more that plea which rises from the depth of the ages and from Bethlehem and from Calvary in a prayer for peace, a peace that prevents armed conflicts, a peace that should have its roots and its guarantees in the heart of every man. The bishops, pastors of Christ's flock from every nation under heaven, will recall the concept of peace not only in its negative aspect, which is detestation of armed conflicts, but even more in its positive demands which require from every man a knowledge and constant practice of his own duties: spiritual values, possession and use of the powers of nature and science directed to elevating the standard of the spiritual and economic welfare of all nations.

The Council desires to exalt in a holier and more solemn form the deeper application of fellowship and love which are natural needs of man and imposed on the Christian as rules for his relationship between man and man, between people and people. Oh, the mystery of divine providence, by which the imminent celebration of the Second Vatican Ecumenical Council once again uncovers the duty of service, a duty which embraces the destiny of all humanity. Oh, the beauty of that prayer in the liturgy, "grant your Christian people peace and unity." Oh, the overflowing joy of the heart on reading the 17th chapter of St John, "that all may be one." One in thought, in word, in work.

On September 27, 1962, I attended a gathering of the Vatican family of cardinals, monsignors, priests, technicians, gardeners and a handful of nuns. They buzzed happily in the Hall of Benedictions and then broke into cheers and applause when the Pope came walking in. John appeared at his best, smiling warmly to right and left as he bounced up to the front of the hall. He settled on a large red throne and flexed his red-slippered feet nervously while Archbishop Pietro Parente, assessor of the Holy Office and right-hand man of Cardinal Ottaviani, paid a homage in the name of all ("I don't know why they chose me to do this") on the eve of the Second Vatican Ecumenical Council. A little breathlessly, John launched into an intimate discourse (he used the "I" form instead of the "we" dictated by ancient usage) and quietly asked his "family" to "live the Council" during the coming days and to pray for it. He also asked them to pray now for an important special intention.

He intended the prayers, I suspect, to shoot up to heaven (John always thought of heaven as "up there," judging from his gestures) and bounce back down to Moscow where, right at that minute, they were desperately needed.

For it was precisely then that Monsignor Jan Willebrands, secretary of the Secretariat for Promoting Christian Unity, was preparing to climb aboard Czechoslovakian Airlines Flight Number 502 heading for Sheremetievo Airport in Moscow. His mission: to talk to the top members of the Moscow Patriarchate, persuade them that John XXIII would like them, as representatives of some forty million Orthodox, to attend his Council where, said Willebrands, they would discover that John's *politique* was not that of Pius. Rome would be friends with Moscow.

Chapter Five

DOWN THE SLIPS

I

FROM every continent they came, from 133 nations, and as they arrived at Rome's Leonardo da Vinci Airport or the Stazione Termini, or the ports of Naples and Genoa, their very presence cried witness to a Church that was in the world as never before.

There was Paul Etoga, a husky native bishop of Mbalmayo in the Cameroons, who had just scraped together enough money to take a boat to Le Havre, hitch-hike to Paris and squeeze into a second-class railway carriage for Rome. There was Minnesota-born Harold Henry, whose missionary order of Columban Fathers had sent him to Korea 29 years ago where he had lived through two wars and become the first Archbishop of Kwang Ju. There was the visionary Jesuit T. D. Roberts, who, foreseeing Indian independence, had renounced clerical colonialism and left his See of Bombay in 1944 to write and lecture (usually on the abuse of authority in the Church).

They came singly and they came in blocs. Ninety-three bishops from Indonesia, Japan and the Philippines, mostly brown and bearded, chased the sun halfway around the globe in a jet, full of uncertainties about the Council—like many more of the 800 other missionary bishops from other parts of Asia, Africa and South America—or their future in it. Eighty-four Indian bishops left a land glowing in rosy neutralism, hardly thinking they would return to a land of war. African bishops, 296 of them, arrived weary and tired after their droning flights up from the long Dark Continent, feeling somewhat shaken by the suddenness of their transport from the bush into ancient Rome. One of them, Bishop Joseph Busimba of the Congo, checked into Fiumicino's customs office with three elephant tusks as a gift for the Pope. Another, Archbishop Aston Chichester, who had been in Rhodesia for many of his eighty-four years, wandered around the Jesuit Curia and listened to talk that only confused him: "Just who *is* this bloke Ottavi . . . Ottaviani?" he demanded.

They poured into the hurly-burly of the Vatican's reception centre on Via della Conciliazione. The Maronites from Tyre and Tripoli, Baalbek, Nisibis, Cairo and Cyprus, led by His Holiness the Patriarch Meouchi of Antioch, proud of their 700 years' resistance to the Turks and Arabs. The Melchites from Aleppo, Antioch, Jerusalem and Laodicea, led by the fiery Maximos IV Saigh, claiming to be the sole representative of the Eastern Church and ready to fight for the ancient ways of the East in a Church he felt was too romanized. And the bearded bishops of other ancient rites: the Syro-Malabars, the Malankars, the Copts, the Byzantines, the Chaldeans, the Armenians.

The European bishops flocked in, more at home than the missionaries. The thirty-three bishops from Catholic Ireland and the ninety-five from Most Catholic Spain, the Spanish feeling themselves on the brink of the future, the Irish full of misty memories of their part in the fight for infallibility at the First Vatican Council; both Irish and Spanish suspicious of the alien theologies of the French and the Germans. The forty-two bishops from England and Wales and the twenty-seven from Portugal, equally insular, equally hoping for an early end to an unnecessary Council. The sixty-eight Germans, nervously fearing themselves too far in front with their projects, the 159 French determined not to push their programme too hard, content to sit back and play a waiting game.

Some 217 United States bishops flew in by jet or sailed over on leisurely Italian liners, each of them accompanied by two or three clerical buddies (whom they called "theologians") and checked into the poshest Via Veneto hostelries like the Excelsior, the Flora, the Eden, the Majestic, the Boston. With scant regard for this nudge to the local economy, one Rome newspaper cracked,"The American bishops are consecrating the Via Veneto." (It is true that they brought a clerical tone to the racy Veneto and added some innocently racy stories to those told in the sidewalk cafés.

One of them concerned an ecumenically-minded bishop who, burdened with all kinds of ceremonial garb in his luggage, checked into a British hotel for a meeting with Anglican clergymen. Late that evening, when he returned to his hotel, he found himself in a double room with his pyjamas laid neatly on one bed and on the other—his lace rochets. Another story had it that a German priest had placed an ad in a newspaper for a housekeeper, "with marriage not excluded after the Council."

In a sense, the United States contingent (roughing it in Rome, after the wall-to-wall comforts of affluent America) illustrated in the concrete how much the Church's power structure had shifted in ninety-two years since the last Ecumenical Council. At that time, the United States group numbered forty-eight bishops and one abbot and represented no more than a struggling missionary Church while the Italian bishops, 285 strong, could impose their special siege mentality on the Church of the rebellious nineteenth century. Because of that mentality, some say, the Church never bothered to enter into the twentieth century—or did so only to judge and condemn it.

II

Some great changes, however, had overtaken the world since Vatican I. In 1962 Pope John felt that the Church did not need a Cassandra crying alarm, but only the presence of grace. In his whole approach, John had (without specifically saying so) rejected the entire *politique* of his predecessor and dared to act as if the Communist world too must fit into the plan of redemption.

Left-wing papers attempted to say the best things they could about Pope John's *aggiornamento*. The right-wing press, for its part, muttered about the "dangers of the Council" and even scorned Pope John for praying publicly "for the same Russian cosmonauts who said they did not see God in space." The neo-Fascist weekly *Il Borghese* stated flatly that "the Council should not have been held at all" and pointed out that "John XXIII, with the help of Cardinal Bea, has succeeded in shaking hands with Protestants and Orthodox and even gained the goodwill of the

Moslems, but has not established concord in the Church of Peter."
The editor, Mario Tedeschi, also wondered just how John would
explain the conciliar absence of the Church of Silence.

Thus, when bishops from Iron Curtain countries, too, began
trickling into rainy Rome in the second week of October, Pope
John began to smile. In a way, it looked as if his *politique* had
broken down walls where that of Pius had only built them higher.
On Monday, Cardinal Stefan Wyszynski, accompanied by thirteen Polish bishops, arrived at the papal chambers a half hour
ahead of schedule, and John, informed immediately, hurried
through his audience with the Cardinal Archbishop of Buenos
Aires, had Wyszynski shown into his library and hugged him
hard. Tuesday, the Pope singled out three Yugoslavian bishops
and two Hungarians from the troops of bishops now crowding
into Rome and gave only them an audience. On Wednesday,
he literally laughed for joy when Vatican officials told him about
the arrival of three Czech bishops and Petras Mazelis, Apostolic
Administrator of Telsiai, Lithuania.

It was clear that something was happening inside the Communist world and that the Communist governments had reacted
enough to John's simple unbelligerent approach to let some
bishops come to Rome for the Council. Could these bishops be the
doves of peace? Could those be olive branches they were bearing
from their homes across the dark red sea? Finally on Thursday,
John received a final joyful confirmation that in its long voyage to
world peace, the barque that eventually would have to sail
through many a rocky channel had succeeded at least in getting
down the runway. He got a telegram from Moscow stating that
the Patriarchate of Moscow was accepting his kind invitation and
was sending two official delegate-observers to his Council.

III

The sun burst through the clouds early Thursday morning,
October 11, and contributed to the general joy of this historic
occasion. St Peter's Square, washed by days of rain, sparkled
brilliantly. Rome was in a holiday mood—obligingly proclaimed

for all by Italy's President Segni. Many a tourist, too, crowded into the square for the historic event—but some of them could not help thinking it just a bit ridiculous that the Council, which John XXIII had called "to rediscover the lines of the Church's more fervent youth," would commence with such a baroque ceremony.

Some 2,381 Council Fathers, in golden mitres and golden piviales, marched out of the papal palace's bronze doors in rows of sixes, swung right across St Peter's Square, then right again up the *scala regia* and into the basilica. From high atop the Bernini colonnade, this all seemed like a fine bit of choreography, something that Cecil B. De Mille could have staged. As a matter of fact, an Italian government-owned film company had thirty cameras poised in and around St Peter's to shoot the show in colour.

When at last the Pope appeared at the end of the procession, he was carried undulantly along on the *sedia gestatoria* by nobles in outrageous red knickers and capes, surrounded by half a hundred young men in blue and orange bloomers, iron breastplates and lace ruffles, and a score of other cartoon characters out of O. Soglow. Some of these hoisted long poles supporting a sort of awning, and two of them flanked the *sedia* with full ostrich feather fans: sobering symbol of the ties binding even a pope with a new vision to the traditions and ancient usages of the past. (Possibly there was a reason for all this. Someone suggested that the curial ceremonialists feared that a more simple appearance of the Pope among his bishops might destroy his primacy. But then, this seemed a little absurd.)

Inside the basilica, however, when the bishops arrived in their seats and looked for the Pope, they discovered he had dismounted at the doors and proceeded on foot up the aisle. To the frustration of chief rubricist Archbishop Enrico Dante, that was not the only change John made. He modified the ceremony of obeisance. He ordered the Gospel sung in Arabic and Old Slavonic as well as in Latin and Greek. He vetoed the placement of the pontifical throne on a spot five feet above the sanctuary floor, and ordered instead a simple brocade chair put on the highest level of the Bernini altar "so everyone can see a little better."

As John made his way up the aisle, some observant bishops saw John look painfully to his right at a bronze statue of Peter the Fisherman, rigged in the same kind of pontifical robes he was wearing and topped by a bejewelled triple crown. The Great Fisherman. John left his own triple crown reposing untouched on the altar during the entire ceremony.

As celebrated by Cardinal Eugène Tisserant according to the Roman rubrics, the Council Mass was a long, tiring rite. But the Pope and the Council Fathers took orders well and followed everything with what appeared to be pious recollection. Behind the altar, however, and in each apse, a couple of thousand spectators played out a comic role. A tribune (or reviewing stand) had been set up behind the altar for the journalists, but somehow a band of local gentry had managed to crowd in, first to boggle, then to chatter, then at the most solemn moment of the Mass, the Consecration, to shout imprecations at an usher who had chosen precisely this moment to hand out souvenir pamphlets of the occasion.

Priests and seminarians from around the city wound up standing like so many cattle in the space below the press tribune. Most of them seemed to ignore the Mass, preferred to renew old acquaintances, chatter about their professors, or snap pictures of the crowd. Some retired to corners of the apse to read their daily Office.

After the Mass, the cardinals and patriarchs (in that order) filed before the papal throne and kissed the Pope's ring in an act of obeisance. John spoke a friendly word to most of them. He could say nothing to the Melchite Patriarch of Antioch, Maximos IV Saigh—because Maximos stayed away from this session in protest against the order of precedence, since, he maintained, patriarchs have rights that were established long before cardinals came to be. In the name of their watching colleagues, two archbishops and two bishops carried out the same act of homage, kissing the Pope's right knee; and two robed representatives of the Dominican and Franciscan orders knelt before John and kissed his slipper.

John read an ancient profession of faith that is made before any great gathering of the Church. "I John, Bishop of the Catholic Church . . ." and every Council Father echoed his response.

The Secretary-General carried an ornate fifteenth-century book of the Gospel to the altar, opened it to the 1st chapter of St John and the Church's 21st General Council began.

IV

When the time came for John to deliver his opening discourse, he flexed his red and white silken slippers somewhat nervously and glanced at the delegate-observers to his right and to his left. The observers had originally been assigned seats in a tribune to the Pope's right, but John decided to move them closer to the altar and himself by having special chairs set up for them on the sanctuary floor—which brought them down to the level of the last remnants of European nobility that had managed to come to the Council.

Past councils were councils of exclusion, effectively setting aside those who would not submit to the Church's authority. This Council was obviously different. Two months before, a French theologian predicted: "When those thirty or forty or fifty observers show up at the Council, they'll have a role that will be psychologically more important than the rest of the Fathers put together."

As John began to talk, it became clear how well that prediction was borne out. After his introductory remarks, the Pope outlined the Church's new orientation, not a defensive one at all, but one that would "look to the future without fear." Optimism was the keynote.

"In the daily exercise of our pastoral office," said John, "we sometimes have to listen, much to our regret, to voices of persons, who though burning with zeal, are not endowed with much sense of discretion or measure. In these modern times, they can see nothing but prevarication and ruin. They say that our era, in comparison with past eras, is getting worse. And they behave as though they had learned nothing from history, which is nonetheless the teacher of life, and as if at the times of other councils, everything was a full triumph for the Christian idea and for proper religious liberty.

"We feel," said John, "that we must disagree with those prophets of gloom, who are always forecasting disaster as though the end of the world were at hand." Some Council Fathers could not help but glance over at the face of Cardinal Ottaviani who was sitting impassively on the Pope's right. If a vote had been taken then and there among the bishops, Ottaviani probably would have won the title as the Church's Number-One Prophet of Gloom, and he is certainly one of the few persons in the world who had daily access to the Pope.

Considering his usual circumspection (and his usual circumlocutions), John could not have been more direct. "In the present order of things," he continued, "Divine Providence is leading us to a new order of human relations, which by men's own efforts, even beyond their very expectations, are directed towards the fulfilment of God's superior and inscrutable designs. Everything, even human differences, leads to the greater good of the Church." In this he was referring quite clearly to "the new political world" of which he had spoken in his radio message of September 11, a world that had waved a fearless good-bye to the Constantinian era. As far as the Church today is concerned, John said, it need not ally itself with the State. "It suffices to leaf even cursorily through the pages of ecclesiastical history to note clearly how ecumenical councils themselves . . . were often celebrated to the accompaniment of most serious difficulties and sufferings, because of the undue interference of civil authorities. The princes of this world, indeed, sometimes in all sincerity, intended thus to protect the Church. But more frequently this occurred not without spiritual damage and danger since their interest in this was guided by the views of a selfish and perilous policy."

Having answered his critics from the political right, John turned to outline what he expected of this Council. "The Church," he said, "should never depart from the sacred patrimony of truth received from the Fathers, but at the same time, she must ever look to the present, to new conditions and new forms of life introduced into the modern world, which have opened avenues to the

Catholic apostolate." But he added quickly, "Our duty is not only to guard this precious treasure (as if we were concerned only with antiquity), but to dedicate ourselves with an earnest will and without fear to that work which our era demands of us.

"The salient point of this Council is not, therefore, a discussion of one article or another of the fundamental doctrine of the Church which has repeatedly been taught by the Fathers and the ancient and modern theologians and which is presumed to be well known and familiar to all. For this a Council was not necessary. But . . . the Christian, Catholic and Apostolic spirit of the whole world expects a step forward towards a deeper penetration and a developing realization of the faith in perfect conformity to the authentic doctrine, which should be studied and expounded through modern research and modern scholarly disciplines." Then John dared to utter something which no progressive theologian would have formerly ventured in mixed company: "The substance of the ancient doctrine of the deposit of faith is one thing. They way in which it is presented is another." In so speaking, John firmly allied himself with those scholars seeking to make the Christian Message more relevant today, and firmly against those who look upon the faith as a polished pearl given to the Church to preserve intact for all time. Said the French daily *Paris-Press*, "We had expected a traditional message of welcome. Instead, John XXIII was determined to give an historical discourse. We knew about his liberalism. But today he affirmed it with a singular determination. There is no doubt that his discourse will go right to the heart of the Catholic world. But it is also certain to arouse agitation in some quarters."

John had further advice for the modern Cassandras in his own cabinet, always so ready to condemn. "Often errors vanish as quickly as they arise, like fog before the sun. The Church has always opposed these errors. Frequently she has condemned them with the greatest severity. Nowadays, however, the spouse of Christ prefers to make use of the medicine of mercy rather than that of severity. She considers that she meets the needs of the present day by demonstrating the validity of her teaching rather than by condemnations. Not, certainly, that there is a lack of fallacious teachings, opinions and dangerous concepts . . . but they are so evidently in contrast with the right norm of honesty and have produced such lethal fruits, that by now it would seem that men of themselves are inclined to condemn them, particularly those ways of life which despise God and his law." John made it clear he included all forms of totalitarianism in this category of self-evident errors. "Even more important, experience has taught men that violence inflicted on others, the might of arms and political domination, are of no help at all in finding a happy solution to the grave problems which afflict them."

The solution, John insisted, is not any union of Church and State or a return to the papal meddling in the political life of nations, but a christifying action in the world through Christians working in society. Through them, the Church can say "to the human race, oppressed by so many difficulties, as Peter said to the poor man begging his help, 'Silver and gold I have none; but what I have I give thee: In the name of Jesus Christ of Nazareth, arise, and walk.' "

John went on to outline his hopes for Christian unity, which he called "a great mystery Jesus Christ petitioned with fervent prayer from his heavenly Father on the eve of his sacrifice." John pointed out that Christ's prayer for unity at the Last Supper was a prayer for all mankind, and that, somehow, the Council, "while bringing together the Church's best energies and striving to have men welcome more favourably the good tidings of salvation, prepares and consolidates the path towards the unity of mankind."

The plain fact of the matter is that neither Pope John nor his most acute advisers could have seen, in the autumn of 1962, just what the ecumenical movement would bring about. But they did not feel particularly worried about this lack of clear goals. As one member of Cardinal Bea's Secretariat put it, "Maybe after one hundred years of living together ecumenically, the problem of unity will pose itself in different terms."

For John this was enough. Enough for the intuitive mind to see only the ultimate goal (the unity of mankind) and the first practical human step needed to reach that goal (making the Good News of salvation more welcome). The second and third and subsequent steps? Time, it would seem, would tell what those steps could be. In the meantime, at least, John and his assembled bishops would concentrate on doing what they could to move the Church *un balzo in avanti*—a leap forward. For him, it was clear to many progressive minds, the Council was to be conciliatory, reformist, creative.

But Cardinal Giuseppe Siri of Genoa, who had come to the Council, along with many other Italian bishops, completely equipped to solve all the problems of the Counter Reformation, offered his own exegesis of Pope John's opening discourse. Interviewed in the Italian weekly *Orizzonti*, Siri said he preferred the judgment of *Osservatore Romano* to that of Pope John when it came to pointing a way to this Council. "One shouldn't forget," said Siri, "that the first task entrusted to the Church of Our Lord is that of teaching the truth. Without this, it is impossible to please God. This hierarchical order of things, divinely established, will also remain, I hold, in this Council. . . . The pastoral sense does not consist in distributing caresses, smiles and acts of condescension anywhere and everywhere. . . . It is absolutely false to say that a pastoral concern can characterize this Council if it implies that other councils did not have the same holy duty."

Siri, at least, gave fair public warning of the stance he would take on the bridge of Peter's barque.

That night, 500,000 persons, by estimate of the Roman police, jammed into St Peter's square for a torchlight demonstration of their abiding trust in the Pope God had given them. If John was having any doubts about his turning the Church outward (some advisers had been telling him for months that revisionist approaches to Catholic doctrine, even its formulations, would disturb the simple faith of the masses), they may well have been dispelled by the presence of that mob. "Dear children, dear children," cried the Pope. "I hear your voices. My voice is an isolated one, but it echoes the voice of the whole world. Here, in effect, the whole world is represented." John was clearly overcome by the crowd, their shouts, their torches, the light of a rose-coloured moon which, he pointed out, was "also contemplating this spectacle."

But he did have the presence of mind to remind everyone that they were united not by the mere formulations of philosophers and jurists, but by Christ himself. "The glow and the sweetness of the Lord take hold of us and unite us." Christ, clearly, was the source of John's optimism. His love was enough.

V

On the next day, having delivered himself of his revolutionary discourse opening the Council, John could reasonably have been expected to let things ride for a while, but he held two more historic meetings, one with the representatives of 79 nations (including the United States Ambassador, G. Frederick Reinhardt) and seven international organizations, and another with the delegate-observers to the Council. In both of them he offered more explanations of what course the Council would take.

Surrounded by the overwhelming rainbow of colour in the Sistine Chapel, John addressed the representatives of the nations who sat three abreast in four rows. "The Council is for the Catholic Church," he began. "It is concerned with the adaptation of its methods so that the teaching of the Gospel may be lived worthily and more readily assimilated by the people. It endeavours also to prepare the way for the coming together of so many brethren seeking after unity. But the Council . . . apart from its religious significance, has also a social aspect which concerns the life of nations."

John then proceeded to explain how the Council could contribute to world peace, "a peace directed to the increasing of respect for the human person and to the procuring of a just freedom of religion and worship, a peace which nourishes harmony between nations." John looked up and added: "And there is no reason why this should not exist, even if it calls for some sacrifice on their part." The Council's task, said John, would be "to make clear to the world the teaching of Christ the Prince of Peace." The natural consequences of this would be "love for one another, brotherhood, and the end of strife between men of different races and of different mentalities. The help which the developing nations need so urgently could thus more quickly be provided to assist them in the search for their true well-being without any attempt to gain power over them." John raised his eyes for a moment from the text. "It is time that something decisive was done. . . . For men *are* brothers and, we say it from a full heart, all sons of the same Father." And then, though the Pope's Curia had done nothing to prepare the Council for any such basic considerations as war and peace, John added: "The Council will certainly help to prepare this new climate and to remove the danger of war, that scourge of nations, which today would mean the destruction of humanity."

At this point, John's voice became more vibrant. "Excellencies, there is here before us in the Sistine Chapel Michelangelo's vast masterpiece of the Last Judgment. The seriousness of it gives one much food for thought. We must indeed render an account to God, we and all the heads of State who bear responsibility for the fate of nations. Let them give ear to the anguished cry of 'peace, peace' which rises up to heaven from every part of the world, from innocent children and those grown old, from individuals and from communities. May this thought of the reckoning that they are to face spur them on to omit no effort to achieve this blessing, which for the human family is a blessing greater than any other."

Since the Italian patriots brought on the suspension of the First Vatican Council in 1870, the Church as an institution had withdrawn from the world. Pope Pius IX had even decreed that any Catholics who dared to participate in the government be excommunicated. Now, as a pope with quite another vision looked out over the representatives of practically all the great nations on earth—many of them good Catholics who had taken an honoured place in their countries' public life—he made an ingenuous plea. "Let the nations continue to meet each other in discussion and reach just and generous agreements that they faithfully observe. Let them be ready to make the sacrifices that are necessary to save the world's peace. The nations will then be able to work in an atmosphere of serenity. All the discoveries of science will assist progress and help to make life on this earth, which is already marked by so many other inevitable sufferings, ever more delightful."

This optimistic view of the world, said John, could not help but answer "the anguished problems of our day," could not help but achieve "true progress of individuals and of whole nations."

VI

One way of measuring John's stature and of understanding his world picture is to contemplate Pius XII. The story goes that a newly-appointed bishop came to Pope John once and told him he felt it impossibly hard to follow his predecessor, an overwhelming personality. He reported that the Pope told him, "Do the same thing I do. I try to imagine what *my* predecessor would have done and then I do just the opposite." Whether this story is true or not, it does help to measure John's approach by comparing him with Pius XII.

Pius XII was a traditionalist, an aristocrat, a Roman, a man whose ecclesiology was founded on the old Augustinian dualism. In his final years, as he stood at the end of an era, he had more disillusionments than consolations. The world was split into two irreconcilable blocs. His efforts to foster biblical and theological research had provoked what he thought was a rebellion against authority, and in 1949 he felt compelled to write an encyclical called *Humani Generis* that brought that research to a demoralizing halt. Towards the end, when he was too ill to govern the Church singlehandedly, he saw the final proof that his ecclesiological thought as expressed in *Mystici Corporis Christi* was inadequate to meet the exigencies of a new world, a world of increasing tensions.

Side by side with his disillusionment went an ignorance of the new dimensions of the one internationalized world. He knew it existed, of course. He even wrote about it. But he could not break away from the old duality. He saw European unity as a bulwark against the East. He saw continued Demochristian political power in Italy as the only viable position for the Church in Italy. He took for granted the fission of the world into two blocs: it had been that way in Augustine's time, it was like that in the time of Innocent III. It was like that at the Reformation and again in 1870. It would always be like that.

In rare moments of vision—forced on him by events of horrendous or world-shaking character (the impact of the first series of thermonuclear explosions, the taking over of China in one big bite by Mao Tse-tung, the continual laicization of the Church in the emerging countries of Africa and Asia)—he did perceive vaguely the outlines of a fresh order and felt the very foundations of the world moving under him. On these occasions he fell back on a *mystique* of providence and invoked the vision of the Church passing through a new Calvary to a fresh Resurrection where her pristine beauty would once more be manifest to the eyes of disillusioned men as they raised their hands to heaven and called for deliverance. But this would be the result of humanly contrived cataclysm, not of a fresh historical evolution.

If Pius XII had succeeded in calling an Ecumenical Council (and he wanted to until he was dissuaded by his advisers), the result might well have been catastrophic. Pius would have wanted to reform the Curia and still keep it Roman. He would have wished to extend a hand to the separated brethren, and yet his concept of the Church would have repelled them. He would have wished to modify the Church's attitude towards science and thereby keep the intellectual laity of Europe within the fold, but he never could have sanctioned the exuberant activity of theologians like Hans Küng, Karl Rahner, Yves Congar, Henri de Lubac, and others, and would have thereby muzzled the only men who could inspire the dialogue so necessary to the age. In other words, Pius XII's Council would have failed.

John XXIII was no Roman, no aristocrat, no intellectual. He was a peasant by origin, gentle, patient and intuitive. He had no formulated theories or prefabricated geopolitics or hereditary class consciousness. He set about his work gently, *piano, piano*, manoeuvring with the intuitive craft of the peasant. He will be the despair of any conventional biographer, since intuitions are not traceable. In this sense he was God's joke on the Curialists who lived in a two-dimensional universe, could not perceive a new social and cultural and political world aborning, who could not see in the papal candidate Roncalli the foreshadowing of their own downfall. All they saw was a run-of-the-mill career man with no intellectual pretensions or political commitments. He could be counted on to continue with the *status* precisely *quo*, to remain the head of a Roman organization, isolated within a juridical framework, hemmed in by a network of traditionalism that tended to make him, the Vicar of Christ in the twentieth century, a quasi-king, cribbed, cabined and confined in Italy, ensconced on a throne, encased in silk from head to toe, flattered and kissed by crowds of courtiers.

But John took over and expressed himself not in words but in action. Instead of proposing dogmatic formulations on the collegiality of bishops, he called them together in Council where forces he recognized would bring on more democratic ways. Instead of drafting a document reforming the Curia, he let the full force of European intellectualism and American practicality play painfully on the Curia. Instead of writing letters to Protestants and Orthodox to return to the fold, he invited his "brothers in Christ" to the Council so they could witness the long-hidden vitality of the Roman Church. Instead of calling on the West to abandon the hard line towards Russia, he brought Russian observers to the Council (on their own conditions) and made sure the Council would exclude any irritating references to the Church of Silence or Soviet atheism. Instead of issuing a document defining the place of "the others" in the Mystical Body, he authorized Cardinal Bea to pray with Moslems, Hindus, Buddhists, Confucianists, Shintoists, Anglicans, Lutherans and the rest in an *agape*. Instead of producing a paper on the rights and duties of Christians in Catholic Italy, he tacitly blessed the *apertura a sinistra* with cunning innocence: "*Sono tutti i miei figlioli, non è vero?*" "They're all my children, aren't they?"

VII

At two modest Roman *pensioni*, delegate-observers from seventeen different Christian bodies were buzzing over the swirl of events. There is a little bit of the tourist in everyone, and the delegate-observers were no exception. They, particularly, were in a fine position to observe what many of them were sure would be long considered one of the events of the century. Since their arrival, the observers were treated as the most privileged characters in a city full of persons who had, at home, been accustomed to the heights of episcopal privilege and deference. Many of them had been met at the airport by Cardinal Bea's right-hand man, Jan Willebrands. Almost all of them were established in one or other of two *pensioni* close to the Vatican, and all were told John would pay the bills. All were given directions by special guides and interpreters from the Bea Secretariat, theologians like the American Jesuit Gustave Weigel, the Belgian Dominican Jerome Hamer, the French Dominican Christopher Dumont. All were established in the best seats for the October 11 opening and promised access to the daily Council Meetings (which excluded everyone but Council Fathers and 201 consulting theologians). They were also given copies of the supersecret *schemata* to be considered by the Council Fathers.

"When I first heard they had the *schemata*," said one American theologian, "I almost fell over." The observers, of course, were pleased at this move (most of them could read the Latin in which the *schemata* were couched), but one of them, Canon Bernard C. Pawley, a special guest of the Secretariat from the Archbishop of Canterbury, merely commented matter-of-factly, "If we didn't have the *schemata* how could we really understand what's going on here?"

The observers and almost everyone else in Rome were also agog over the arrival in the city of the two representatives from the Moscow Patriarchate. At three o'clock on Friday, October 12, reporters gathered at Fiumicino Airport to meet the delegates. First man off the plane was the Archpriest Vitali Borovoi, 46, and behind him came the Archimandrite Vladimir Kotliarov, 32. Both wore black cassocks and the high round Byzantine hat, both wore beards and golden pectoral crosses, both wore inscrutable smiles. Borovoi had been serving as the permanent delegate of the Moscow Patriarchate to the World Council of Churches in

Geneva, and Kotliarov as the vice-chief of the Patriarchate to Jerusalem. Both men were in New Delhi for the World Council meeting in November of 1961 and in Paris for the World Council's executive meeting in August, 1962. When reporters approached them at the airport, they stopped good-naturedly, but explained that they spoke only Russian and a little English, and told reporters only the obvious. "We're here," they said, "to follow the work of the Ecumenical Council." Tight-lipped Jan Willebrands, there to meet them, said the usual. Nothing.

Reactions to this news came quickly from every quarter, Communist, anti-Communist, right, left, centre, Catholic and Orthodox.

In Athens, Archbishop Chrysostomos called the action "a grave blow to Orthodox unity." A fundamentalist paper in Spain remarked that "a Council directed by the Holy Spirit is surely not the place for two committed members of a religious communion which is allied to godless Marxism." An Irish wit cracked in his weekly column, "to integralists, traditionalists and all diehards, the Council is becoming like a Papini nightmare in which Old Nick appears in clean spats and carrying a Missal." A spokesman for the Maronites in Beirut sniffed, "This is the proof of the obvious. Orthodoxy is split down the middle and it sets the Byzantinophiles into proper perspective."

On the morning the Russian observers arrived, I entered the bustling press office on Via della Conciliazione and there encountered one of the world's busiest anti-Communists, Dr Carl McIntyre, president of the International Council of Christian Churches, a large and powerful group of fundamentalist Churches set up to oppose modern ecumenical movements around the world and to support John Birch-type movements in both North and South America. McIntyre, who seemed proud that his instincts had brought him to Rome at this particular time, made his feeling about the Russian observers perfectly clear. "These men are the agents of Communism," said McIntyre. "Borovoi is a favourite of Nicodim and he's the man who took the place of the Soviet secret agent Nicolai," explained McIntyre darkly. "I don't know Kotliarov," he concluded, "but he has the same job in Jerusalem that Nicodim had before he went back to Moscow."

McIntyre said that his group did not want to have anything to do with the Ecumenical Council but explained his presence in Rome as a sort of one-man watch and ward society. He stayed less than a week, then left for the United States.

The Italian right-wing press saw the arrival of the Russian observers in the perspective of the centre-left government of Premier Amintore Fanfani. *Il Borghese* denounced "this complicity of Catholics in the work of Marxism, progressively destroying those divine and human, moral and civil values which in twenty centuries have formed the Christian West." *Il Borghese* editor, Mario Tedeschi, is a beautifully mustachioed young man who told me he really did not have any religion himself, but nevertheless considered "*la chiesa cattolica romana*" as the best bulwark against Communism and Socialism. He maintained close communications with Cardinal Ottaviani throughout the session.

VIII

Official cries of amazement came also from Istanbul where, just a few days before, the Synod of Constantinople had decided not to accept John's invitation to send observers to the Council. The Patriarch, His Holiness Athenagoras I, had wanted to come, in fact had often expressed his private opinions on John's hopes for unity. In March 1962 he told the Catholic news service *Kathpress* in Vienna he was willing to join a united Christian front. "That is why we wish to visit Rome, so that we may embrace each other, weep over our long separation, express our pain about the past and our happiness for the future." He then added, half jokingly, "Theologians should be locked up on an island for a few years and we should come to an agreement. The speed of world events and the recession of Christianity does not permit us to wait for their decisions."

As it turned out, however, Athenagoras was kept waiting, not for the decisions of Orthodox theologians, but for the decisions of the Orthodox Patriarchate of Moscow which was meeting with Monsignor Jan Willebrands from September 27 to October 2. During those days, the synod listened to Willebrands, to his explanation of what the Council would be, his assurances that it would undertake no anti-Communist polemics, his discussion of the role observers would play. At the end of the talks, the synod said it was all very interesting, but that it could not make any announcement then about sending observers to Rome. Did the Moscow Synod want to wait and consult with Constantinople, according to an earlier agreement? It did not. The Moscow Synod (or the Soviet government to which it is tied legally and financially) decided to play a bit of one-upmanship and underline its *de facto* precedence over the more ancient Patriarchate of Constantinople. Some forty million Orthodox owed allegiance to Moscow, while Constantinople could claim only 270,000. Clearly, here was a chance for Moscow to assert its ecclesiastical independence.

Willebrands returned to Rome on October 3 with the official answer of Moscow: "The Moscow Patriarchate does not see its way clear to announce the sending of observers to attend the first session of the Second Vatican Council." Both he and Bea understood the answer. The Russians were coming in their own good time. On October 4, Bea sent a telegram to Moscow's Archbishop Nicodim, president of the Bureau for External Church Relations: "I thank Your Eminence for the reception given to our secretary. Today we are sending an official invitation to His Holiness, the Patriarch, to send two or three observer-delegates to the Council. With spiritual respect, Cardinal Bea."

Out of courtesy, Bea sent a message to Athenagoras, the only thing he could send him: the official, carefully worded message that Willebrands had brought back to him from Moscow.

On October 7, Athenagoras sent the last in a series of telegrams to Moscow, asking what the synod's intentions were. Moscow tersely answered: "Nothing new to report." Athenagoras weighed the implications of the answer. He suspected the worst: that Moscow was sending observers without consulting Constantinople or any of the other Orthodox synods that, in their 1961 meeting in Rhodes, had agreed on Orthodox unity at all costs.

From his palace in Istanbul looking out over the Golden Horn, Athenagoras summed up the situation realistically. Maybe, he thought, it would be better to let Moscow win this battle of nerves, only one of a long series, he knew, past and future. He would lose face with his friends in the West by not sending an observer to Rome, but his own synod strongly opposed such a move, and rumours had come back to him that perhaps two-thirds of its members would attempt to depose him if he did. He also recognized with some sympathy that the moves of the Moscow Patriarchate itself were agonized actions carried on within the monolithic state and part of a struggle for the continued life of Orthodoxy within the Soviet Union.

On October 10, the Holy Synod of the Russian Orthodox Church met under the Patriarch Alexei and decided to accept the invitation, named two observers, set down rules for them in Rome (they were to report not less frequently than once a week, and send printed matter from the Council), and commissioned Archbishop Nicodim to handle reportage.

On October 11, the Council opened. On the 12th, observers arrived from Moscow. And when the news arrived in Istanbul Athenagoras sat down in his study and penned a cordial letter to Alexei in Moscow, expressing his "love and understanding."

IX

In Rome, Cardinal Bea refrained from any public expressions of delight, in view of the official Orthodox reaction. John XXIII also refrained, but no one doubted he was pleased and happy. When I talked with John XXIII in August, I learned he was hoping mightily for this breakthrough, not because he wanted to play the part of an international politician, but because he had found himself cast, all of a sudden, in the role of a father to all mankind, and he could not be content as the father of only one-sixth of humanity He did not hesitate to be photographed greeting the Russian delegates at the reception which he held in the Hall of Consistories on the evening of the 12th for all the observer-delegates. With characteristic simplicity and an eye for effect, John ordered a wooden armchair placed for him at one end of an oval of observers, referred to himself in the first person singular, and won the goodwill of many observers with what some understood to be a soft-pedaling of papal powers asserted so often by predecessors. "Insofar as it concerns my humble person," said John in French, "I would like not to claim any special inspiration. I content myself with the sound doctrine which teaches that everything comes from God." As for the observers' presence at the historic opening of the Council, John confessed, "I devoted all my attention to the immediate duty of preserving recollection, of praying and giving thanks to God. But my eye from time to time ranged over the multitude of sons and brothers, and suddenly as my glance rested upon your group, on each of you personally, I drew a special comfort from your presence."

With a figurative glance over his shoulder at the Holy Office, John continued, "I will not say more about that at the moment, but will content myself with recording the fact. Blessed be God in each day as it comes. Yet if you could read my heart, you would perhaps understand much more than words can say."

John recalled his ten years at Sofia, ten more at Istanbul and Athens, and his work in Paris. "I had frequent meetings then with Christians of many denominations," he said, "and I cannot remember any occasion on which we were ever divided on principle nor had any disagreement on the plane of charity . . . . We did not haggle. We talked together. We did not argue. We loved one another."

In August at Castel Gandolfo, I learned that John was impressed "with the need for all to come down from the throne—everyone." He expressed the same feeling to the observers: "Your welcome presence here and the motion of our priestly heart (the heart of a bishop of the Church of God, as I said yesterday before the assembled Council), the emotion of my beloved fellow workers and, I am certain of it, your own emotion, too, combine to show you that there burns in my heart the intention of working and suffering to hasten the hour when for all men the prayer of Jesus at the Last Supper will have reached its fulfilment."

John conceded the fact that the way to unity might be a long one but insisted that the Church is now taking steps "with patience and prudence," implying that the only practical way was one firm step at a time. And then he added immediately, "It is now for the Catholic Church to bend herself to her work with calmness and generosity. It is for you to observe her with renewed and friendly attention."

After the audience, the observers reacted with as much enthusiasm over the meeting as anyone could expect since their reactions had to be considered official reactions. Dr Joseph Jackson, president of the National Baptist Convention, Inc., of Chicago, spoke of the obvious "goodwill on both sides." Dr John Moorman, Anglican Bishop of Ripon, said, "We had the impression of being members of one family, even though together for such a short time." Prior Roger Schutz, of the Calvinist community of Taizé, France, said, "We are full of hope for unity." And his colleague from Taizé, Max Thurian, spoke of the Pope's simplicity: "This simplicity, this cordiality. He said these things, he spoke like a priest."

X

On the following Monday night, the observers met on the third floor of what was in 1362 a Roman domicile for a special order of priests called *Penitenzieri* whose job it was to absolve pilgrims from certain Church censures. Now that building is called the Columbus Hotel, and the observers heard no talk of censure, for although they represented seventeen "non-Catholic" bodies, they were special guests at a reception held in their honour by Cardinal Bea. He leaped a theological chasm when he found a better way to address the observers than the one John's theologians had imposed on him (John had called them "Chers Messieurs"—dear sirs). Bea's choice: "My very dear brothers in Christ"—a title, he hastened to explain, that "plunges us immediately into the profound consciousness of the incommensurable grace of baptism, which has established bonds that are indestructible, stronger than all our divisions."

Bea asked the observers for their co-operation in the Council. "I ask you to grant us complete confidence," said Bea, "and to tell us very frankly, above all during the sessions specially organized for you by the Secretariat, everything you dislike." He was not asking them for their complaints about the Roman weather (which was rather wet) or the Roman cooking (which they found delicious anyway) but about the "ecumenical thrust" of the Council—the acceptability or unacceptability to them of what was said on the Council floor. "Share with us," urged Bea, "your positive criticisms, your suggestions, and your desires. Of course I cannot promise to find a solution for every problem. But I do assure you that we shall be grateful to you for your confidence, that we shall try to consider everything sincerely in Christ in order to do, as far as we are permitted, everything that can be done now and in the future." (It was clear that neither Bea nor the Pope excluded the possibility that the Holy Spirit could speak through the observers.)

Immediately, Dr Edmund Schlink, a delegate from the Lutheran *Evangelischee Kirche in Deutschland*, and professor at the University of Heidelberg, sprang to the microphone and thanked Bea and the members of his Secretariat for all their kindness, and offered the first public reaction to Pope John's talk that opened the Council. Said Schlink: "Naturally, all those gathered here are aware of the great and deeply rooted obstacles by which we are separated from each other. However, I should like to draw your attention to two points which encourage us when hoping for a true dialogue among all of us.

"The first one," Schlink went on, "is the idea frequently expressed by Cardinal Bea in his addresses during the last two years and mentioned again in the Pope's opening address at the Council. It is absolutely necessary in all our words and in all our actions to recognize ourselves to be bound by the truth revealed to us. At the same time, however, a distinction must be made between the substance of the doctrine and its linguistic formulation. I am convinced that separated Christianity possesses more common substance than can be recognized at first sight when looking at the various formulations.

"The second encouraging fact," continued Schlink, "is that Cardinal Bea himself is an important representative of the science of exegesis and that this science since the encyclical *Divino Afflante Spiritu* has seen a great revival within the Church of Rome. As however the Bible is our common good, and as the science of exegesis of today is unthinkable without inter-denominational co-operation, there is sufficient reason to set great hope on the development of the research work done in this field."

The members of the Secretariat noted Schlink's words, and one of the members, Bishop Emile Josef Marie De Smedt of Bruges, Belgium, pondered them carefully. Later, during the Council debate on Scripture, De Smedt would convey some of Schlink's ideas to the assembled Fathers. All of this, noted one of the members of Bea's team, was a far cry from the spirit of the First Vatican Council that could move a vociferous majority of Council Fathers to hoot and cry "anathema," when Bishop Josip Georg Strossmayer of Bosnia suggested that many Protestants were men of goodwill.

Canon Pawley, too, noted the difference in climate. He said we were witnessing "a thaw in four hundred years' duration of icy non-co-operation and hostility," and though he was "sure that many things will be decided upon at the Council that we may not agree with, still he rather liked the idea of both Catholics and Protestants "rethinking the Reformation."

XI

By the end of the Council's first week, with the coming of a third official observer from Moscow, Nicolai Anfinoguenov, the number of observers had reached 39. They represented all of the major Christian groups except the fundamentalist sects and the Baptists (who had, at their August meeting in Stockholm, failed to reach a majority agreement to send observers). Nevertheless, even the Baptists had representation in the pleasant person of Dr Joseph Jackson of Chicago, who was a special guest of the Bea Secretariat. Bea had requests from many other individual Baptist bodies for invitations to the Council, but, anxious not to offend the World Alliance, Bea referred them to the Stockholm decision. Why then was Jackson at the Council? Because he was a Negro representing 5,000,000 United States Negroes? No, it was simply because when the Pope met Jackson in 1961, he told him he would have to come back for the Council. Jackson came—as a personal guest of the Pope.

Other bodies, too, had unofficial representation in Rome for the Council. Dr Carl McIntyre looked on (as much as he could from outside the walls of the basilica) for fundamentalist Christians who number at least seven million in the United States alone. Dr Zacharias Schuster, head of the Paris office of the World Jewish Congress, made frequent trips to Rome during the Council to keep himself and his organization posted.

The Churches that were represented officially inside the Council were, in the order released by the Bea Secretariat: Russian Orthodox, Egyptian Copts, Syrian Orthodox, Ethiopian Orthodox, Armenian, Catholicosate of Cilicia, Russian Orthodox Church Outside Russia, Old Lutheran World Federation, World Alliance of Reformed Churches (Presbyterian), Evangelical Church in Germany, World Convention of Churches of Christ (Disciples), Friends' World Committee for Consultation (Quakers), International Congregational Council, World Methodist Council, World Council of Churches, International Council for Liberal Christianity and Religious Freedom (Unitarian-Universalist). Special guests of the Secretariat represented somewhat less officially the French Calvinists and Waldensians and, through Dr Oscar Cullmann of Basle, the Protestant biblical scholars.

The observers had very little free time in Rome. They kept mornings for Council Meetings, intently watching the parade of bishops to the microphone, and did a great deal of meeting among themselves, comparing notes, discussing issues, writing reports back to the organizations which had sent them. Some of them squeezed in a little sight-seeing, others visited scholars of various Roman colleges, and many attended dinners and receptions in the evenings. As often as necessary, they received briefings from members of the Bea Secretariat or experts brought in by the Secretariat. The first of these briefings was misinterpreted by the

Associated Press mainly because the Secretariat (which would have been helped by public relations assistance during the Council) failed to inform the press corps about the scope of the meetings. The Associated Press was trying hard to please when its wires carried this story in October:

"Quietly, with utmost secrecy, Roman Catholic churchmen and representatives of at least 12 other Christian denominations made history here. They sat down together to start a joint search for closer contacts between their churches. The unheralded meeting came within 24 hours of Pope John's dramatic call for Christians to 'work actively' for Church unity. It lasted 2½ hours and was conducted in great cordiality. The historic event occurred in the seclusion of a Rome hotel room. Assembled were men of many faiths. . . . They sat shoulder to shoulder with seven men of Rome, the Pope's envoys—just 200 yards from the great Basilica of St Peter's. Never before in modern times had so many Catholic churchmen sat down with so many representatives of so many different non-Catholic churches in a formal examination of joint aims. Some high sources said the meeting was without precedent in the annals of Christianity . . ."

When one London newspaper read this cloak-and-dagger story, an editor phoned one of the English observers, Dr John Moorman, Anglican Bishop of Ripon, and demanded to know what sort of negotiations were going on, refused to believe him when he answered flatly (and sleepily), "No negotiations. We're just trying to keep informed about what's going on." Which was exactly the truth.

The Secretariat hastily released a communiqué to the official press office saying, "To amplify on the discussions of the Council, the Secretariat has foreseen special meetings with the observers every Tuesday afternoon in the Columbus Hotel. The study meetings are strictly private. As everyone knows, the Secretariat has the job of caring for the relations between the organism of the Council and the observers and offering them information necessary for following more easily the work of the Council."

Other observers had similar chilling encounters. Dr Kristen E. Skydsgaard, delegate of the World Lutheran Federation and professor of theology at the University of Copenhagen, was approached by one American reporter and asked if he knelt during the opening ceremonies of the Council. "I don't think that's any business of yours," said Skydsgaard. "How many observers knelt during the ceremony?" persisted the reporter thickly. The professor turned away.

In spite of such awkward situations, I found many observers willing to talk with me when they discovered I was not aiming at sensational headlines but rather at a certain *sense* of the play and interplay of the Council. Some talked under the condition they would not be quoted. Others spoke more freely. One of these was Dr George H. Williams, Winn Professor of Ecclesiastical History at Harvard University and a delegate from the International Congregational Council. "We've felt the partitions have been taken down," he told me over *cannelloni* at Il Passetto, "and we're living off the joy of the *rencontre*. To be isolated is a deadly thing, you know, but, until John XXIII, the Roman Catholic Church thought isolation was a strength."

Williams was still glowing from his meetings with the Pope. "Now Pope John sees the whole thing not in terms of the past, but in the language of the apocalypse—a future reference. For the Church, this is something new. And Pope John isn't setting himself up as someone above us. He is with us. When he spoke to us the other night, did he sit on a throne? No. He sat on a chair—with the throne behind him. And at the end of the talk, he turned to the Russians and said in Old Slavonic, 'Lord have mercy on us.' On us. He's not sitting on the throne but lumping himself in with us."

With his academic traditions, Williams could obviously speak more freely than many other observers some of whom were understandably reluctant to speak to the press for fear they would be misquoted or misunderstood at home. But perhaps the text chosen by another observer, Dr John Moorman, at his first sermon in Rome's Episcopal Church of St Paul, summed up the general feeling on all sides. "There is a time to tear and a time to sow," quoth Moorman, and added, "This is a time to sow."

Chapter Six

A NEW CREW

I

IT was at a reception three days before the opening of the first general congregation of the Council that I first encountered Bishop Thomas K. Gorman of the Dallas–Fort Worth Diocese. Since he was a former episcopal chairman of the United States bishops' press section, I found him as good a man as any upon whom to pour out my complaints about the velvet curtain I had found surrounding the official sources of information on the Council. Gorman listened with admirable patience for a time, then lit a foot-long cigar and said flatly (in a tone calculated to moderate my outrageous zeal), "You're not going to see many headlines coming out of this Council." A story in *The New York Times* two days later, carrying a by-line by Paul Hoffman, seemed to confirm Bishop Gorman's scepticism about the news value of the Council. "*Traditionalist Tendency Prevails Among Delegates*" is the way the copy editor put it, and Hoffman wrote, "The dominant trend is averse to radical changes in Church doctrine or policy."

In a cable to New York, I questioned this. "Let's wait and see," said I, attempting to head off my editors at the pass. I was just naïve enough to believe most of the things that John had been saying about the Council and his intentions to use it as an instrument of bringing the Church "up-to-date," that he actually did have a "most intense inspiration of the Lord" to give through the Council "an answer to the expectations of the whole world caught up in the complexity of this modern era."

And I had an idea that perhaps the power structure of the Church had shifted slightly since 1870. The faces I saw in that Thursday morning procession bespoke a tremendous variety of experience. With Patrick O'Donovan of the London *Observer*, I saw "executive faces and kindly faces and imperious faces and ascetic faces, and faces that have known good tables." I saw black faces and yellow faces and brown faces and white faces and faces that had set themselves against pain and deprivation. The Church may not have been "of the world," but these bishops were certainly in it, and I could not imagine the Council Fathers, the successors to those of Nicaea and Ephesus and Trent, now gathered from Borneo, Little Rock, Fukuoka and Madagascar, coming to the Council to rubber-stamp the curialist view of the Church and the world. Nor could I quite see how the missionary bishops from the exploding Orient, 374 strong, nor the 296 bishops from throbbing Africa could possibly leave the push towards Church decentralization to a handful of German, Dutch, French, and Belgian conciliar Fathers.

Then, too, when I obtained copies of the names, addresses and telephone numbers of various national hierarchies in Rome, I began to realize that somebody was underestimating the number of the German, Dutch, French and Belgians. Yes, it is true that there are only nine bishops in the Netherlands, but the mimeographed pages listed seventy-six. "How could this be?" I asked. "You forget," smiled the young priest in the Netherlands press centre, "you forget the missions." Similarly, there were only fifteen Belgian bishops at the Council, but the Belgian list contained fifty-nine names. The French and the Germans also claimed a good many missionaries. Now the missionaries were returning to give their mission witness to the universal Church. Some Curialists referred to them with contempt as *periferisti*, and it is true that many missionaries stepped into Rome fresh from the bush with next to no knowledge about the Council or the preparation that had been made for it. They did have cultural ties to the transalpine bishops, however, and were aware that in the past decade, ever since Europe turned the corner into the prosperous 'fifties and 'sixties, they had received considerable mission help—most of it direct help—from the bishops of northern Europe. Unknown bishops kept popping up at Cardinal Josef Frings' temporary home in the German College to thank him for the school he had built, or the church, or the new seminary, and then to add, not unnaturally, "What's happening at this Council?" And then Frings would say, "Well, young man, since you have asked . . ."

Young man. No one has worked out the average age of the average missionary bishop, but many of them have been in the episcopal college for only a short time. Bishop Vincent McCauley of Fort Portal, Uganda, told me he was number 1803 in seniority, and he had been a bishop for less than two years. That meant that 578 bishops (many of them natives from the new nations) had been consecrated since then.

The astute Paulist, Father James Sheerin, editor of *The Catholic World*, warned me, "Don't underestimate the missionary contribution to the Council. The missionary bishops are the conscience of the Church." And Archbishop Eugene D'Souza of Nagpur, India, told me, "Our minds are effervescing now." But if the missionary bishops were to be the conscience of the Council, the transalpine bishops would have to spur it on. On the wet, wet night of October 12, news came to them that the Curia was attempting to rig the election of commission members—in a subtle way, yes, but rig it nonetheless. Cardinals Suenens, Alfrink, Frings, Doepfner, Koenig, Liénart and Bea conferred by phone. What to do? Would it insult the Pope to demand a recess? No, came the answer, it would not.

II

The next morning, to the intense satisfaction of many, Cardinal Liénart and Cardinal Frings blew the Holy Office list of commission candidates into figurative bits before the eyes of all. The meeting was adjourned in fifteen minutes.

The session was supposed to proceed with the nomination of the 160 members who would make up the ten commissions of the Council. The Pope had already named the cardinal-president of each committee, the conciliar Fathers would elect sixteen more, and the Pope would select another seven. According to the Council rules, the task of the commission would be to prepare and amend the *schemata* for decrees and canons in line with the opinions expressed by the Fathers. It would be up to the commissions to codify all the additions, corrections and opinions expressed by the bishops during the floor debates, submit them back to the Council for vote, incorporate the agreed changes into the text, and reintroduce it for final approval. Since some of the *schemata* on the agenda were very long (the first one on Liturgy ran forty-five quarto pages of succinct Latin), the procedure could be a long one, but it did have the merit of allowing the Fathers of the Council complete freedom to speak their minds on the matters under discussion.

It was obvious that the Fathers had no intention of waiving that freedom. As soon as the session opened, Cardinal Liénart asked for the floor. Speaking on behalf of all French bishops, Liénart proposed that voting on the commissions be postponed. The Fathers could not rightly be expected to vote yet, he said, since they did not know the candidates. "It is necessary," said the Cardinal, speaking in Latin, "that there be a preliminary consultation, especially between the members of the forty-seven various episcopal conferences." A great silence fell upon the assembly, and two young bishops at the east end of the basilica looked at each other with a wild surmise.

Cardinal Frings took the floor to second Liénart's motion. He stated that he spoke on his own behalf "with the consent of" Cardinal Doepfner of Munich (who is president of the Bavarian Episcopal Conference) and Franziskus Koenig of Vienna (president of the Austrian Episcopal Conference).

Then, with the realization of what was happening, the applause began. It boomed in the back of the basilica, among the younger bishops of South America and Africa and Asia, and it broke in a wave up to the table of the ten-man presidential board. The board needed no vote to understand the mind of the Council and called a hasty meeting right there. (It was the first time they had ever met, a fact that demonstrated clearly Secretary-General Felici's feeling of confidence in his own private Curial directorate.) The presidents called Felici over. "Tell them," said Cardinal Tisserant, the president for the day, "tell the Fathers the elections are postponed until Tuesday."

Felici told them.

Although the official press office shed little light on the turn of events, the Roman breezes were soon full of rumours and reports of conversations on the Council floor. I felt the whole thing significant enough to cable New York (beyond deadline time). *"So-called liberal minority aren't going to have anything crammed down their throats by Italian Curia. Today demonstrated they have strength to avoid that possibility. This clearly going to be real parliament of Church."*

III

"BISHOPS IN REVOLT" screamed the headline in more than one European daily. Was this a rebellion against the Pope? In fact this display of conciliar independence was exactly the opposite. It was the first dawn of Pope John's hope for a real Council, a Council that could help him move the Church into the world.

John could look at the world of 1962 and see that it was, certainly, shrinking and, because it was, tending towards an ever-greater unity. Towards a geographical unity—probably; towards a political unity—possibly; towards a greater sharing of ideas and ideals among men—certainly. When the two Soviet cosmonauts went into their simultaneous orbital flight on August 12, 1962, John said such undertakings could become "an expression of true, peaceful and well-founded progress towards human brotherhood."

Where would the Church fit into this progress? Would it remain, as it had for centuries, on the periphery of things? Would it remain choked inside its insular haven, keep the world at arm's length, and suffer through it as it became, for lack of faith and hope and charity, progressively poorer?

John's problem was largely a practical one. How get the Church into the world? The answer he finally found was one inherent in the very nature of the Church itself. Christ founded the Church on his Apostles. John would restore and renew that Church through the successors to those Apostles. To lever the Church and Christianity out of the sloughs of irrelevancy and isolation and back into the main current on the sea of the world, John would call on his bishops.

The story goes that John's oldest brother Saverio paid a visit to the Vatican during the Council preparations. "What about this Council?" Saverio asked. "You're going to have an enormous number of bishops, archbishops, and cardinals, aren't you?"

John answered Saverio in language his brother could well understand. "What I am doing," he explained, "is imitating the farmers up at our place. You see the farmer bending over his plough, drawn by two horses, ploughing the uplands and the plains. A trinity of toil. Now, I am the ploughman, my bishops are the horses, and together we can plough the uplands and plains of this world for Christ. I need all the bishops because we must work for the world."

In effect, then, by calling the Council, John yoked himself with all his fellow bishops and with God in a trinity of toil.

The figure is, of course, only a figure. A good comparison as far as it goes. John didn't think of the world's bishops as his slaves—he called them his brother bishops too often for that—but he did see them as the potential (and at that stage *only* a potential) force that could help him make the Council more than the banal and churchy event the Curialists wanted, and something instead that would put the Church into the world.

If once they were in Rome he could encourage them to exercise their "collegiality," that special group charisma which he knew they possessed, then he would have a real Council. But would he succeed? Hadn't the bishops been trained in quite another tradition? Hadn't they lost, somewhere along the line, the sense of their collegiality? Hadn't they been trained, first by their professors in the seminary and then by the Curialists in Rome, to think of a bishop as a functionary of the central government?

Certainly many bishops from the United States, who had been trained in this latter day tradition, fully expected to come to Rome and place their rubber stamp on the *schemata* drawn up by the Roman Curia. One of them told his people he would probably be back in three weeks. Even if an American bishop favoured radical reforms, he did not expect to see them passed in the Council.

IV

The world's daily press tended to overemphasize political categories in decribing the ensuing Council action, but it was given ample excuse by the bishops. It is a fact that on Sunday, October 14, and Monday, October 15, various national groups of bishops met to hammer out lists of commission candidates. On Sunday the French met at Villa Bonaparte, the French Embassy to the Holy See, the Germans, Austrians and Swiss at Santa Maria dell'Anima, the Dutch at a hotel on Via Crescenzio, the Belgians at the Belgian College on the Via del Quirinale, and the Italians at the Domus Mariae on Via Aurelia. On Monday, the Spanish, surprising many by not meeting en bloc with bishops from South America and the Philippines, intensified their contacts with the Dutch. Both the African and United States hierarchies were told by different curial cardinals not to hold any meetings at all "lest the world mistakenly think the Council was dividing along nationalistic lines." The Africans, for the time being, ceded. But the United States bishops complained to the Cardinal Secretary of State, Amleto Cicognani, that they had been planning for months to have their annual meeting in Rome, so Cicognani said to go ahead and have their meeting, "but keep it *quiet.*"

For their part, the Italian bishops could not agree on what sort of list to draw up for the 160 commission seats. The Italian bishops had set up a national conference with the approval of Pope Pius XI, but their first scheduled meeting was cancelled when Pius XI died in 1939. Pius XII never favoured its resurrection and the Roman Curia looked on it as nothing more than a threat to their power in Rome. Until October 14, 1962, then, the full Italian bishops conference had never met. The effect of this policy was not lost on some sardonic observers who could see that precisely when the Curia needed help to raise its own sails its Italian crew of more than 400 did not know a halyard from a swab. What is more, they were not united. Cardinal Siri of Genoa proposed naming four or five Italian candidates for each commission and doing a little horsetrading with other episcopates. Cardinal Urbani of Venice thought they ought to draw up a list of 160 candidates representing the countries and continents of the world on a proportional basis. Cardinal Montini of Milan offered a third view—that the Fathers not choose on the basis of geography at all but think first of the culture, experience and piety of the nominees. In the end, the Italians produced a mixed list of 160.

The Germans, Austrians and Swiss drew up an international list of men they considered progressive, but they named only one or two German bishops to each proposed commission list. This group had considered naming no Italians—with 430 persons at the Council and control of the palace guard, Italians could be expected to take care of themselves—and insisted on naming extra cardinals on each commission to counteract the influence of the Italian cardinal already named by the Pope to head each commission. But after messengers had crossed and recrossed Rome several times on Monday night, the German–Austrian–Swiss bloc finally joined forces with the French, Dutch, Spanish, Belgians, Luxembourgers, Yugoslavs and Poles and together agreed on a list of wide geographical distribution. It contained only two of the twenty-eight names listed by the Italians and proposed five other Italians who had not been named on the Italian list—including Cardinal Lercaro of Bologna, and Bishop Gargitter of Bressanone, both of whom were elected anyway, and Bishops Carraro of Verona and Guano of Livorno, both of whom were later appointed to commissions by the Pope. In other words, the transalpine bishops really had no objections to Italians as such—because the issues they hoped to treat in the Council were not national but theological. No matter how much the pundits talked about national blocs, the fact was that the Council would soon be—in fact was already—split along progressive and reactionary lines. "Perfectly natural," said an editorial in *Osservatore Romano* that was surprising in its calm, "for a council where the extremes of the authority-freedom paradox are seen in close association. Authority is at the service of freedom, freedom at the service of authority, and both are at the service of truth. It is quite natural that, within the Council, there should emerge something which would be called, in parliamentary jargon, 'parties of the centre, right and left.'

But these parties or oppositions arise out of the need to seek and express the truth. A council, though it has divine aid, is carried on through free discussion between men. A council would be completely without value if projects, opinions, proposals and expressions aimed at clarifying truth were to be suppressed."

Much of this editorial, in fact, effectively supported the forces and counterforces that began to emerge in the Council, that were, in fact, necessary to the Council if it was going to find its own way. Many bishops had long thought of themselves as the Pope's messenger boys (what else had they been taught, either in the seminary or in their dealings with the Roman Curia?). But Pope John, by the very act of bringing the bishops to a Council and setting them on their way, was expressing a silent wish that they would discover their collegiality and establish their own imprint on the Council of the twentieth century.

America's once-popular television star, Bishop Fulton Sheen of New York, took up the cudgels against the press for reporting what was happening at the Council (and no more). He pooh-poohed the idea of forces within the Council, talked about it as if it were some kind of miraculous divine intervention that came down to grip the Fathers "who go into the Council 2,500 fallibilities and come out as one infallibility." Warming to his subject, Sheen attempted to reduce current newspaper accounts of the Council to absurdity by "rewriting" scriptural narratives of the First Council of Jerusalem in newspaper language.

He concluded this tour de force with, "Now go back and read the report of the Council in the Acts of the Apostles. Did the pre-council press reports of conflicts, blocs and groups ever materialize? Not a one!" If Bishop Sheen had reviewed his Acts, he might have seen the inspired version of the story: "And when there had been much disputing . . ." (Acts 15:7).

But if the newsmen were using their own familiar political categories to explain the play of force in the Council, Sheen himself could not help injecting his own philosophical categories onto the scene. His major objection to the press accounts of conflicts at the Council: they presupposed a Hegelian (read: Communist) dialectic, "a spirit of tension, conflict, opposition and disdain of truth . . . no concern for the objective truth, but for the setting in contrast of two contrary ideas, or points of view."

What really bothered many others, however, was a far more real danger—that this Council would fall into the pitfalls of the earlier councils of Basle (1431–45) where nationalism motivated an anti-Italian drive by the German princes, and the Council of Constance (1414–18) where nationalism motivated an anti-Italian movement aimed at the primacy of the Pope.

At Vatican II, however, the Spaniards headed off any possibility of such a repetition by quickly appointing a committee of three bishops and charging them with maintaining "public relations" with the bishops of other lands. The French followed their lead and opened their conferences to the representatives of other groups. French theologians Congar, Daniélou and De Lubac spoke before conferences of Africans, South Americans, Canadians. The German Jesuit liturgical scholar, Josef Jungmann, and the great Innsbruck Jesuit, Karl Rahner, spoke to Africans and Asians and South Americans. Cardinal Suenens himself talked to many English-speaking bishops, and there was a great interplay among all the nations of Central Europe. One thing was clear, however: the discussions, the lobbying, the riving of the Council into force and counterforce captured the attention of the world. The pomp and the ceremony were over, and logically the world could have been expected to forget about the Council. It did not and could not because there were lively things happening there.

Tuesday, the Fathers arrived at St Peter's and found printed leaflets containing names of candidates proposed by different episcopal conferences, with the understanding that every Council Father was free to choose the members he wished, even those not appearing on the lists distributed. After a brief discussion on whether "winning" candidates needed a two-thirds majority (they did according to the rules) or merely a plurality (they did not, according to Cardinal Ottaviani), the Fathers were told to fill out their ballots in the basilica or take them home and finish them, then bring them back to the Council Secretariat in the evening. Until the 400,000 possible votes had been counted and the presidency announced, the Council could not go on, and the

Fathers were told to come back Saturday. No one, apparently, thought of beginning the discussion of the first *schema* while the votes were being counted. This was the first indication to me of avoidable delay, if not outright bungling, on the part of Felici's Secretariat. Perhaps he had been stunned by the force of the "barbarians" from the North—and the South—and the East—and the West. Still and all, there was something engaging and human about this assembly at that early period. The Pope, for his part, seemed to delight in watching the Council find its way. On Wednesday, October 17, he told a group of 15,000 pilgrims that they should not worry if things dragged a bit because *"chi va piano, va sano e lontano"* (he who goes slowly, goes safely and goes far). And members of at least three different continental groups received discreet phone calls from those closest to John reminding them that a vote against the Curia is not necessarily a vote against the Pope.

When the Fathers reconvened on Saturday, Felici announced the results of the voting on seven commissions. (Others were still being counted by seminarians from the Roman College and the Propaganda College.) To those who understood that the men at the top of the list had received the most votes (this was never stated officially), it was clear the transalpines had cornered powerful blocs of votes. Their candidates stood at the top of every commission list. Of the five Italian bishops mentioned above who had not made the Italian list (but had been placed on the transalpine list) two were elected. Bishop John J. Wright of Pittsburgh who was not nominated by the United States bishops, was discovered on both the transalpine and Italian lists, and was also elected.

All in all, the progressives could only look at the election results as an astounding victory. The Fathers did not elect a single Curialist and chose sixty-eight "unknowns" from places like Barquisimeto, Ernakulam, Winnipeg, Melbourne, Milwaukee, Léopoldville and Atlanta. According to the rules, Pope John was supposed to appoint eighty persons to fill out each commission to the required strength of twenty-five. But the vote had really thrown a huge balance to what everyone predicted would be the liberal "minority." And so the Pope made an obvious effort to even the forces, because, as the old proverb goes, it is just as bad to lean over too far backwards as it is to fall flat on your face. The Fathers had elected only nineteen Italians (and some of these were not conservative). At the next meeting of Italian bishops, on October 24, they got into such a row over what they should have done or should not have done on the election issue that they disbanded, never to meet again during the first session. Rumour has it that Cardinal Montini held his own meetings of progressive Italians in his apartment in Vatican City (which John XXIII had put at his disposal).

John raised the number of Italians to forty-two and then broke his own rules by appointing another ten—the staunchest conservatives in the Curia, the ten executive officers of the ten major curial congregations. This brought each commission's strength to twenty-six.*

At this there was a good bit of grumbling by the progressives—at first. Then they realized that John did not want any pyrrhic victories. Before the Council, John had read every scrap of material he could find on the First Vatican Council. Above all, he wanted to avoid the dictatorial methods of Pio Nono who never arranged to give the liberal minority even a tiny representation on the commissions of that Council. Long after it was over, liberal partisans would point to that fact as an argument against the validity of its major dogmatic decree.

V

On October 20, when the commission voting was finished, the Council Fathers produced, as if by magic, a "Statement to All Humanity" that certainly did not sound as if it came from a conciliar body of the Roman Catholic Church. It mystified the press so much that editors could hardly believe it and shunted it in

* The English-language communiqué stated that the Pope appointed the latter curial ten to give each commission an uneven number for voting purposes, but this obvious guess (that is all it was, since none of the day's communiqués in other languages carried that speculation) did not include the commissions' presidents who are voting members of their respective commissions.

truncated form to inside pages, making room instead for a picayune story that Pope John had forbade any death-bed pictures of
himself. But it was an important measure of the Council tempera-
ture and evidence of a new conciliar tone.

In the United States, John J. Ryan, a layman, had written
before the Council: "God the Father has spoken to us, His
children, through the prophets and His Son, in the language of
poetry. He expects to be thought of, appreciated, prayed to, in
terms of this language. Might not the Council say as much
expressly and then, by their own speech, testify to their Christlike
distaste for literal-mindedness and legalistic frigidity? If it is all
right to say to a scholar that 'grace is created actuation by un-
created act,' it is better to speak of grace to everyone else as food
that nourishes the starving, water that cleanses and quenches, oil
that soothes and strengthens, health that frees from paralysis and
restores the sight, life that raises from the dead. Maybe the Council can speak less in the mode of a Renaissance Cicero and more
in the mode, in this apocalyptic era, of St John."

Before he came to the Council, Cardinal Julius Doepfner had
written along the same lines: "We must offer all peoples the
revelation of God by presenting it in its scriptural simplicity and
in the profound awareness of our faith."

When the Council Fathers, then, were presented with this
proposed "Statement to All Humanity," it was, in the deepest
sense, an answer to the pleas of many that the Council would indeed speak to humanity in human terms, and a boldly simple
statement of what this Council was up to. Behind all the pomp
and glory of the Council opening, which the Council Fathers
realized had been carried to the ends of the earth by all the
sophisticated efficiency of the mass media, the Council Fathers
merely wished to point out that they, 2,300 scattered successors
of the Apostles, were in Rome to remind millions of Christians
and hundreds of millions of others that Jesus Christ is still with us.

Ninety-two years ago, the First Vatican Council became, in
the words of one of its bishops, "lost in all kinds of childishness"
and finally produced what seemed to many Catholics and almost
all Protestants a highly unnecessary declaration of the Pope's

personal infallibility. Now, right at the outset of this Council, the Fathers, with a clear vision that went right to the heart of things, affirmed their conciliar intentions: to become "the increasingly faithful witnesses of the Gospel of Christ."

"We believe that the Father loved the world so much that he gave his Son to save it, and that he freed us from the slavery of sin through this same Son, 'to reconcile all things unto himself, making peace through the blood of his Cross' (Col. 1:20) that we might be called and truly be his sons. Moreover, we receive the Holy Spirit from the Father that, living the life of God, we may love God and our brothers, with whom we are united in Christ. We, therefore, who are the followers of Christ are not estranged from earthly concerns and toils. Indeed, the faith, hope and charity of Christ urge us to serve our brothers in conformitywith the example of the Divine Master who did not come to be served but to serve. 'He hath laid down his life for us: and we ought to lay down our lives for the brethren' (I John 3:16)."

A Catholic priest-journalist later told me he thought this statement was "too Protestant" because it was "too biblical"and "not doctrinal enough," and added, "If I hadn't known where this statement came from, I would have said a Protestant minister wrote it." His puzzlement, of course, struck me at the time as symptomatic of the disease in the Catholic Church which the Council was called to cure, for the only thing that made the statement "Protestant" was its biblical tone and its emphasis on the Church born, not to rule, but to serve. That sense of service, now so largely forgotten both by supercilious clergymen and a sycophantic lay people, was part of the very fibre of the early Church, which conceived of its authority as a *diaconia* or service. Later Christians thought of the Church as a "community" in which God often made his will known through the humblest and least esteemed of his children. In the early Middle Ages— the age of Constantine—the Church became identified with political society and political power, and the false notion of a "Christendom" (with all its horrendous concomitants) was born. In the late Middle Ages, there was added to the Church's authority a legalism that was out of keeping with scriptural, patristic, and liturgical usage. The trend favoured the idea of the priest "governing" his parish, of the bishop and the Pope as "judges," of the Pope as a "sovereign." Since (and because of) the Protestant Reformation, a *mystique* arose in the Church that tended to identify God's will completely with the institutional form of authority, resulting in a clergy that has hidden under a false cloak of absolutism and presented an essentially juridical conception of the Church. Now, says an archbishop from France, "the bishop is reputed to be a sort of prefect, priests functionaries, sacraments the residues of magic rites, religion a group of laws to which one submits because of a feeling of exterior discipline and from which one escapes without understanding their true value, as happens with the laws of the State." It is because of this mentality that bishops think of themselves as "heads of dioceses," which is really a legalistic designation, while Pope John continually referred to visiting bishops as "head of the *Church* of Florence," "head of the *Church* of Bologna," "head of the *Church* of Vienna"—a pastoral concept.

It was precisely this notion of a "serving Church" that the Council's "Statement to All Humanity" was trying to underline, so that the Council could give "a happy impetus in favour of human welfare . . . the findings of science, the progress of the arts and of technology, and a greater diffusion of culture . . . to peace among peoples . . . and social justice. We proclaim [the statement continued] that all men are brothers irrespective of the race or nation to which they belong . . . ," asserting the Church's need "to denounce injustices and shameful inequalities, to restore the true order of goods and things so that, according to the principles of the Gospel, the life of man may become more human."

The statement echoed Pope John's words of October 11 in which he embraced even non-Christians in his world view: "Humbly and ardently, We invite all to collaborate with Us to establish in the world a more ordered way of living and greater brotherhood. We invite all, not only Our brothers of whom We are the pastors, but all Our brothers who believe in Christ and all men of goodwill whom God 'wishes . . . to be saved and to come to the knowledge of the truth' (I Tim. 2:4)." And it ended with an optimistic wish that such a re-entry of Christ into the world (through his members on earth) would make "the kingdom of God shine even now upon the earth almost in anticipation of the eternal kingdom."

This "Statement to All Humanity" was largely an attempt on the part of Council progressives (John XXIII among them) to set a new conciliar tone. John had taken the new tone much earlier, of course, by his great cordiality to each and every one of the "separated brothers"who appeared in his apartment to greet him. (Dr Arthur Mervyn Stockwood, Anglican Bishop of Southwark, who visited John on April 7, 1962, commented afterward in the light of that visit: "I think that a coming together among the Churches will not result from changes in doctrine, but from a change of attitudes.")

And so, at the beginning of the Council, the papal documents were there in black and white and they indeed set a new tone: John's radio message of September 11, and his three talks of October 11 and 12 to the Council Fathers, to the extraordinary missions and to the delegate-observers. By producing their "Statement to All Humanity," the Fathers demonstrated that they had listened well to John's ideas, had caught his new spirit and intended to carry it through. The liturgical *schema*, which was written in the same tones, had already been selected by Pope John to carry on the new motif.

The fact that the "Statement" could have passed on the Council floor so easily was an encouraging sign, considering the source of the "Statement." The men who wrote the original draft were Dominican theologians Yves Congar (whose troubles with the Holy Office, since he wrote *True and False Reform in the Church*, in 1950, have been unending) and M. D. Chenu, former provincial of the French Dominicans who was removed from his post in the early 1950's and even had one of his works, *Une École de Théologie: Le Saulchoir,* put on the Index of Forbidden Books. Congar and Chenu put the "Statement" in the hands of the French bishops who took it to the Council presidency. They took it to the Pope out of courtesy and had it printed by the Vatican press *cum approbatione Summi Pontificis* and proposed it to the Fathers without warning, gave them a half hour to study it, then asked for comment. Five cardinals spoke (among them Poland's Cardinal Stefan Wyszynski who in answer to one proposed amendment saw no need for mentioning Communism in the statement), Melchite Patriarch Maximos IV Saigh, and thirty-one archbishops and bishops. Two bishops proposed adding the name of "Mary, the mother of Jesus." Some thought it too long. Others thought it too short. Archbishop Denis Hurley of Durban, South Africa, said it appeared it was being railroaded through and that argument had some appeal to fair-minded bishops who were accustomed to good parliamentary procedures. One angelic creature said he thought it contained too much emphasis on the "temporal order." Someone else objected to a statement in the original draft that the world was *always* far from peace because of the threats engendered by scientific progress itself, which was marvellous progress but *not yet* intent on the supreme law of morality. He suggested that the *always* be changed to *still* and the *not yet* to *not always*—which the presidents thought was a point well taken and they made that change, added Mary's name and asked for a standing vote. Very few persons remained seated, and the Council passed it.

With the tone of that statement set, John and his progressives were ready to consider the liturgical *schema*, the only one of the seventy *schemata* that really came to grips with the modern needs of the Church, the only one that rejected the juridical formulation of the Church's latter and sadder days. On the eve of the liturgical debate, a theologian told me, "This will set a new tone for conciliar decrees. After they pass this, the Fathers of the Council can't go back to the old way. They will have to produce the rest of their formulations in language that means something to the modern world."

Chapter Seven

CHARTING NEW WATERS

I

THE pomp and glory of the Council's solemn opening faded and the intrigue of the Council's elections vanished. The *Life* photographers jetted to Yemen where an inter-Arab war had broken out between republicans supported by the United Arab Republic and the royalists backed by Jordan and Saudi Arabia; and to Iraq where an earthquake had snuffed out several thousand lives. The journalistic eagles of the British press moved to Monaco, where De Gaulle was putting pressure on that suddenly too independent principality and to Geneva where the nations of East and West began the *n*th round of bombsmanship, a dreary game in which each side attempted to force the other into exposing its desire for war.

The reporters who had to stay for the rest of the Council (the wire service men, a reporter from *The New York Times*, the *Herald Tribune*, the *Baltimore Sun*, and an assorted band of priests and laymen representing the Catholic press, to name the principals) took a deep breath and faced up to the task of trying to explain something called "the liturgy debate" to a world which their editors told them was "a hell of a lot more interested in the Council than we thought they'd be." The reporters, a competent group with solid goodwill, gave the bishops the benefit of the doubt—2,300 bishops would not have funnelled into Rome for *nothing*—but, for the newsmen, it was an impossible job to understand what the "liturgy" was in general, why it was an issue, or what the debate was all about.

To them it appeared to be a great amount of talk about Catholic rites of worship.

As it turned out, this debate underscored: (1) the strength of the

Council's progressive wing; (2) the collegial awareness of the conciliar Fathers; and (3) the unreality of the curial Counter Reformation mentality. It also gave the delegate-observers a chance to see that the Church was not a monolithic monster but a body of bewildering diversity.

But all of this was hardly apparent to the average reporter at the Council. "Pretty hard to cover when you can't get inside, isn't it?" remarked one United States bishop with a heavy sarcasm that might have been directed either at the press efforts in general, at the conciliar secrecy in particular, or at the incongruity of the juxtaposition.

Official communiqués were rather less than useless (see Chapter Nine) because they avoided getting even close to the core issue involved in the liturgical reforms proposed to the Fathers. "Reform" obviously implied that there was something that needed reforming, but no one would dare say in public what it was in the Church's life of worship that needed reforming.

The official communiqué implied rather, by avoiding the matter, that any kind of reform was unnecessary, and it concentrated instead, day after deadly day from October 22 to November 13, on a variety of picayune and churchy matters.

But the discussions (through fifteen plenary sessions and 328 speeches) were far from pious. In them, one could see the drama of an expanding Church now snapping the chains of an unnatural immutability and demonstrating a vitality that few had suspected possible. In the liturgy debate, one could sense the conflict of two opposing forces on the bridge of Peter's barque, the one looking only to the internal organization of the ship, and the other worried where the vessel was going.

On the surface it appeared that the Council could not have begun on a safer, less controversial *schema*. It was, the Pope thought, precisely the thing that would give the Fathers a good start; a subject they all knew something about.

The authors of the liturgical *schema* thought they had made a fine start by formulating it in the most intelligible language they knew. The introduction and first chapter, said one of them, Aimé Martimort, who is also a director of the French Centre of Pastoral

Liturgy, were determined by the general orientation of the Council and were written therefore in "a new theological language" which he contrasted with other *schemata* couched in an "old scholastic style." The new style, he said, was "biblical, patristic, wholly oriented towards the pastoral, understood by the people and will touch them deeply, all men—Orthodox, Protestants and even pagans."

As for the means of liturgical renewal, the authors of the *schema* declared, Pope Pius X had put a liturgical movement in motion exactly sixty years ago. Since then, liturgical scholars had been engaged in exacting historical research, first verifying what the *substance* of the liturgy was, clarifying the meaning of liturgical symbols, signs, gestures and words.

They had tried to see how intelligible the liturgy was for modern man, and then, in a spirit of adaptation to the times, save the substance and enhance its relevance, avoiding, as Pius XII warned in the encyclical *Mediator Dei*, "two extremes in regard to the past, a blind acceptance and a total scorn." The scholars had for years been hard at work on a practical application of the programme enunciated by John XXIII in his October 11 discourse: "The substance of the ancient doctrine of the deposit of faith is one thing, the formulation of it is quite another." And now, after sixty years of work, this most mature of all modern movements in the Church had formulated some answers. It had redesigned churches, putting the altar in the centre and gathering the people close. It had administered weddings and funerals in the language of the people. It had experimented with dialogue Masses. In some places (the upper Midwest of the United States, for one), the liturgical movement had advanced. In others, it had stood still. Unaccountably, Italy itself was at best still immured in the merely devotional.

The Council itself was not expected to provide specific answers, however. Members of the Preparatory Liturgical Commission had incorporated many specifics in a 400-page tome (as yet unpublished) for the benefit of bishops who wanted to know more about specifics. The liturgical movement had only succeeded in getting piecemeal, reluctant, and minimal approval from the

Sacred Congregation of Rites* and the Supreme Sacred Congregation of the Holy Office. What was needed was a conciliar decree establishing the higher principles (*altiora principia*) of a reform in worship and giving the world's bishops the power to apply them in their own lands. What the *schema* asked for, in effect, was the end of the period of ecclesiastical colonization and a recognition of a healthy pluralism within the unity of the Church.

II

Predictably enough, the missionary bishops (more and more conscious of the excellence of the native cultures) spoke strongly for adaptation. They knew the potential value of the liturgy in their educative work and could only nod vigorously whenever they heard a liturgical scholar like Father Josef Jungmann point out that the liturgy was the principal method, in fact one of the Church's first methods, of catechesis. Archbishop Eugene D'Souza of Nagpur, India, asked for the vernacular in the Mass and sacraments which he called "a must, for the simple reason that beautiful rites are completely lost on our people if they are in Latin formulas which they do not understand. The Church will not be perfect until it succeeds in incarnating itself where it exists." Bishop Lawrence Satoshi Nagae of Urawa, Japan, said that "Liturgy must not be elaborated in a language which people do not understand, nor must it use pomp and ceremony which have no real meaning for modern man. Modern Japan considers the Catholic religion outdated and defunct and will continue to do so until the liturgy becomes simple, the approach more direct and the people able to participate more immediately with the priest." Bishop Willem van Bekkum of Ruteng, Indonesia, whose

* Progressive strategists decided not to attack the congregation, which certainly deserved its lumps, but to set up radical liturgical renewal as part of a plan that had been carried out steadily since Pius XII wrote *Mediator Dei*. Thus, progressives distributed at the Council lists of "indults" granted to particular countries for sung Mass in modern languages, for dialogue Masses, for the Mass in Chinese, for the Gospel and Epistle in the vernacular, for administration of the sacraments in Italian, Hindustani, Konkani, Marathi, Portuguese, Spanish, Japanese, English, Gaelic, French and German.

expertise in the liturgy was, according to a story in *Osservatore Romano*, "not born or developed in dusty wanderings through a college library," made a strong appeal for adaptation of native rites and customs—including the native dances—in the Church's sacramental system. "In this," said van Bekkum, "we convert all culture to Christ. If you put Christ into any action, it is not pagan any more. I hope the tongues of the Papuans and the Indonesians become sacramental tongues."

African bishops were caught in a paradox. They eagerly favoured adaptation of the liturgy to the native customs of their peoples, but could not generally approve of the "vernacular" at this stage of their history. In most areas, there was no "vernacular" or common language as such, but fifteen or fifty vernaculars in a single diocese. Still, they spoke strongly for the possibility of the vernacular at some future date.

Bishop Louis La Ravoire Morrow of Krishnagar, India, remarked simply that the liturgy was only a means to an end, the good of souls, and, as presently communicated in Asian countries in a Latin the people did not understand, fostered a "magic mentality." Bishop Enrique Rau of Mar del Plata, Argentina, asked the Fathers, "If the liturgical movement is a work of the Holy Spirit, how can the Council fail to listen to his inspiration?" And Bishop Clemente José Carlos Isnard, of Nova Friburgo, Brazil, added: "The liturgy is a sign: it ought to be understood."

Others from non-missionary lands, but possessed of the same missionary spirit, spoke in the same accents. Bishop Willem Bekkers of 's-Hertogenbosch, the Netherlands, declared: "To reach the people we must be able to organize the structure and language of the liturgy in our own territories. The door should be open. What we ask is the possibility, not the obligation, of making necessary ten-year experiments—and this should last for at least a century." Monsignor Henri Jenny, Auxiliary Bishop of Cambrai, asked, "How can they understand what Jesus says if the Gospel is read in an incomprehensible language? How can they really pray if they do not understand what they are saying? Let us not deprive the world of the Word they are thirsting for."

Archbishop Paul Hallinan of Atlanta, Georgia, elected by the

Council to the Liturgical Commission, spoke for bishops "of various lands" some of whom were, presumably, bishops in the United States. He pointed out later in a press conference that "a liturgy that can be understood would provide a new avenue to our separated brethren who often find the Latin language an alien element and would provide a living contradiction of the popular American myth that 'religion is a private affair.' " (Some press reports said the United States bishops were "not interested in the liturgy." But on Sunday morning, October 28, more than 150 United States bishops attended a study session of the liturgy conducted by the American liturgist Father Frederick McManus, and they all indicated a general enthusiasm for the reforms outlined in the *schema*.)

Maximos IV Saigh, Melchite Patriarch of Antioch, Alexandria and Jerusalem, a man who has been fighting Roman centralism all his life, read the Fathers a lesson in language and liturgy:

Christ, after all, talked in the language of his contemporaries. It was also in Aramaic that he offered the first sacrifice of the Eucharist, in a language understood by all the people who heard him. The Apostles and the disciples did the same. It would never have occurred to them that in a Christian assembly, the celebrant should hold the scriptural readings, or sing the Psalms, or preach, or break bread, in a language other than that of the gathered faithful . . . . The Roman Church used Greek in her liturgy up to the third century, because it was the language used by the faithful in those times. And if then she started to abandon Greek in favour of Latin, it is precisely because Latin had become the language of the faithful. Why should the same principle not apply today? The East never had a problem on the subject of liturgical language. Every language is, in effect, liturgical. We in the East never imagined that the faithful could be brought together to pray in a language which they do not understand. The Latin language is dead. But the Church remains alive. And language, the vehicle of grace and of the Holy Spirit, should be clear and alive. It is for men and not for angels.

III

What opposition could anyone possibly put in the way of the *schema*? How could anyone argue with the ideas of a Van Bekkum, a Hallinan or a Maximos?

It seemed incredible at the time that anyone would speak against the *schema* in general, since it was billed as a genuine *aggiornamento* (a fact which the Fathers would later confirm by overwhelming vote), but on the very first day of the debate, four worthies did exactly that.

"There are several theological errors in the *schema*," said Egidio Vagnozzi, Apostolic Delegate to the United States, to the assembled Council Fathers. "For example [he referred to a particular passage in the *schema*] it says here that our worship is Christ-centred. Now we all know it's God-centred."

Cardinal Ernesto Ruffini of Palermo, Sicily, did not reject the whole *schema* outright, but took the approach of a Southern Congressman in the face of civil rights legislation and suggested a host of complicating amendments.

World-travelling Cardinal Francis Spellman used what one wag described as "the time-worn argument from tourism." "No matter where you go on the face of the earth, the Latin Mass is a sign of Catholic unity."

And Vatican secretary of the Sacred Congregation of Rites, Archbishop Enrico Dante, seeing in the *schema* a threat to every rubric he had ever memorized, complained, "Everything has been ordained by tradition, and now you want to change it all?"

But surely these could not be the only arguments against the *schema*. Surely its opponents within and without the Curia had better reasons than this to oppose it. They did have them but, unused to giving reasons for saying "no," it took them some time to articulate them. When they did, however, it became plain that they opposed this *schema* for two principal reasons, one disciplinary and the other doctrinal. In effect, the real issues were (1) decentralization of authority and (2) the vernacular.

Clause 21 of the *schema* called for an application of liturgical reform to various regions according to the conditions in those regions—which would be judged by the bishops on the scene and not by canonists in Rome. Clause 24 of the *schema* opened up the possibility for Mass to be said in English, or French, or German or Iapanese or Swahili or Papuan. The first issue resolved itself into a fight (on a practical level) over authority in the Church. The second into a theological problem that has been puzzling the Church since its Founder began to set aside "divinely instituted" laws of the Jewish theocratic state.

Every evidence points to the fact that the Curialists saw in clause 21 a real threat to their great power in Rome. And in clause 24, many bishops at the Council, curial and non-curial alike, saw a threat to the faith which they and their predecessors had so carefully codified. The missionary mentality tended to concede the first point and deny the second. Since, despite rumours in Rome to the contrary, I did not attend the debates in St Peter's, I can only piece together the scraps of the reasonings, both pro and con.

First the theological problem. Although the Roman Mass had long since ceased to teach the faithful, the standpatters feared that, if it were put into the vernacular, it really *would* teach them— and teach them incorrectly. Better and safer, they said, to keep it in Latin. The official communiqué, always on the lookout for the best conservative arguments (because of the curial orientation of the man who composed it daily), put the case for no change in this manner: "Latin has not only traditional values but a true unifying effect. Furthermore, because of its logical precision, because of its concrete phraseology of legal terms, it is particularly suited for theology and dogma." Progressives could howl over this argument and did. One man pointed out that the Mass was not a law course and not a lesson in dogma, and another, a missionary, said the argument did not help him solve the problem of helping his people take a more active role in their community worship. But these were only practical arguments. The conservatives were actually concerned over a deeper problem—a problem that every religion must face sooner or later.

This problem, a Jesuit professor of liturgy at the Gregorian University told me, was the crisis of immutability. "If you look at the history of religions," he said, "you see that most of them consider themselves to be somehow always the same. They cannot change, because, they feel, it is the one eternal, immutable God they have to express." All religions, said the scholar, seem to reach a certain formalistic stage. When they do, the custodians of the religion see their first duty very clearly: essentialize what is basically non-essential. With their gaze riveted loyally on the immutable God, they forget that they are men who either grow and lose their formalism or get mired down in a morass of non-meaning.

A missionary bishop from Indonesia put the matter more simply: "If we do not grow," he said, "we atrophy."

Ultimately, then, the conservatives' problem at the Council could be resolved into their understanding of the Incarnation. Did the Second Person of the Blessed Trinity actually become man in the full sense of the word? If he did, what did that mean? Did it mean that human nature was changed? How? Did it mean that from that time on, Christ's followers would have to wear seamless robes like their master? Wear a beard? Not marry? Speak Aramaic? Keep the Jewish Law as he did?

The First Council of Jerusalem met to try to resolve this problem. It did—up to a point. The Council of Chalcedon attempted it again in another context. It came up with a formula, but the Church has been struggling to understand it ever since.

But could the faith survive in other surroundings? The lessons of history seem to prove that it can. The teachings of Jesus were relayed in Aramaic, then in Greek and finally, when the power of Rome extended over the civilized world (as it was known then), in Latin. But, of course, even then the missionaries carried the Good Tidings to other peoples in other languages. The Church grew and worshipped in Old Slavonic and Malabar and Coptic and a host of other tongues. Yet somehow the Roman spirit, always an exclusive thing, seemed incapable of considering that fact. It insisted on Roman uniformity, on Roman law as a tried and true safeguard against the incursions of heresy. At the time of the Reformation, the Church, to defend itself, had to opt for the Roman solution. Since then, immutability has been considered the ideal way to preserve the faith. For the latter-day Roman spirit,

preserving the faith means preserving the predominance of the
Roman Curia.

IV

Thus, the second real cause for battle in the liturgical *schema*, the
proposal to decentralize. If the liturgical *schema* passed, it would
mean the beginning of the end of curial power. Once the Pope
could find a way of delegating his power to regulate the liturgy
not to the curial congregation, which has been responsible for it
for so long, but rather to the bishop in the field (who, as a successor to the Apostles, seems to have much more of an inherent
mandate directly from Christ), then what could stop him from
delegating it in other matters? In the matter of marriage and the
Church's courts that regulate it so strictly? In the matter of educa-
ting the clergy? In the matter of keeping the faith of Christ? In
the matter of censorship and academic freedom and scholarship?
In the matter of collecting money for the missions? This is the
only explanation for the great resistance of the Curialists. If the
liturgical *schema* passed, it would mean the beginning of the end
of their power. A poor and celibate cleric does not enjoy the
challenges of a business career or the consolations of family life.
He can sublimate the lack of these in a drive for power, and who
but God can say whether he makes power an end in itself or the
means to a greater goal? The very definition of papal infallibility
was really motivated by a curialist fear that papal power would
somehow be taken away by the Italian *risorgimento* or French
Gallicanism. Though the definition did not prevent Italian patriots from seizing the Papal States, the Curialists stood in the
glow of that pale light and, considering themselves extensions of
papal infallibility, looked out from the Papal States to the whole
world. With the beginning of modern means of communication,
the world, in a sense, grew smaller; the Curialists imagined their
power over it grew greater and greater. Encased in ecclesiastical
preferment and attendant security, they wielded from their invisible and inaccessible Roman offices a power which could make
the parish priests of Pernambuco tremble and which could ex-
plode ecclesiastical bombs in San Francisco or Sydney.

Faced with the possible loss of that power, they found themselves opposing liturgical reform. One night at a meeting of papal diplomats, Archbisop Egidio Vagnozzi told them to oppose this reform and "fight for the Curia."

Thus some Curialists could and did find insignificant things to say against the *schema*; many concentrated on what seemed the most compelling argument based on the "unity" of the Church—by which they meant uniformity. Reputedly the most brilliant of the Curialists, Bishop Dino Staffa, secretary of the Sacred Congregation of Seminaries and Universities, pointed out the theological consequences of an "adapted liturgy." On October 24, he told 2,337 assembled Fathers:

It is said that the Sacred Liturgy must be adapted to times and circumstances which have changed. Here also we ought to look at the consequences. For customs, even the very face of society, change fast and will change even faster. What seems agreeable to the wishes of the multitude today will appear incongruous after thirty or fifty years. We must conclude then that after thirty or fifty years all or almost all of the liturgy would have to be changed again. This seems to be logical according to the premises, this seems logical to me, but hardly fitting [*decorum*] for the Sacred Liturgy, hardly useful for the dignity of the Church, hardly safe for the integrity and unity of the faith, hardly favouring the unity of discipline. While the world therefore tends towards unity more and more every day, especially in its manner of working and living, are we of the Latin Church going to break the admirable liturgical unity and divide into nations, regions, even provinces?

In the face of the most bewildering variety of the Council's bishops, languages, and liturgical rites, which were celebrated one by one, according to Pope John's wish, day by day before all the Council Fathers united in an Ecumenical Council, that was quite a statement. The very Mass that opened the Council that morning was concelebrated by Philippe Nabaa, Archbishop of Beirut, two priests, and one deacon in the Greek and Arabic accents of the

Greek Melchite Rite. Apropos of that Mass, Cardinal Montini wrote his people of Milan:

This beautiful but mysterious ceremony has given the Council in an unexpected way the experimental proof of the need for the liturgy to be understood and followed by the congregation. It has given the Council an equal opportunity to appreciate the beauty and the richness which the variety of rites confers on the Church. The unity and the spiritual communion of diverse tongues and manners of expression seem to result in such a variety, not less marvellous and powerful than that resulting from a rigorous uniformity of rites in which everyone can participate with profit. Catholicity, which is multiform, ought to be a rich argument for the unity of the Church.

This seemed like a rather direct refutation from Montini of Staffa's statement that "the universality and unity of the sacred liturgy are most important in my humble opinion, especially in the sacrifice of the Mass which confirms and demonstrates the unity and catholicity of the faith."* Staffa then added what to him must have been the unanswerable argument—a favourite but question-begging† one that was repeated time and time again by the Curialists in other contexts: "Moreover, we must beware if taking anything away from the supreme authority of the Roman Pontiff, for Canon 1257, backed up by the encyclical letters of many Roman Pontiffs, reserves to the Holy See alone the right of 'ordering the Sacred Liturgy' and the Constitution *Mediator Dei* repeats the same prescription in weighty tones, interprets it and carefully confirms it." His real argument was a disciplinary one. Staffa concluded with the illogical notion that the whole liturgical *schema* be sent to the Holy Office for a theological scrubbing.

---

* Some days later, a Father argued against the "unity argument" with a citation from St Paul's Epistle to the Ephesians: "Careful to keep the unity of the spirit in the bond of peace. One body and one Spirit . . . One Lord, one faith, one baptism. One God and Father of all." But, the Father added, not one language.

† Because it ignores the fact that a Council speaks with greater authority than the Pope alone.

I.C.—5*

V

The framers of the *schema* had not intended to make the constitution a theological matter—but merely a pastoral and practical application of principles to the problems at hand. They were content to let the theological and dogmatic basis for their *schema* remain implicit. The Preparatory Liturgical Commission declared that in the proposal "it wished to define nothing dogmatically."

But to Cardinal Ottaviani this was a theological problem. And no wonder, really. The *schema* implied in its whole and in every part that Christ was incarnate in time and, therefore, a force in the world. It hit right at the core of every integralist's view of Christ as a historical figure who lived on the planet for thirty-three years, was crucified, died, was buried and rose from the dead—after he had set up a juridical body called the Church to "keep the faith pure and undefiled." To the integralist, the Incarnation was a historical fact. To the progressive, the Incarnation was not only a fact by an ongoing process carried on through Christ's members in time. The one view was static, the other dynamic. The one was an outgrowth of the Old Two Cities idea, comparing the faith to a walled city; the other an older idea developed out of modern research into the Epistles of St Paul and measured against insights into the history of cultures. The one was a theology of pessimism and fear; the other a theology of optimism and hope. Both of them were based not on any specific dogma but rather on totally different ways of looking at the reality of the Church in the world.

That world was a changing thing. At one time, when all was wonder and the world was filled with magic, the Mass could be a mysterious thing and something not quite right (or at least necessary) for the man in the pew to understand. Today, when all the sophistication of modern science destroys none of the wonder in the world but merely opens new mysteries, many think the Mass can be understood and yet be an object of wonder as well.

And if the Church was going to be "in the world," the Mass would have to be properly understood by the people as the corporate worship of their community. John XXIII's encyclical *Mater et Magistra* had already laid down the most current commitment of the Church to social reform—especially in the new nations of Asia, Africa and South America—not merely to save the great masses from atheistic Communism (which system also relies on apparently the same kinds of social reform to create a new world), but because this social action should be the natural action of its members. Those members raise their heads and hearts to heaven, but they walk and eat and breathe on an earth that Christ redeemed and is supposed to go on redeeming through them. This kind of double citizenship, however, has its dangers. In the medieval Church, a commitment to the world-as-it-was-and-could-be contributed to a confusion of the secular and the sacral (which amounted to clericalism of the worst kind and a too exclusive concentration on the things of this world, so that even the popes ended by living the life of Eastern potentates). In the modern Church, there could be a similar danger: that in their social action, the Church's members could become too earth bound.

If the Church is going to plunge into the hurly-burly of the world (and it seems clear that this was the vision of John XXIII and shared by many in the Church) without becoming a mere society of do-gooders, then its members must continually relate their communality to the Trinity. Fortunately, the Church does not really have to look around for some special way of achieving that relevance. Christ himself, the liturgical scholars point out, gave his followers the Mass—a form of corporate worship which, if understood, gives them the real reason for their social being: their dependence on God, their elevation to a supernatural destiny, their realization of their blessings in the teaching of Christ, their common acceptance of the cross of Christ, their common offering of themselves with Christ to the Father in a continuation of his redemptive action in the world.

The Council's concentration on the Mass (and other sacramental forms of worship), therefore, was aimed at providing precisely the balance needed in a Church that was beginning to commit itself to the Atomic Age, to the re-creation of a new world. The problem for the Council was to get the majority of the

Church's members off the periphery of mere devotionalism (where a certain kind of centrifugal force had propelled them) and into the heart of Christ's spirituality.

During the liturgical debate, more than one Father scored the substitution of private devotionalism for the central mysteries. One day a Spanish prelate asked the Fathers how much longer the Church would have to put up with such "relics" as the Virgin Mary's milk, her veil, St Joseph's sandal and the like. He urged they "be reverently buried and heard of no more." More than one Father suggested that the Italian Church might be one of the worst offenders in this. "Nearly everywhere in Rome," noted Father Robert Rouquette, a French Jesuit journalist at the Council, "the congregation attends the Mass, but doesn't participate in it . . . the preaching goes on while the Sacrifice is celebrated, the people chatter and joke . . . People get into this habit from their childhood. It's certainly very pretty to see the *bambini* playing freely under the eyes of Our Lord during the Mass in the broad central aisles of the church, and the beautiful polychrome floors may be a fine gift of God for playing hopscotch. But as sweet as these dances before the ark might be, we must say they hardly contribute to a sense of the sacred."

Many more of the Fathers expressed a desire to right another imbalance in Catholic worship. Since the day of the heretic Pelagius, who insisted on the self-sufficiency of men themselves in their struggle for salvation, the Catholic Church had to emphasize the objective value of the Mass apart from the dispositions of the faithful. The grace of the sacrament, it was said, works *ex opere operato*, that is out of the Mass itself, and not *ex opere operantis*, or because of the dispositions of the man in the pew. Many catechisms put such a stress on this fact that the inevitable happened: the faithful tended towards a sort of mechanical rationalism, a feeling that it did not matter what they did in the pew as long as the priest continued to mumble the right words up on the altar.

When Christ became man, he became man in every sense. He had Jewish parents. He ate their food, he spoke their own words, thought their thoughts. For a time, his Apostles believed they had to garb their faith and the faith of all his followers in the same vestments. The First Council of Jerusalem, as described in Acts of the Apostles, grappled with the problem of freeing the word of God. As Archbishop Denis Hurley of Durban, South Africa, put it, "At Jerusalem the Apostles, under the guidance of the Holy Spirit, had to decide whether or not the Christian Faith would be presented to the world in Jewish garb. The Second Vatican Council at the dawn of the Space-Atomic Age must decide what new vesture must replace the garments the Church has worn through medieval and post-medieval times.... The infallibility of the Church is not called into question, but the infallibility is a last-ditch defence. It prevents us from falling over the cliff. The knowledge that there is a guard-rail is comforting. But it would be a betrayal of God's Word to cling to the guard-rail and not venture with that Word into the vast, unfolding vistas that cry out for its presence."

But Cardinal Ottaviani, as always, opted for no change. On October 30, the Fathers settled in for round two of the liturgical debate, a discussion of chapter two, the Mass. Theoretically, all 2,257 of the Fathers could sign up to speak again. Many of them did. Cardinal Godfrey spoke first (against the vernacular). Then followed Cardinal Gracias of Bombay (for the vernacular), Cardinal Bueno y Monreal of Seville (against), Cardinal Alfrink of Utrecht (for). As they spoke, Cardinal Ottaviani waited near the microphone in front of the cardinals' section, his face a picture of holy mortified recollection. But that expression soon changed when he launched into a passionate diatribe against those Fathers who talked of any changes in the Mass. The Canon of the Mass, he said, had not been changed since the seventh century, and who were they to dare change it? The Fathers, he said, were leaning towards heresy with all this foolish talk. Finally, after a full seventeen minutes, when his stream of Latin became almost completely incoherent, the president reminded Ottaviani that he had already exceeded his time limit by five minutes (politely giving him an extra two minutes). Ottaviani continued, his voice rising to a falsetto. Finally, Alfrink cut him off. When the Fathers realized what had happened, they broke into applause. Ottaviani flushed, then returned to his seat, clasped his hands together and closed his eyes. His left foot trembled. Two more cardinals spoke. One of them, Cardinal Bea, suggested the Fathers were getting bogged down in details and would be better advised to leave the specifics to committee. And then Cardinal Ottaviani left his seat— not to return for two weeks.

Ottaviani's aides at the Holy Office offered no explanation for his absence, but some of the sidewalk theologians had the perfect story. It was not a true one, but somehow it caught the spirit of the occasion. The very next morning, went the story, Ottaviani came out of his apartment and found no chauffeur. He quickly hailed a cab, told him, "To the Council," and the driver drove him to Trent.

VI

Meanwhile, at the Council, the Fathers continued to address themselves to this problem of renewing and adapting the liturgy, most of them agreeing to the necessity of leaving the door open for Mass in *their* language. Among them were Olaechea Loizaga of Valencia, Spain; Medeiros Delgado of Maranhão, Brazil; D'Souza of Nagpur, India; Garcia, Coadjutor Archbishop of Oviedo, Spain; Marty of Rheims, France; Father Aniceto Fernandez, Master General of the Dominicans; McGrath, Auxiliary Bishop of Panama; Rolim of Cajazeiras, Brazil; Kémérer of Posadas, Argentina; Devoto of Goya, Argentina; Kobayashi of Sendai, Japan; Thiandoum of Dakar, Senegal; Pildáin y Zapiláin of the Canary Islands; Melas of Nuoro, Italy. Still others included De Vito of Lucknow, India; Schoiswohl of Seckau, Austria; Weber of Ichow, China; Saboia Bandeira de Mello of Palmas, Brazil; Muldoon, Auxiliary Bishop of Sydney, Australia; Carraro of Verona, Italy; Ferrero di Cavallerleone, prelate of the Grand Master of the Knights of Malta; Vielmo, Vicar Apostolic of Aysén, Chile.

But some Fathers began to grow impatient. Still others continued to add their own embellishments to the *schema*. One bishop from Yugoslavia suggested adding St Joseph's name to the Canon of the Mass. Many of the progressives stopped talking and merely handed their observations to the Secretary-General in writing, believing that the case for reform had been sufficiently well made and confirmed from every point of the compass. Some feared that the other side was determined to filibuster the *schema* to death. On October 30, almost 200 Fathers had signed to speak on the second chapter alone.

Cardinal Cushing, nervous and irritated with the irritation of a good politician who knows poor organization when he sees it, left for home, where, he said, he could do more good for the Church by raising money for the missions.

Some pointed out that the Secretary-General's experience in writing Latin odes did not necessarily qualify him to run the world's biggest parliamentary assembly. But that did not lessen the annoyance of many who felt the Council was wasting time. Father Gregory Baum wrote in *Commonweal*, "No one knows exactly who determines the agenda of the Council. No one knows who lays down the order of discussion, who determines when the voting is to take place, and how the working commissions are to operate. No one is able to say what will happen next or at what office such information is available. . . . This obscurity in the procedure leads to annoyance and lack of confidence on the part of the bishops. Everyone speaks about 'they': 'they' have announced, or 'they' have decided; or 'they' have not yet made up their minds —and nobody knows who 'they' are."

At dinner tables in the *ristoranti* and *trattorie* of Rome, those coming from countries with a parliamentary tradition hashed over ideas for quickening the pace. Someone suggested that separate national hierarchies choose their representative bishops and let the rest of them return to their dioceses. No, another objected, that would not work because that would put Italy with 450 bishops on the same plane as Germany with sixty-eight. And if you gave each nation proportional representation, would you appoint the older and senior (and possibly more conservative) bishops to speak for their younger colleagues? Someone else suggested grouping the Council Fathers into standing committees. But that would destroy the idea of a General Council, they said, and the results could be capricious.

Douglas Woodruff, editor of *The Tablet* of London, thought he had discovered one source of the creeping progress. "It has been the great weakness of the powerful group headed by French and German bishops," wrote Woodruff, "that, while they are full of ideas, they seem to think ideas can make their own headway, and that they tend to underestimate the importance of procedure."

Actually, neither the Pope nor his progressive bishops collaborating with him in the wings were terribly worried about the pace or the procedure. The Pope wanted to exercise his authority with the greatest discretion, and the transalpine progressives wanted to give the Fathers more time to breathe in the air of change and adaptation before they moved on to more serious matters.

The Pope wanted his bishops to realize that this was their Council, and that they were here not as simple counsellors of the Pope, but authentic teachers, judges, witnesses of the faith. In the silence since Vatican I, the impression was too widespread that the Pope was everything and the bishops were nothing. That was patently wrong, in John's view, and he let them go on discovering in the liberty of the Council action itself what no document could have told them with as much force: that they were the representatives of the universal Church.

As practical-minded Pope John sat up in his fourth floor apartment watching the debate on closed-circuit television, he saw another value in the leisurely pace—an educative one. Members of the various national hierarchies in turn called on the Pope, and he found they were learning many things at the Council. If they said they were not learning, he challenged them . A group of bishops from the Far East paid a visit one day, and John turned to one of them, a tall bearded fellow. "La Barba," said John (his name was not La Barba), "what do you think of the Council?" "Not much," said the bearded bishop bluntly. "Why not?" demanded John. "We're not doing anything," replied the bishop. "Ah," said John, "you sit down there in St Peter's and you listen, and I sit up here in my apartment and I listen—and we both learn something."

The Fathers indeed learned, especially those from the mission lands, who had not had time to keep informed on the progress of the Council, who had not been reading the theological reviews, who had not received the *schemata* until a few days before their departure for Rome, who feared they could contribute nothing. They learned what the issues were by talking to other bishops— and to the theologians and scholars. In the leisurely Roman atmosphere during these first weeks, they discovered that a great deal of progress had been made in the years since they left the seminary. The entire weight of all the Catholic scholarship that had been in motion since the end of World War II seemed concentrated in Rome in the persons of theologians like Karl Rahner, Joseph Ratzinger, Yves Congar, M. D. Chenu, Henri de Lubac, Edward Schillebeeckx, Hans Küng. All of them were theologians on the march, men well equipped with the ideas that dovetailed neatly into the needs of pastors around the world. The joint effort of bishops and theologians together in group conferences and dinner conversations had an incalculable effect.

Whatever the effect, Cardinal Ottaviani suspected it would not help his "defence of the faith." He went to Pope John and expressed his concern over what he had been told was a very active ferment of new theological ideas in Rome. The Holy Office had its eye on men like Congar, Chenu, de Lubac and Rahner. In fact, Ottaviani had tried three times to have Rahner's work on the episcopacy and the primacy condemned, but had succeeded only in persuading the General of the Jesuits to have all Rahner's books censored by Jesuits in Rome. Now he found Rahner in Rome, lecturing bishops, even writing critiques of his commission's *schemata*. He asked the Pope to send Rahner back to Innsbruck—and also to keep the Jesuits from the Biblical Institute away from the innocent foreign bishops. The Pope's reply was classic. He suggested Ottaviani discuss Rahner with Cardinal Koenig of Vienna, and said he did not see how anyone could tell a bishop whom he should or should not talk to. Rahner was Koenig's private theologian, and Koenig was hardly in the mood to send him away.

The bishops were learning, too, about the intellectual bankruptcy of the Curialists in Rome. When they held conferences with the integralist theologians, they found them a defensive lot, inclined to rely not on reasonable argument but on wild charges.

One of them, Monsignor Francesco Spadafora, told a group of Mexican bishops that Rahner was a "formal heretic."

VII

Despite the good effects of this snail-like pace, however, many felt there ought to be some kind of limit on debate. The speakers droned on. Archbishop Heenan later noted that "many of them had nothing to say."

By the end of the discussion on the *schema's* preface and first chapter, someone calculated that the Council had gotten through one-eighth of the liturgical project which was only one of seventy different *schemata* fitting into the Council's *aggiornamento*.

Thus, after three weeks of meetings, the Council had finished no more than 1/552 of its work. At this rate, the Council would last thirty-two years—if there were no recesses at all. Few of the bishops present on October 11, 1962, could hope to be alive in 1994.

The Presidency met on October 26 to see what could be done to speed up matters. They could not agree on a thing. Finally when the Council recessed for four days, the bishops took stock of the situation.

Cardinal Montini reflected the general uneasiness of this period in a letter to his people. "What kind of theological plan can there be for this immense and formidable discussion? There does not seem to be any established plan. Will it be possible to establish one now?"

"What these people need," said a New York priest with a solid backbround in ward politics, "is a good Irish politician and a parliamentarian."

When the Fathers returned on November 4, after a four-day recess, the Secretary-General reminded them that "given the great number of those who have signed up to speak, the President and the Secretary-General recommend being brief, avoiding repetition and getting together beforehand so that one can speak for many who think the same way."

By practical necessity, therefore, the Secretariat had come around not only to tolerating the existence of "blocs" at the Council but to encouraging them.

The Africans banded together for the first time in history, and from then on, whenever an African spoke at the Council, he spoke for "Africa, Madagascar and the Islands." Other national conferences followed suit. The power structures were shifting, and that was the sign the Pope was waiting for.

What the Council clearly needed was some sort of cloture rule to shut off debate, but the history of Vatican I gave the Pope pause. On June 3, 1870, the Fathers of that Council invoked closure on the infallibility debate, but a minority of eighty, including Cardinals Schwarzenberg, Mathieu and Rauscher and some of the leading archbishops of Germany, Austria, Hungary, France, Northern Italy and North America, lodged a vigorous protest. Dom Cuthbert Butler reported that "application of the closure—the only one—was one of the critical events of the Council, the one which more than any other gave rise afterwards to criticisms and attack outside on the validity of the acts of the Council and of the definition of infallibility, on the ground that the closure was an unlawful suppression of rightful liberty of speech."

But certainly things could not continue this way. "If they do," said one Father, "we'll be going on into the next century." Finally, on November 6, the Pope decided to put a decision on cloture up to the Fathers themselves. He authorized the presidency to call for a standing vote on the advisability of such a move. "All those in favour please stand," cried the Secretary-General. The Fathers rose to the motion with a roar of approval. "All those not in favour . . ." said Felici, not without a sense of humour. The Fathers greeted this with a roar of laughter. "If anyone had stood up for that," recalled one particularly weary archbishop, "we would have torn him limb from limb."

The president of the day, Ignazio Tappouni, Syrian Patriarch of Antioch, promptly asked the Fathers if they wanted to close the discussion on the second chapter of the liturgy, with the stipulation, of course, that any Father who was shut off could submit his intervention in writing to the Secretary-General. Tappouni got a unanimous reaction to this, too, and the Fathers immediately began discussion of the third chapter.

The Fathers were now on their way. On November 7 they disposed of chapter three, on the Sacraments. On November 9 and 10 they disposed of chapter four, on the Divine Office. On November 12 and 13 they lumped chapters five, six, seven and eight together and finished them off, ending with a standing vote to proceed with the next item on the agenda (as suggested by the Pope), the *schema* on the sources of revelation.

On November 13 the Pope sent the message to the assembly that he was adding the name of St Joseph to the Canon of the Mass. This shocked some of the Fathers who thought that the Pope should not have taken such unilateral action and should have left such a decision up to the Council. By doing this with a snap of his fingers, however, the Pope was really demonstrating two things: (1) that the Council should worry itself about more important things. (One theologian had told me days before, "Half the world doesn't even believe in God and we worry about St Joseph.") And (2) that there is nothing the matter with change in itself. (The Canon of the Mass had remained unchanged since the year 603 but, to John, that did not mean it could not be changed now for good reason.)

After that silent sermon, the Pope and his cadre of progressive cardinals resolved to test the temper of the Council. On the next day, November 14, they called the first general vote of the session. They asked whether or not the Fathers wanted to approve the general lines of the liturgical reform so that the Council's Liturgical Commission could get some kind of general mandate to guide them on a final draft. They did not ask them to vote on specific points at issue, neither on the decentralization which was clearly going to be the only practical way of making any cultural adaptation, nor on the adaptation itself to the language and customs of peoples as diverse as the Twi-speaking tribes of Africa and the Papuan peoples of Indonesia. Both decentralization and adaptation, however, were the solid supports of this plan. If the Fathers could be induced to approve these first, it would be an easier matter to build the entire structure later.

The Fathers demonstrated their intentions by what was, considering the drawn-out liturgical debate, a ridiculously lopsided vote in favour of the *schema*. Only forty-six out of 2,215 Fathers voted *"non placet,"* which immediately proved that the Curialists led by Cardinal Ottaviani were in a very small minority indeed, though before the vote some progressives thought their cause was highly uncertain. It was just the sign the Pope had hoped for before he moved the Council into the scriptural debate, which he planned to be not only a consideration of scientific biblical studies today, but also, in effect, another test of the Council's attitude towards the modern world.

By its vote, the Council showed that it was ready to recognize the world as something that extended beyond the Roman lake of the Caesars. It recognized the world as a complex of customs and cultures that may possibly look very strange indeed to a Vatican clerk, but not, for that reason, any less redeemed and redeemable by a Christ who was crucified for all. In this project, the Council effectively came to grips with the problem of the Church and the cultures of man. In the next project it would come to grips with the problem of the Church and the mind of man.

Chapter Eight

THE WINDS OF CHANGE

I

THE world, it seemed, was a world caught up in a kind of spiral movement towards a universal society. It was a world of men become more sapient, learning, at an exponentially quickening pace, how to apply their minds to the problems of life and death, of space and the psyche, of weather and hunger and disease and a myriad of things that had, up to a short time ago, always beeen considered the exclusive domain of the divine, and "solvable" only by prayer.

What possible light, what possible life could Christ be in a world so glowing with the efforts of its own creation that scientists could light a city for a dozen years on the tappable energies latent in a pail of water, or televise *Swan Lake* from New York via outer space to New Guinea—in colour? Was the Incarnation totally irrelevant to the life of men in their creative and re-creative work in the world? Was the "life of Christ" a mere historical thirty-some years spent in a corner of the earth, or was it his energy poured out on the world, filling all times, transcending each one of them, uniting together the whole course of mankind? And where did the barque of Peter fit into this plan? Was it, the supposed bearer of Christ to all nations, intended to keep his light locked in the hold? How long would the deck officers fear to let Christ through his extensions in time, suffuse the sciences with his light?

In a large sense, the Council's scriptural debate was the occasion for a re-appraisal of the whole relationship between the Church and science. Though the official Church has never really condemned scientific investigation, its directions have been largely negative. Too often it looked through the telescope of Galileo and saw only danger to the City of God. Pope Pius XII, of course, jogged many of the old suspicions about learning with his messages on the positive values of the sciences. And John XXIII saw in each of the scientific disciplines "the beautiful *tesserae* of an enormous mosaic." But the fact remains that a long history of anti-intellectualism cast its shadow on Catholics and that this attitude could no longer prevail if the Church, the entire body of Christians, was going to be a conscious and willing part of the new world aborning.

For the official Church, obviously, the most basic science is theology, and, though the Church claims to rejoice in the protective presence of the Trinity, its theology, as science, greatly depends on another science—that of Sacred Scripture, God's inspired word. Many Council Fathers came to Rome in 1962 troubled over this science. Many had been told that it, too, was a danger to the City of God. They were given a *schema* that embodied these fears and were asked to approve it. If they did, they would set back the biblical sciences another century. If they did not, they would, in effect, open the Church out to a new and confident presence in the world.

Compared to the adolescent sciences like anthropology or psychology, scriptural science is an infant. It was not really born, as far as Catholics are concerned, until the twentieth century. An obscure priest named Richard Simon tried to father a Catholic, scientific, biblical movement in seventeenth-century France, but he appeared just long enough to be condemned by the Inquisition of the day. He left no Catholic progeny. English Deists picked up his intellectual seed in the eighteenth century, and the German rationalists followed in the nineteenth. Then, under the German stimulus, Catholic theologians with a scholarly bent attempted to apply the dangerous proposition that knowing is better than not knowing and began their scientific inquiries just in time to run into the chilly drafts of the Catholic "modernist" crisis at the beginning of the twentieth century. The leader of the Catholic exegetes, Father Marie Joseph Lagrange, the founder of the Dominican *École Biblique* at Jerusalem and the brightest luminary on the horizon of Catholic exegesis, was suddenly struck by a senseless decree from Rome on June 29, 1912. The decree forbade him to continue teaching at the *École* and banned all his works in all Catholic seminaries of the world. He returned to France and there marked time writing New Testament commentaries until he died some twenty years later.

Then, in 1930, Pope Pius XI approved the appointment of Augustin Bea as rector of the Pontifical Biblical Institute, and charged it with the task of forming future professors of Sacred Scripture in Catholic seminaries and universities. For a time, the institute made solid, if unspectacular, progress, but, soon after Pius XII took over the pontificate, Curialists began to play the old anti-modernist tune and attacked the orthodoxy of the whole biblical movement. Pius XII promptly answered these attacks with the encyclical letter *Divino Afflante Spiritu* (drafted by the Jesuit Bea) and that, everyone thought, was that.

In the letter, Pius XII finally gave the scholars the charter they needed to plumb the depths of the Scriptures with all the scientific tools at their disposal. These included ancillary sciences like archaeology, palaeontology, and Semitic languages and literature. In particular, the Pope dwelt on the use of what he called "literary forms" and considered the type of historicity contained in the Bible. The violent attacks of rationalism in the nineteenth century had all been based on a narrow, myopic conception of history, "Just as it really happened"—*wie es eigentlich geschehen ist,* to use the famous phrase of the German philosopher. But the recounting of facts as they happened, the building up of a pattern of events by the careful collation of documents and eyewitnesses, the strictly chronological recounting of a passage of history—these are modern concepts and a modern idea of how events should be presented. This is not the kind of historicity we find in Scripture, said Pius XII. To demand a modern conception of historicity from writers in the last millennium before Christ or indeed from the New Testament authors would be as reasonable as demanding an account of the Galileo universe from Strabo or depth psychology from Plato. The fact is that both in the Old and the New Testament, historical events are recounted in ways and in forms which were in usage at the time of the composition of these books. As a result of this sound approach, the Catholic doctrine of inspiration and its important corollary, inerrancy, are defendable, and, indeed, find their proper expression.

Under the guidance of Pius XII, the biblical scholars came to a deeper understanding of how God, through specific events, personalities, and human utterances, has intervened in human affairs. As the Jesuit biblical scholar, David Michael Stanley, has put it, the history in the Bible is a particular "genre of history, which we call salvation-history or *Heilsgeschichte*. [It] is the story of God's self-revelation to us, and its aim is obviously very different from that of modern scientific history which is written without reference to the divine point of view. . . . The evangelists propose, in their written accounts of Jesus' life upon earth, to give their readers not merely an exposition based upon ocular testimony. They aim at writing salvation-history. They offer an insight into the meaning of the mystery of Jesus Christ."

Modern biblical scholars, therefore, can say that the Bible is full of particular literary forms, all of them varyingly "historical" in the modern sense. Among these special literary forms: the genealogy, the eyewitness account, popular traditions, family reminiscences, externalized representations of interior experiences, the midrash.

Once the *genealogy* is seen to be an art form and not strict "history," then there is no need to "reconcile" the age-old "conflict" between the genealogies of Matthew and Luke, since those genealogies are deliberately incomplete and have different aims. Luke attempts to convey the idea that Jesus was the Son of God, and therefore uses the Greek genealogical phrase "X who was of Y" in ascending order—which thereby permits him to employ the same expression for Adam's relationship to God as for Seth's relationship to Adam. On the other hand, the chief purpose of Matthew's genealogy is to show the link between esus and the salvation-history of his people; Matthew therefore descends from Abraham and employs the biblical term "generated" to show that Jesus is from seed of Abraham.

Eyewitness accounts (which are seen to be obviously that from their vividness) also go beyond mere surface reporting. In 3:9–22, Mark goes beyond sense impressions to testify to the divine mystery of the person of Jesus. Matthew obviously reports the words of Jesus so as to keep their semitic idiom and flavour, but other evangelists, especially John, express Jesus' sayings in their own style and terminology.

Popular traditions are those old stories told especially by the peoples of the Near East to explain the nature of things. Scholars say that God was pleased to use even these as the vehicle of his revelation. Among them they instance the story of the Magi and possibly the story of the strange happenings in Jerusalem after Jesus' death (Matthew 27:51–53).

Family reminiscences are seen, say the scholars, in certain parts of the Matthew and Luke infancy narratives.

Externalized representations of interior experiences? Scholars cite the heavenly voice at Jesus' baptism apparently heard by no one else (Matthew 3:16), Jesus' triple temptation (Matthew 4:1–11), possibly the annunciations to Zachary (Luke 1:11–22), to Mary (Luke 1:26–38), Joseph's dream in Matthew 1:20–21. Other expressions related to this genre: attempts to describe supernatural phenomena which defy human expression, for example, the Pentecostal "tongues *as if* of fire" and "his sweat became *as it were* drops of blood."

The *midrash* is a pious reflection on a past event which brings out with greater clarity the salvific aspect of that event. For example, Elizabeth says to Mary, "Why is this granted me that the mother of my Lord should come to me?" This is, say the scholars, obviously a reflection of II Samuel 6:9, "How can the ark of the Lord come to me?" By putting these words in the mouth of Elizabeth, say the scholars, the evangelist Luke could reveal a whole new dimension of the Virgin Mary in the economy of salvation.

As long as this kind of probing is done "with the eyes of faith," the Christian world can only become all the richer for it. Cardinal Alfrink once said, the Catholic exegetes "work in all sincerity to bring out more clearly the profound meaning of the Word of God." The Christian intellectual community must applaud such activity. As the Jesuit rector of Rome's Biblical Institute once told me, "Some talk about the masses taking scandal from our scientific work. I think it is the intellectuals who take the greater scandal if we do *not* engage in it."

But what impact can the modern biblical movement have on the average Christian? It has had and can have in the future an increasing impact on Christian unity with all that that implies. And, as it takes an increasing hold on the average teacher and priest, it could bring the Christian out of his abstract religious world into the world he lives and loves in. Redemptorist Father Bernard Häring, one of the Church's leading moral theologians today, believes that "the biblical movement has helped to put the faith into a real historical context. The very methods of literary form criticism imply that men are not abstractions and that God does not choose to deal with them as if they were. Men exist in a concrete environment and God speaks to them in that environment. By going to Scripture, we see how God presents the Good Tidings. He does not speak in abstract terms. He speaks to men in their actual situations. The moral message of the Gospel is not therefore an abstract, legalistic, juridical message. It is integrated in the Good Tidings." Such an approach, said Häring to me in a private conversation, implies an "intense involvement of the Church in religious sociology. After learning the essential message," said Häring, "we learn from the Word of God how to speak. But then we have to look at the concrete situation today to see how to apply this message. We can either give the people the old formulas or we can attempt new answers. We may run the risk of making some mistakes in this attempt. But we will surely be wrong if we attempt to keep using the old formulas. Life is not a formula. Much less a formula that was conceived in the seventeenth century."

II

In spite of the obvious contributions made by the biblical scholars, however, and the great promise of much more to come (as in the field of nuclear physics, most of the biblical scholars are young men trained since World War II), Curialists and other reactionaries united for the separation of action and intelligence soon busied themselves in a campaign to blunt the scientific thrust that was launched, in a burst of inspiration, by Pius XII.

Overt rumours were started in Rome that the Biblical Institute was teaching heresy. They were traced to two curial monsignori, Paolo Igino Cecchetti and Antonino Romeo, but Cardinal Giuseppe Pizzardo, then the secretary of the Holy Office, assured the worried rector of the Biblical Institute that he had given them personal orders to cease and desist. They did not. Both men continued to write and speak publicly against the biblical movement. An anonymous article even appeared in *Osservatore Romano*, on July 2, 1958, aimed against an *Introduction to the Bible*, the second edition of which was being prepared under some guidance of Bea himself, then a consultor of the Holy Office. Pius XII made an avowed answer to that article with a letter to the International Catholic Bible Congress in Brussels at the end of August. The two monsignori stopped their public attacks but enlisted the aid of another monsignor from the Holy Office, Antonio Piolanti, plus the forum of the Lateran University review *Divinitas*. In December, 1960, *Divinitas* published a violently passionate attack against the Biblical Institute by Monsignor Romeo. A great furor arose. Members of the Pontifical Commission of Biblical Studies, including Cardinal Achille Liénart, protested strongly, and the rector of the Bibilical Institute countered with refutations of the Romeo charges which he called, "systematically deformed calumnies."

Nevertheless, these attacks had their inevitable effect. Bishops everywhere began to have their doubts about the biblical movement. American bishops who had not heard of the charges via the ecclesiastical grapevine soon found the attacks being exported to the United States by the Apostolic Delegate Egidio Vagnozzi. Vagnozzi appeared at Marquette University in June of 1961, and in perhaps the most widely publicized baccalaureate address of the spring expressed "a necessary caution to those who allow themselves to be overcome by the glamour of that which is new and by the allurement of that which is calculated to startle rather than to enlighten." (This was Vagnozzi's own later description of his talk that attempted to score, one by one, the Catholic intellectual in a secular society, reform of the liturgy, the vernacular in the Mass, liturgical art and recent developments in scriptural studies. He did all of it, he later explained, "as the representative of the Holy Father in this country."

Needless to say, Vagnozzi's remarks did not sit well with Catholic intellectuals or with Catholic biblical scholars in the United States. One group of laymen replied through an open letter that was carried in some few Catholic weeklies. Vagnozzi replied in kind, putting the laymen into their "proper place in the Church" where they have their "proper good to contribute to the life of Christ's Mystical Body." However, said Vagnozzi, "the layman has not been constituted as teacher of the *magisterium* nor as admonitor of the hierarchy. When, after mature deliberation, one wishes to inform those in authority of the problems and inspirations of the people, he can do it directly, rather than by sending critical letters to the press."

Soon after Vagnozzi's talk at Marquette, on June 20, the Holy Office issued a *Monitum* on biblical studies. Some Catholic newspapers interpreted the *Monitum* as a stern reprimand to biblical scholars (one paper offered the explanation that an unnamed Catholic exegete had denied "the historical accuracy of the Incarnation"), but the scholars themselves saw in the *Monitum* an encouragement to further investigation and "a most reasonable and restrained call for all biblical teachers and writers to exercise due prudence and reverence."

However, the *American Ecclesiastical Review*, ever eager for action at the sniff of heresy, seized upon the *Monitum* as fresh material in its standing campaign against the biblical innovators. The Rev. William S. Schneirla, of St Vladimir's Orthodox Theological Seminary in New York, concluded, after studying the *Review* for some months running, that it aimed to present Roman Catholic scriptural scholars as "dilettantes engaged in a field of investigation that is suspect and perilous in itself, [who] subvert tradition and the analogy of faith to their highly personal and Bultmannian exegesis, neglect prayer for misguided study and promote each other in a neo-Modernist cabal."

Archbishop Vagnozzi used the same *Monitum* in an August

address to religious superiors at Notre Dame University where he advised them that subjects "pursue their studies in a spirit of humble faith, not vain rationalism or self-seeking . . . forming fo your institute religious who are strangers to the self-assurance o. subjectivism . . ." Vagnozzi then added: "In this regard I wish to call your attention in a particular way to the recent *Monitum* of the Holy Office regarding biblical sciences. This *Monitum* did not originate in the personal worries or limited views of a small group of Vatican officials. Nor was it issued without serious and weighty reasons. It comes from that sacred congregation which is supreme among the authoritative organs of the Apostolic See and of which the Holy Father himself is the head and prefect. A *Monitum* is only a warning, but it is designed to prevent the adoption of stronger and more direct measures."

At the end of August, the Catholic Biblical Association of America met at Norwood, Ohio, and found a place in its busy agenda to pass a resolution proposed by the Jesuit John L. McKenzie rejecting unwarranted attacks on biblical scholars in America. The association sent the resolution to the National Catholic Welfare Conference in Washington, but the NCWC News Service, preferring prudent inaction to reporting the news, suppressed the story.

The *American Ecclesiastical Review*, however, suppressed nothing and used the rest of its numbers preceding the Council in full-throated and triumphant cry for the hide of the vulpine "scrip-turists." It was owing largely to the editorial guidance of Monsignor Joseph Clifford Fenton that American bishops were aware of the charges being levelled on their side of the Atlantic. The editor, a faculty member of the Catholic University of America, wished to convince the bishops that the modern scriptural movement aimed deliberately at dismembering the Church of God.

If anyone came to the Council unaware of these attacks but able and/or willing to read Italian, he soon found he could catch up on the most virulent charges. Each and every Council Father was presented upon his arrival in Rome with a jaundice-coloured, 36-page pamphlet by Monsignor Francesco Spadafora, entitled

"*Razionalismo Esegesi Cattolica e Magistero*," "Rationalism, Catholic Exegesis and the Magisterium." Spadafora carefully specified that this work was "meant for the most reverend Council Fathers only and strictly reserved to them alone," but the work turned out to be an unrevised reprint of two articles already published in an Italian review called *Palestra del Clero* and a previously unpublished third article entitled "Criticism and the Gospels." In this pamphlet, Spadafora attacked the exegetical method called *Formgeschichte*—Form Criticism—as practised by non-Catholic biblical scholars and, he said, currently being taught without reservation by the Pontifical Biblical Institute. Spadafora explained his purpose—to prove that the Pontifical Biblical Institute is an instrument being used "to try to introduce into the Church, or to make the Church accept, the principles of criticism used by rationalism, the evolutionist theories of Wellhausen and Gunkel for the Old Testament, and of Form Criticism for the New Testament." He recommended to the Fathers that they make "an explicit, express condemnation of such a system" and look for positive guarantees "to prevent young priests coming to Rome to study Sacred Scripture from losing all that they had learnt during their theological studies."

Spadafora's attack was no mere theological dispute. If it had been that, if it had remained on a scientific (if impassioned) level, the world of scholarship would have stood to gain in the end. Spadafora's attacks, however, were directed against the Biblical Institute's two senior New Testament exegetes, Stanislaus Lyonnet and Maximilian Zerwick. Spadafora charged Lyonnet with perverting the sense of original sin as taught by the Council of Trent, and Zerwick with having denied the historicity of Matthew 16: 16–19, the classic text used to prove the promise of the primacy to Peter. Both charges were proved false, and it appeared that Spadafora's charges would die, but unaccountably and without explanation, the Holy Office demanded the end of Zerwick's and Lyonnet's exegetical careers and the pair were teaching ancient languages when the Fathers arrived in Rome in October. On the night Lyonnet and Zerwick were dismissed, some Curialists had a victory celebration at the Pensionato Romano.

"This time, we shall break the monopoly," one of them shouted.

Those who were puzzled over the apparently great power of a chubby Italian monsignor (who had once said that Pius XII was "a cretin who knew nothing about exegesis") soon learned that Spadafora was only a front man for Monsignor Antonino Romeo, an *aiutante* in the Congregation of Seminaries; Monsignor Antonio Piolanti, the Rector Magnificus of the Lateran; Cardinal Ottaviani; Cardinal Pizzardo; and Cardinal Ruffini. Ruffini, an old student of the Biblical Institute, momentarily came out of the wilds of Palermo on August 24, 1961, to pen an article called *"Generi letterari e ipotesi di lavoro nei recenti studi biblici"* that ran, to his everlasting chagrin, on page one of the *Osservatore Romano*. There, as the author of an engaging *New Yorker* series on the Council has pointed out, Ruffini undertakes a point-for-point refutation of a central passage in Pius XII's encyclical, *Divino Afflante Spiritu.*

Said Pius XII:

In the words and writings of the ancient Oriental authors, the literal sense does not appear with as much clarity as it does in writers of our times. What they—the authors of the Bible—intended to signify by their words cannot be determined solely by the laws of grammar or of philology. It is absolutely necessary that the exegete go back to the manner of thinking of the Orient in those far centuries, so that, helping himself with the resources of *history,* of *archaeology,* of *ethnology, and of the other sciences,* he may discern and recognize what literary genres the authors of that ancient age wished to use or actually did employ. ... The exegete cannot determine *a priori* what were the forms of speech and expression used by these authors. He can only do this by the attentive study of the ancient literatures of the Orient.

Ruffini, seriously concerned, no doubt, that the Church might have to admit that logically some of its interpretations these many centuries have been "wrong", wrote the following:

How can anyone suppose that the Church has during nineteen centuries presented the Divine Book to its children without knowing the literary genre in which it was composed, if this is the key to exact interpretation? Such an assertion becomes all the more absurd when one takes into account that a large number of these superior-minded critics not only call for new applications of the theory of literary genres in regard to the inspired books but remit to the future a definitive explanation; that is to say, to the time when one will come to understand better, through the study of *history*, of *archaeology*, of *ethnology*, *and of the other sciences*, the manner of speaking and writing of the ancients, particularly the Orientals.

The New Yorker article, needless to say, was required reading in Rome by the bishops who were eager to learn, even if it meant learning from *The New Yorker's* mystery man, Xavier Rynne.

III

However, most bishops did not depend on such material for their real theological insights. As a matter of daily routine, at lunch in the afternoons, at dinner, into the night, the conciliar community was treated to an intensive programme of lectures, panel discussions and conversations from and with other bishops and theologians from all over the world.

If any bishops were wondering what the proper relationship was between bishops (*the teaching Church*) and expert theologians or historians (officially and juridically the Church *to be taught*), he received ample evidence at the Council of the practical necessity for the teaching Church to listen to the voices that come, charismatically, from ... wherever the Spirit wished them to come from. As one bishop from Canada put it, "The episcopal office consists not only in speaking to the people but in listening to the forms and expressions of the Christian faith."

Thus, in the weeks before the scriptural debate, theologians from varying schools of thought were asked by the bishops for their opinions on the biblical movement.

I.C.—6

Cardinal Bea wrote a special fifty-nine-page article on the historicity and inspiration of the Bible, had it translated into four languages and distributed around Rome. Cardinal Ruffini gave a talk to the Spanish bishops and Karl Rahner gave one to the South American bishops, and he and his close friend and collaborator Father Joseph Ratzinger, wrote a *schema* on Scripture that many bishops hailed as a possible replacement for the *schema* that was produced by Cardinal Ottaviani's Preparatory Theological Commission (it was said that the Ottaviani *schema* amounted to an outright attack on the biblical scholars and their methods); Rahner and Ratzinger also wrote a critique of the Ottaviani *schema* that listed twelve other reasons why *"hoc schema non placet."* The chief among them, as far as I could see, was the complaint that it was not pastoral, that is, it laboured under the old assumption that the Scriptures were not really for the people. It is no secret that many Catholics consider Bible reading "rather Protestant." Monsignor Arthur Elchinger, Coadjutor Bishop of Strasbourg, pointed out in one press conference during the Council, "In most Catholic homes, you don't find a Bible—or if you do, it doesn't have a place of honour." During the liturgy debate, Cardinal Antonio Bacci of the Roman Curia asserted that *"nuda scriptura non est pro popolo"*—in other words the Church should no more encourage reading the Scripture to the people in their own language than promote prep-school excursions to the *Folies Bergères*. Elchinger said statements like this "bespeak a minimist conception of the word of God."

Not the least popular among the theologians in Rome were the Jesuit Fathers of the Biblical Institute who scattered around the city, each of them a legate to the bishops of his own tongue. When Ottaviani heard this, he furiously hied himself to the papal apartments to protest against these missions, but the Pope's answer was that if the bishops wanted to inform themselves about the biblical movement, shouldn't they really talk to some of the Jesuit professors?

Thus, as the Council Fathers became more *au courant* with the biblical question (and more bored with the liturgical debate), they became psychologically "ready" for the fireworks of November 14th. The day before, a theologian told me (when I said how much I would like to get inside for that one day), "You may not have to get in. They may blow the roof right off St Peter's."

On the eve of the debate, Cardinal Montini wrote his people in Milan: "Everyone can understand how fundamental such a theme is to our faith and everyone can understand that the Council will speak of it with the seriousness and solemnity which it deserves. But only those who are acquainted with the development of theology, of the progress in Biblical studies, and the heat of the controversies on these questions, inside and outside Catholicism, can appreciate the apprehensions, the hopes, the fears which this new argument brings to the conciliar assembly."

An official took the occasion to warn journalists "to treat this subject with care, caution and the discretion which it requires." The stage was set.

IV

After the conciliar Mass on the 14th (Paul Cheng, the Auxiliary Bishop of Taipeh, Formosa, celebrated, and the 2,215 Fathers present made it a dialogue Mass when they joined in the responses), the Secretary-General announced that the president for the day would be Cardinal Eugène Tisserant, dean of the College of Cardinals. Tisserant, seated at the presidents' table at the head of the aisle, corrected Felici. "This morning," said Tisserant, "I'm *legatus a latere* of the Pope."

This meant that the Pope had given Tisserant full power, on this important morning, to speak and act, if necessary, in the name of Giovanni XXIII himself.

Tisserant then nodded to Cardinal Ottaviani who had at last broken his fifteen-day boycott of the Council and come to present the first fruits of his Preparatory Theological Commission's three years' labour. "The teaching of truth," began Ottaviani, "is always and everywhere the same. . . ." It was his job as president of the Theological Commission to present the *schema* to the Fathers, but, remembering the rebuke he had received the last time he spoke in the Council, and reminding the Fathers of his blindness, he called upon one of his assistants in the Holy Office, Monsignor Salvatore Garofalo, "to explain the project."

Garofalo said the *schema* did not intend "to renew doctrine but give it increase," told the Fathers how much work went into its preparation, and outlined the *schema*'s five chapters: (1) the two-fold source of revelation, (2) its inspiration and the literary composition of the Scriptures, (3) the Old Testament, (4) the New Testament, and (5) Sacred Scripture in the Church.

Then Tisserant leaned into the microphone and read from the list of Fathers who had signed up to speak: "*Loquatur Eminentissimus Dominus Achilles Cardinal Liénart Archiepiscopus Lillis: accedat ad microphoniam Dominus Josephus Cardinalis Frings Archiepiscopus Coloniae in Germania.*" The Council Fathers, well aware that both Liénart and Frings were graduates of the Biblical Institute and biblical scholars in their own right, leaned forward expectantly.

"*Hoc schema mihi non placet,*" began Liénart bluntly. "This proposal doesn't please me."

Liénart said he thought the whole *schema* hopelessly inadequate and that it failed to take into account the tremendous progress made in scriptural scholarship during the last forty years, by Protestants as well as Catholics.

Frings was almost poetic. "Truth is like music," he said. "This *schema* belongs to the wrong class of music. It's too rigid. It's immature."

Next man at the microphone was Cardinal Ruffini, the bell-wether of the Roman reactionaries (he spoke thirteen times during the first session, twice as much as any other single man). Ruffini launched the reactionaries' only real argument of the debate and predictably it was an argument from authority. "This is the Pope's own *schema*," claimed Ruffini. "By what authority does the Council presume to attack it?"

Two more conservatives rose to defend the *schema*. Cardinal Giuseppe Siri of Genoa said it "guarded the Church against the danger of modern heresy." Cardinal Fernando Quiroga y Palacios of Santiago de Compostela agreed with Siri but allowed that the *schema* could use a few modifications.

But from that point on during that historic day, the cardinals rose one by one to plead the impossibility of the whole thing. Paul Emile Léger of Montreal said the *schema* was plagiarized from some textbooks and some pretty out-of-date textbooks at that. Franziskus Koenig of Vienna said it avoided the important questions. Bernard Jan Alfrink of Utrecht refuted Ruffini directly but good-naturedly and said that the conciliar Fathers were really showing reverence to the Pope and the Pope's plans for the Council by engaging in discussion. Léon Joseph Suenens of Malines-Brussels said that one part of the *schema* "*non placet*" and another part of it "*minus placet*"—one part of it did not please at all and another part was even less pleasing.

Joseph Elmer Ritter of St. Louis said the *schema* should be rejected (*rejiciendum est*) because it did not fit modern needs and had a "pessimistic, negative tone."

By this time, it was apparent to even the most ancient abbot in the house that something historic was happening. The Council's coffee bar, normally filling up by this time each morning during the liturgical debate, was completely empty when Augustin Bea approached the microphone. As president of the Secretariat for Promoting Christian Unity and also the Council's ranking biblical expert, Bea's words rang out clearly and simply. "This *schema* does not fit the needs of this Council, which was called to bring the Church up-to-date and to promote Christian unity," said Bea, and added that its adoption "would close the door to intellectual Europe and the outstretched hands of friendship in the Old and the New World." What the Council needed, said Bea, was an entirely new document which would be "clear, concise, modern and ecumenical."

Maximos IV Saigh, the Melchite Patriarch of Antioch, speaking in French (his usual open protest against the Latinization of the universal Church), said the *schema* was "negative, polemic" and seemed to derive from some "theological bickerings which the Council should avoid." Maximos scored the "condemnatory tone" and the "outmoded formulas of the Counter Reformation and anti-modernism," asked the Fathers to help Christians find ways of strengthening their Christian life and prepare the way for an ecumenical dialogue. He also asked the Council to have confidence in the Church's great scholars and theologians and leave them "an open field."

Archbishops Gabriel Manek and Albert Soegijapranata, both of Indonesia, spoke against the *schema*, and Archbishop Morcillo Gonzalez of Saragossa, Spain, proposed some substantial modifications.

And that was how the hole was dug for the burial of the first Ottaviani *schema*.

After the meeting, I stood in front of the Holy Office, just to the south of St Peter's, and watched the bishops stream by. Their faces were aglow now that the battle of the Lord had at last begun. A New Zealander said, "Now the gloves are off." Maximos IV said, "The big fellow got 'em [he was referring, I found out later, to Cardinal Bea] and I got 'em too." One Irish bishop was visibly shaken and told a friend (who reported it to me): "We've had a mistaken idea that Cardinal Ottaviani represents the Holy See. My God, we'll have to revise our ideas of what the Holy See is."

Cardinal Ottaviani stubbornly told a consoling colleague, "*Sumus semper cum Petro et sub Petro etiam in summo periculo*"— "We're always with Peter and under Peter even when he's in the greatest danger."

But in his apartment on the other side of Vatican City, Pope John saw it differently. "*Adesso comincia il mio concilio*," said he. "Now begins my Council."

V

The Bishop of Nantes, Jean Joseph Villepelet, later told his people why this day was so important. "We heard a dozen of the Church's most representative cardinals," he wrote, "expressing their opinions freely and strongly on the most delicate questions so far. Our meetings had never attained such greatness. No more little details, like the ones we heard in the liturgy debate—even though they did have an importance. But here we came to the summit of our Catholic faith, its need of being formulated for the modern world, always in light of the pastoral view which is the great preoccupation of the Second Vatican Council."

And Monsignor François Charrière, Bishop of Lausanne, Geneva and Fribourg, said, "Like a jet plane taking off, the conciliar assembly suddenly reached the exhilarating air of doctrinal heights. It was profoundly moving."

The official communiqué, of course, gave little hint of the overwhelming conciliar dissatisfaction with the schema.

It read: "The various positions were outlined: the first favourable to the project, the second unfavourable, and the third asking for its re-working. All agreed that the work of preparation had been very accurate. All, however, admitted that the project on the whole must be perfected."

That was all the communiqué said. Given the bias of the official press office, that is about all it could have said. Anything more would have been treason.

VI

On the second day of the debate, ten cardinals, nine archbishops, one bishop and an abbot got up one by one to voice their difficulties over the schema. Not one of them favoured it as it stood. Cardinal McIntyre of Los Angeles, however, did say he agreed with the schema's treatment of the biblical movement and the biblical scholars "who have confused both pastor and the faithful." For McIntyre, this was, as were all of his interventions at the Council, an honest statement. His Eminence casts a long shadow over the West Coast, but it is owing more to his financial than intellectual stature. Theological discussion does confuse him. Dom Christopher Butler, Abbot-President of the English Benedictines, inserted a typically English suggestion, born of a parliamentary tradition, that since there seemed to be so many objections to the schema, it really ought to be withdrawn.

But the others took the occasion of this debate to articulate their own increasing realization of how the Church's scholars could enter the twentieth century—which was, after all, one of John's principal aims. Archbishop Ermenegildo Florit of Florence pointed out the Fathers' increasing awareness of the value of recent biblical research. It fitted so well, he maintained, into the deepening biblical-liturgical movements of the last decade, which in themselves have had the effect of bringing Catholics closer to some of the "separated brethren." The latter, he pointed out, have been working along the same lines. "It is almost as if the Lord has been discreetly indicating the ways towards that desired Christian unity."

Archbishop Emile Guerry of Cambrai spoke for all the French bishops and refuted the notion that the Fathers speaking against the *schema* somehow wanted to soften Catholic teaching. "Pastors," he said, "know well that their first duty is to teach doctrine in its fullness. But they do want to find the best way of presenting this doctrine and making it better understood and more desirable."

Later, in an interview with the French daily *La Croix*, Guerry amplified on the statement. "You can't separate '*la doctrine*' from '*la pastorale*,'" he declared. "But you can talk about a different approach in a Christian land and a missionary land. In a Christian land, the first care of a pastor is to guard the doctrine, to denounce the errors which threaten his people, to protect them against dangerous influences." (I seriously doubt that there is any such "Christian land" today. In Italy, Spain and the so-called Catholic countries of South America, a process of de-Christianization has been going on for decades but only recently have their pastors decided to face the fact. However . . .) "But in a mission land," said Guerry, a man who thinks of his own land, Catholic France as a missionary land, "the pastor's great preoccupation is to find a way of communicating the doctrine of salvation to all. He feels gravely responsible for the salvation of all. But this does not mean that he is less careful about doctrine or that he is failing in his duty of teaching his Christian people. It means, on the contrary, that his missionary duty obliges him to dig deeply, to assimilate the doctrine so well that he can even present it to the unbelievers, to the indifferents, in a form which is understandable, living, attractive." But in this effort, in this reflection on the truth, said Guerry, legitimate currents will appear in the Church. "The living magisterium of the Church respects this diversity and liberty of investigation and expression, but only on the condition that one of these schools does not attempt to become so exclusive or totalitarian that it considers itself as the only valid interpreter of the Church's teaching or foment suspicion and anathemas against the other."

It was precisely this exclusive mentality, of course, that the Fathers could see in the Ottaviani *schema*. For the "defenders of the faith," the task was simple: preserve what had been handed down. But the archaism of this approach simply did not commend itself to the bishops assembled, members of a living body. In the United States, at least, and in many other countries, I suspect, much has been made of the fact that the Catholic doctrine is "unchanging." Even at the Council, one could hear this kind of reassuring talk from bishops who would turn right around and talk excitedly about the newest discoveries of the biblical scholars or the liturgical scholars or the patristic scholars—even about the new perceptions in depth of the great continental theologians like Rahner, Congar, De Lubac, Schillebeeckx. The fact is that the faith is changing in almost every way because it is growing, and growth is change of the best sort.

Or, as Guerry himself put it in the *La Croix* interview: "We believe that the best way to safeguard the doctrine is to open it up to new penetration [*est de lui ouvrir de nouveau champs de pénétration et de rayonnement*] as the Holy Father explicitly demanded in his opening discourse. . . ." The task is a large one, said Guerry. "Think of all the work to be done on a theology of earthly and human values: the body, love, work, money, art, technical culture, science. Think of all the international social problems, and of ecumenism. . . . We need a dynamic theology but we cannot have it without that Christian optimism that breathes hope, stimulates courage and frees us from our paralyzing fear and our defensive attitude."

From the Ottaviani side came only the defence that the *schema* "was prepared by bishops and learned priests, approved by the Central Commission which was composed of a majority of cardinals."

But on the third day of the debate, both Ottaviani and Pietro Parente, assessor of the Holy Office, got up to push the juridical argument to its limit. Ottaviani claimed that the *schema* was not his own work but that of the Theological Commission which was composed of men from many lands. Parente cited Canon 222 which reserves to the Roman pontiff alone the right of establishing the matter which should be examined at a Council. In other words, the cardinals and bishops who wanted a new *schema* were breaking the law. At this point, the president of the day, Cardinal Norman Gilroy of Sydney, called the attention of all Council Fathers to Council Rule 33 which stated explicitly that "every Council Father can express his opinion on every *schema* presented, to ask for its adoption, its amendment, or its rejection." Ottaviani asked for the floor to protest, but since he had already spoken that morning, he was ignored.

Parente went on to say that he personally thought that not everything he had heard on this subject of Scripture was free from error since the Church had already pronounced on the questions of the two sources and settled this long ago.

Cardinal Doepfner demurred and said he thought the *schema* represented only one school of thought. Bishop Hakim of Akka added that it really only represented one school of one region, since it failed to accord with any Eastern viewpoint which had always been against any disjunction between Scripture and tradition. Bishop Charue of Namur narrowed the source of the *schema* down even further, claiming it represented only one small city in Christendom, Rome, and then took an even longer view of the proceedings and emphasized the possible impact on the modern world of a biblical science that was really scientific. "The best means of entering the modern world is to encourage the scholars," said Charue, and added that if the Church did not do precisely that, it would regret the day as much as it now regrets its silly position on Galileo. Monsignor Jean Baptiste Zoa, Bishop of Yaoundé and secretary of the Pan African Bishops Conference, rejected the whole *schema* and suggested it be given to a work committee of bishops and theologians—which was in a way a cruel blow to Archbishop Parente who had taught Zoa at the

Propaganda College not too many years ago. That afternoon, Parente called on Zoa and asked him if he really believed the things he had said in the Council. Under the inquisitorial gaze of his old teacher, Zoa replied evasively, "I don't think that matters, does it?" Zoa soon found that Parente had talked to other African bishops about Zoa's orthodoxy, and Zoa noticed he himself was later regarded with some suspicion (or at least treated standoffishly) by his African colleagues.

Cardinal Ottaviani, too, was worried about the course of the debate. Each day his face seemed to grow longer, and, after the cardinals had finished speaking each morning, seeming able to hear no more, he would heave a sigh and shuffle out of the basilica. He went to the Pope and told him how concerned he was over the evident dissension among the Fathers. John could see, of course, that Ottaviani was not worried so much about dissension as about the fate of not only his *schema* but the whole future of the Holy Office itself. But he contented himself to take Ottaviani's words at face value. "Dissension?" he is reported to have told Ottaviani. "Dissension also troubled the First Vatican Council and the Council of Trent. Why the discussion at Trent became so heated that at one point an Italian bishop tore the beard of a Greek bishop. Even so, the Council of Trent is remembered today as a great event."

"Well," countered Ottaviani, "if this goes on much longer, the dignity of the Roman dicasteries is in danger. I may resign."

"You will stay," said John. "There will be no humiliation."

Later that day, November 18, Cardinal Bea heard from John. "They are beaten," said John, "but there must be no humiliation."

That night the Bea forces tried to figure out how they could scuttle the *schema* without scuttling Ottaviani. They were still far from any assurance that the Fathers as a whole understood why the *schema* was, in the context of the Council, an impossible document, but they finally decided to present a compromise solution and, at the same time, read the Fathers a lesson in ecumenism.

The next day's debate began with Cardinal Gracias of Bombay

making it very clear that the Pope did not "approve the *schema*" but merely received it from the Central Commission (whose amendments were ignored by the secretaries handling it) and passed it on to the Council. Cardinal Rugambwa compared the by-this-time-battered *schema* to a house that had fallen into ruin. Better, he said, to tear it down and build a new one than to try to repair it. Then Cardinal Albert Meyer of Chicago, a former student of Bea's at the Biblical Institute, said it was clear to him that no general accord could be reached as long as the Council held on to this *schema* and proposed that a new one be written with the co-operation of theologians and exegetes from all nations and all tendencies that would "retain those points that corresponded with the scope of the Council and add those points that it lacked." He also asked for a vote of confidence in the labours of the Catholic exegetes, who should in turn continue to follow the norms for interpreting Scripture laid down by Pius XII.

VII

Cardinal Meyer's intervention was conciliatory and at this point it was just what the Council needed. But how could this *schema* be rewritten in a way that would correspond to the scope of the Council? The Fathers got one more lesson in the continuingly increasing awareness of the direction of this Council. It came from Bishop Emile Josef Marie De Smedt, a member of Bea's Secretariat for Promoting Christian Unity.

"I speak for the Secretariat," began De Smedt, rolling his eyes over the assembly with the pinpointing magnetism of the born orator. "Perhaps you would like to hear from our Secretariat (which is charged by the Holy Father to handle ecumenical problems) what precisely is required before a proposition can be designated ecumenical?" De Smedt paused to let the impact of his words sink in: this was the voice of John's ecumenism about to speak.

Then the speaker rapidly sketched the problem and proposed a solution. Like all great ideas, it was a simple one. De Smedt proposed no change in substantial Catholic doctrine, but he did ask for a change in manner—reiterating, in his own way, Pope John's inaugural statement.

The problem is this: what is required in the teaching and style of any *schema* so that it can better serve the dialogue between Catholics and non-Catholics? I answer that our salvation lies in what Our Lord has communicated to us. To this deposit of faith, to this one fount we all turn, Catholics and non-Catholics.

He glanced up at the faces of the observer-delegates, catching the staring eyes and craned necks, seeing that for them he had come to an essential point.

But when there is a question of how we approach Jesus Christ, then there is a difference. We are all brothers separated from one another. And we have been for many centuries. We know that this discord is against the will of Christ. But when will this division of ours ever cease? For many centuries we have both felt that a clear explanation of our teaching was enough. But each of us explained in his own terminology, from his own viewpoint. Neither of us understood the other and in this way we made no progress. As a matter of fact, prejudice, suspicion, disputes and battles increased on both sides. But in the last ten years a new method has been introduced—ecumenical dialogue.

This dialogue regards not only the truth but also the way in which the truth is explained and it aims at understanding. The ecumenical dialogue is a calm, objective, lucid, apt witness to the faith.

We can use this method now in our Council. Our conciliar teachings can have this ecumenical spirit and can favour the ecumenical dialogue if we use the means that will help our separated brethren understand more clearly how the Catholic Church sees and lives the mystery of Christ.

To express ourselves ecumenically is not easy. We must exclude every kind of indifferentism, to illustrate faithfully the complete and entire Catholic doctrine on any particular matter. How can non-Catholics find out what Catholicism teaches if the doctrine we present is stunted, twisted, or confused? It has been said in this hall that the ecumenical mode of speaking is opposed to an integral exposition of the truth. Whoever feels that way does not seem to have really understood the nature of the ecumenical dialogue.

De Smedt is a superb orator. Those inside the basilica recall that the Fathers poured out of the coffee bar to catch his obviously inspired words. De Smedt went on to underline the conditions for ecumenical dialogue:

1. Understand the present-day teachings of the Orthodox and Protestant Churches. We must be well acquainted with their faith, their liturgical life, their theology.

2. Know what opinions they have about our teaching, the points they understand correctly and the points they do not understand.

3. Know what non-Catholics feel is missing or not sufficiently explained in Catholic doctrine—for example the teaching on the word of God, on the priesthood of the faithful, on religious liberty.

4. Examine whether our manner of expression contains statements or ways of saying things difficult for non-Catholics to understand. We should point out that the scholastic mode, this quasi-professorial method, is often the origin of misunderstandings and prejudice, and that our abstractions are not understood by Eastern Christians. On the other hand a biblical and patristic way of speaking in itself would avoid and should prevent difficulties, prejudices and confusion.

5. Select our words, images, figures of speech with a regard to the reaction they are likely to produce in the minds and sensibilities of non-Catholics.

6. Weigh our judgments and look at them in a context that will be acceptable to non-Catholics.

7. Present our arguments (with citations and reasons) in a persuasive manner.

8. Avoid any sterile polemics.

9. Indicate errors in a way that is not offensive to the persons who are in error.*

But if this sort of approach would have made the *schema* "ecumenical," why, considering the scope of the Council, as repeated time and again by the Pope himself, why was not the *schema* written ecumenically? De Smedt explained why.

"The Supreme Pontiff established the Secretariat for Promoting Christian Unity and appointed to it experts, bishops and theologians who have experience in ecumenical matters. The Pope commissioned the Secretariat to help other preparatory commissions, especially the Theological Commission, to help make every proposal ecumenical. Our Secretariat offered its help to the Theological Commission but the commission (for reasons which I must not judge) declined. We proposed setting up a mixed subcommission, but the Theological Commission responded, 'No, we do not want this.' So the Theological Commission alone finished the difficult work of giving an ecumenical character to the Council *schemata*. With what success?

"Well, we have heard the judgment of many Council Fathers. Those who live among Protestants or in the East say the *schema* lacks an ecumenical spirit. Other Fathers, most of whom live in Catholic regions, have spoken otherwise. To them, the *schema* does not seem to lack an ecumenical spirit. We humbly ask these Fathers to consider whether they have sufficiently examined the true nature of the ecumenical dialogue, its conditions and consequences.

"Most venerable Fathers, this hour is a providential one. But it is a serious one, too. If these *schemata* of the Theological Commission are not written in another way, we will be responsible for the fact that this great Second Vatican Council will have annihilated an immense hope. I utter the hope of all those who, led by John XXIII, wait in prayer and fasting for at long last a serious step forward in the direction of the brotherly union of all those for whom Christ Our Lord prayed 'that they may be one.' "

* De Smedt actually presented only five points on the Council floor, but he released a text that contained nine.

The applause for this speech began in the back of the basilica, among the Council's younger bishops, and crackled up the length of the hall, even though the presidency had asked the Fathers not to applaud. One of the younger bishops later explained. "We couldn't help ourselves," he said.

After the session, the presidency stayed on into the lunch hour. Clearly they had to do something. But they came to no agreement. Again, a parliamentary impasse.

That afternoon, Pope John told the entire group of cardinals, archbishops and bishops of France, "Yes, there's an argument going on. It's all right. It's necessary. There is a need to do it with brotherly feeling. It will all work out. *Moi je suis un optimiste*." He had by then determined to call for a general vote on the acceptability of the *schema*.

VIII

To the 2,211 Fathers assembled on November 20, most of whom were more in the dark about the course of events than the newsmen in Rome, it appeared that the scriptural debate would, like the liturgical affair, go on forever. More bishops began to speak: Cabana, Echeverria Ruiz, Garcia, Klepacz, Nicodemo, Quarracino, de Proença Sigaud, Carli, Costantini. . . .

Finally, Archbishop Pericle Felici took the floor and put a motion to the Fathers in Latin. Then it was repeated in Spanish, French, English, German, and Arabic. Would the Fathers continue discussion on this *schema*? *Placet* or *non placet*?

Many were confused over the motion. The Fathers were asked to vote "yes" if they did not approve of the *schema* and "no" if they did. Despite the confusion, however, the usher-seminarians in white surplices hurried up the aisles to distribute large punch cards, and the Fathers marked them with magnetic pens and signed their names. While they were voting, Cardinal Ruffini leaped to his feet to explain the import of the vote. If the Fathers voted to drop the *schema* now, he said, it was finished for good at this Council. His interpretation was greeted with shouts of "No! No!" Others, following Ruffini's lead, cried "Yes! Yes!" Some bishops called for second ballots so they could change their vote. Finally the ushers collected the cards and passed them to the electronic calculating centre behind the Secretary-General. Minutes later, he announced the results: 1,368 voted to end discussion; 822 voted to keep going. Twenty-one ballots were null, probably because they were inscribed with regular ball-point pens and not the special magnetic ones.

According to the Council rules, it would have taken a two-thirds majority—or 1,460 votes out of the 2,211 assembled—to stop the discussion. And so, although 62 percent of the Fathers were not even willing to continue talking about it, the discussion, Cardinal Ruffini pointed out, would have to go on.

The daily press had a difficult time reporting the events of this day. Almost without exception, the wire services and great papers of the world took the vote to mean defeat for the progressives. And no wonder. The official communiqué was totally deceptive. "The majority of the speeches of the day were in defence of the project, once more underlining the positive reasons which had been advanced in the preceding days. Among other things the opinion was expressed that to reject the project in its entirety would signify that it contains errors, which no one admits." This was the first time that the communiqué had indicated whether opinions expressed at the Council were predominantly pro or con. On the first day of the debate, for example, the most highly regarded cardinals spoke out eleven to two against the *schema*, but the official release covered that up quite effectively. In this communiqué, the statement summarized a few of the arguments very briefly, then explained that the Fathers voted on what amounted to a cloture motion, and announced the results like this: "The results of the ballot, which were made known shortly before the conclusion of the assembly, indicated that the discussion of the single chapters of the project will continue in the following days." That was all it said. It gave no figures. It gave no explanation.

Many reporters wrote glum stories about the defeat of the progressives (the reporters were almost all on the progressive side, probably because they instinctively realized that although Christianity was the same, its message had to be adapted to the progress of history, while the motto of Cardinal Ottaviani, "*Semper Idem*," carried to its logical conclusion, would put the Catholic press out of business tomorrow). But some progressives themselves rejoiced at the vote. "No, we didn't get the two-thirds," a famous French theologian told me outside St Peter's, "but the *schema* is done for." Another theologian gave his interpretation: "After all, by a majority of more than 500, the Council Fathers don't even want to discuss this draft. When the Pope sees this, he'll have to do something." And at an American Embassy reception that night for all the United States bishops, another theologian explained, "This vote was tremendous. Five days ago, we never would have gotten half these votes. The Fathers have come a long way."

The next day the obvious happened. The Secretary-General announced that Pope John had decided to set up a special commission "composed of several cardinals and some members of the Theological Commission and the [members of the] Secretariat for Promoting Christian Unity . . . to rework the project on the source of revelation . . . [and] submit in due course the new project for the examination and vote of the Council Fathers."

Discussion then continued on the first chapter of the *schema* on revelation which was called *de duobus fontibus revelationis* (the two sources of revelation). Sixteen Fathers spoke against the chapter, pointing out the impossibility of separating Scripture and tradition and the need for an interpenetration of the two. But they did so rather softly. "It would have been like beating a dead horse to go on," said one American theologian. Anyway, hardly anyone was listening—except Cardinal Ruffini, who was taking his turn as president for the day and, therefore, forced to sit there. Most of the other Fathers trooped out to the basilica's two coffee bars, the Bar Jonah and the Bar Abbas, where they buzzed excitedly about the winds of change in the Church.

In that afternoon's *Osservatore Romano*, one could see that the new winds had penetrated even there: in reporting the day's events, it referred to the disputed first chapter, not by the name

Ottaviani had given it, "on the two sources of revelation," but simply as "on divine revelation."

IX

Once they had won their victory, the progressives avoided any gratuitous crowing about it. But that vote and the Pope's reaction to it represented a decisive victory over old (but not ancient) ideas, and defensive mentalities and, frankly, over the men who had been keeping the barque of Peter in dry dock for centuries. "It isn't a matter of doctrine that separates Christians," a Canadian priest told me before the Council. "We can always work out the doctrine. It's Romanism. It's Vaticanism. That's the trouble." And nowhere in all the seventy *schemata* for the Council did one find more "Romanism" than in the *schema* on revelation. It was negative, condemnatory, polemic, anti-intellectual and, to quote Cardinal Tardini, "a few other things besides."

Before the Council, some delegate-observers said, after a look at the *schema*, that if it were adopted, they would have no choice but to leave the Council in protest. "If tradition is going to be put on the same level with Scripture," one of them said, "then it's clear that this Council isn't interested in renewal." His point was, I think, that modern Catholic theologians had been making progress, not by spinning out new doctrine from post-Tridentine lectures and treatises, but by returning to Scripture and the earliest history of the primitive Church for wisdom and inspiration. The French called this a *resourcement*, by which they meant the very kind of scientific research being pursued at places like the Biblical Institute in Rome, the *Ecole Biblique* in Jerusalem, the University of Louvain and the *Institut Catholique* of Paris, whose efforts were generally condemned in the *schema*. If the Fathers had accepted the *schema*, they would have, in effect, trimmed the scientific sails of the barque of Peter.

But, of course, that did not happen. The Fathers rejected the *schema* on revelation and, by implication, the other theological *schemata* as well—on the deposit of faith, on matrimony, on the moral order—none of which, as prepared by Cardinal Ottaviani's

Preparatory Commission, was universal enough or sufficiently representative of the whole Church to be discussed by the Fathers.

These other *schemata* were full of condemnations—the kind Pope John said on October 11 the Church could do very well without—conjured up by the Church's lugubrious prophets of doom. The *schema* on the deposit of faith, in a chapter on the evolution of the world, betrayed the old static view of the Two Cities, shuddered with an anti-scientific bias, and attacked the theories of French Jesuit palaeontologist Pierre Teilhard de Chardin. The *schema* on the moral order tilted at windmills, failed to come to grips with the real problems posed by situation ethics and ignored the moral implications of the latest sociological and psychological research. The *schema* on matrimony was almost completely negative, ignored the social and human character of marriage to concentrate almost exclusively on its biological "primary end." It also deplored marriages between Catholics and Protestants and implied that such marriages are somehow worse than marriages contracted between Catholics and atheists. All of which served to demonstrate to many annoyed Fathers that, thanks to the exclusiveness of the Preparatory Theological Commission, the three-year preparatory period had not been enough to furnish them with the basic documents they needed to make their Christian witness to the world.

When the Pope effectively ended the debate and set up a joint commission to rewrite the whole *schema*, some journals of opinion were a bit put off by what seemed to be an arbitrary action of the Pope from outside the Council against a majority vote. *The Times* of London tried to justify the Pope's action as "an effort to readjust the balance between the rival schools of theology within the Council." But, as Father Gregory Baum pointed out in *The Commonweal* on December 21, 1962, "the Pope did not act from outside the Council. He did not affirm his supreme authority over the Council. On the contrary, he acted as president of the Council, and he upheld the majority. The intervention of the Pope prevented the smaller party from imposing its will on the larger party." And, far from "balancing" two schools of thought, the Pope set up a committee that weighed two to one in favour of the progressives. He determined that the committee should include all twenty-five members of the Theological Commission voted at the beginning of the session, all twenty members of the Secretariat for Promoting Christian Unity, five other cardinals, Cardinal Ottaviani and his secretary, Jesuit Sebastiano Tromp, and Cardinal Bea and his secretary, Monsignor Jan Willebrands. It is generally believed that of this group of fifty-four, Ottaviani can definitely muster only eighteen votes. Obviously Pope John did not feel, as Father Robert Graham suggested in *America* on November 24, "that Church leaders must balance off the yearnings and anguish of a small but sensitive élite, which registers the spiritual hunger of a new world aborning, against the rather prosaic and unimaginative, but profound piety and faith of the great masses."

Both *La Croix* and *Le Monde* saw the implications. "The importance of the Pope's decision cannot be overemphasized," said *Le Monde*. "It represents not only a turning point in the official theology of the Church, but in a certain sense the end of the Counter Reformation era. By acknowledging the right of a theology centred in the biblical tradition, and by integrating the findings of contemporary exegesis into its doctrine, the Church is freeing itself from an attitude of self-defence against the movement of the Reformation which goes back to the Council of Trent, and is entering an era of dialogue and perhaps of convergence with Protestants, who, on their part, are endeavouring to deepen and to purify their own heritage." *La Croix*, only a bit less exuberant, sensed "a new atmosphere at the Council. These painful days will not have been in vain, because they have shown up the retrogressive and anti-ecumenical character of a clan which is really hostile to the *aggiornamento* of the Church which is the Pope's aim. The situation is cleared now. It will remain so if the Council continues in the future to show vigilance and firmness, as everything leads one to suppose it will."

La Croix knew, of course, what the Church might expect from the "retrogressive clan" in Rome. As soon as they saw which way the wind was blowing, they began to fill up with the fear of all the devils. They planted the idea in the Italian press that the great debate was really only a feud between two Roman universities, the Lateran University and the Biblical Institute, which was one way to belittle its significance, for the Italian Church at least. In January I chatted with a country priest of Verona about the scriptural debate and discovered that the poor simple fellow believed this interpretation because, after all, what other information did he have?

The retrogressive clan also tried to discredit Cardinal Bea. Rome's *Giornale d'Italia* came out on November 22 with a four-column story on page two, revealing that the Ukrainian bishops at the Council had gathered and drafted a statement protesting against the seventeen-year imprisonment in Russia of the Ukraine primate Archbishop Josyf Slipyi and their extreme displeasure over the presence at the Council of the three observers from the Moscow Patriarchate. The fact of the matter is that, while the fifteen Ukrainians (two of them now active in the United States), had prepared such a statement, they were dissuaded by both Cardinal Cicognani and Cardinal Bea (who were, at that very moment, covertly working to have Slipyi released), and the statement was withheld. However, a Holy Office assistant somehow got his hands on the document and revealed its contents to the *Giornale d'Italia*. Bea, fearing that this blast could undo all the patient work of the last two years to open the Council to the Orthodox world, called an immediate press conference for one of the Protestant observers, Dr Oscar Cullmann, and took the occasion to slip in his own casual statement that the Secretariat was very pleased with the presence of all the observers. Since then, Rome's extreme right-wing press (some journals and reviews are even so bold they call themselves "Fascist or "Neo-Fascist") has been picking at Bea or members of his Secretariat whenever they find anything they can twist to what they suppose is Bea's discredit. One highly-placed official of Rome's *Movimento Sociale Italiano* (neo-Fascist) confided to me at a dinner party that if I ever wanted to know what Cardinal Ottaviani was thinking, all I need do was consult *Il Tempo* every day, or *Il Borghese* every week. Both organs have been carrying on obviously inspired attacks on the progressives since the first session ended.

The fact is, however, that such tactics were precisely the wrong things to use in a Rome that was full of hard-working bishops intent on matters of the greatest pastoral concern.

The conservatives finally went so far as to publish a special red tome of 640 pages and deliver it to every Council Father at his Rome residence. The book was called *Complotto Contro La Chiesa* and was written under the nom de plume of Maurice Pinay. A yellow paper band encircled the book and said, "Fathers should read especially the introduction and table of contents. This book not for sale." The book was an obvious rehash of old anti-Semitic literature inside a special introduction and final chapter written for the Council. The special message: that cardinals, archibishops and bishops of the Council's progressive wing are part of a gigantic Communistic, Masonic, Zionist plot to destroy the Church.

Why did the Ottaviani camp attempt such chicanery? Surely they must be more intelligent than their actions indicated. My neo-Fascist friend offered the explanation of every losing football coach: We just don't have the horses. "The Holy Office," he said "is full of a lot of second-raters." This may or may not be true, or may be part of the truth. A famous theologian from Western Europe explained the gaucherie of the retrogressive clan this way:

In many of the *vota* received during the preparatory phase of the Council, bishops of many lands, especially of mission countries and of South America, had insistently demanded the internationalization and decentralization of the Curia. It is understandable that a group of administrators so ancient and so settled in its ways immediately felt itself threatened. This fear hardly brought them a sense of well-being. They reacted from the first day with acidity and even aggressiveness. They defended themselves even before being really attacked. They put off a lot of bishops who previously had been too well behaved and too passive to dare say anything against the Curia.

They constantly identified themselves with the Pope, as having been named by him, acting in his name, directly approved by his authority. At the same time, they sought to push policies quite different from those which the Pope continually suggested in his speeches. This, too, greatly irritated the bishops. It is hard to understand how a body of diplomats with such long experience in diplomacy allowed itself to commit one blunder after another.

The sole explanation is fear, always a bad counsellor.

Chapter Nine

THE SMOKE SCREEN

I

WITH the end of the scriptural debate, the Fathers needed something to relax their tensions. They found their sedative in a soporific *schema* concerned with the Church and mass communication media, but which turned out to be an assertion of clerical "rights" over the press, radio and television of the world. The Fathers spoke rather desultorily about the *schema* for two and a half days, then decided it was not really worthy of an Ecumenical and General Council and voted to bind the whole thing up and publish it later as sort of a Council by-product. It will make, say those who have seen it, a fine anti-quarian relic of the curialist mind at work in 1962, its defensiveness, its clerical view of the Church, its abstract view of the press. "If nothing else," commented one of the observer-delegates, "the *schema* demonstrated how much the Council needed the presence of lay experts."

The fact that there was a *schema* on mass media at all, of course, was astonishing. It was included because Pope John ordered it, rightly believing the mass media should fit somewhere in his overall effort to put the barque of Peter onto the sea of the world. Evidently, the Curia did not see it in the same perspective. Nor could it see the real value of another project of the Pope—setting up the first official Vatican press office in the history of the Roman Catholic Church. The story of that office is an amusing one. A wag has said that the only one who kept the secrets of the Council was the chief of that office, Monsignor Fausto Vallainc. And one can see the basic truth of the remark when one reflects on the fact that the efforts of that amiable monsignor resulted in clouds of information—smoke screens of inconsequential fact intended to camouflage the event. If in this chapter I seem to descend to some unpretty particulars, I do so only because I believe they serve to demonstrate in the concrete that the official administration of the Church was, in 1962, a long way away from a genuine recognition of the human dignity of its members and their right to know. The Secretary-General's press policy was a ludicrous flim-flam that bespoke a contempt for the world's press and the public it represented. It was also an insult to the Council Fathers.

Monsignor Vallainc wrote to a Paris journalist some months before the Council: "We do not need the press." This attitude was not new. It was the expression of a long-standing clerical disdain for the press as belonging, somehow or other, to the opposite camp, to the Other City, the City of Mammon. During the First Vatican Council one of the curial secretaries, a Frenchman named Louis Veuillot, bitterly complained to his diary about the press coverage of that Council. The coverage, in fact, was poor, since no one would tell the few reporters working out of Rome just what was happening inside the basilica. Veuillot did not see the press as representing the peoples of the world, or, if he did, did not think the Council concerned them in any way. "What difference does it make to the Council," wrote Veuillot on January 11, 1870, "what the journalists write about it? Journalists are the waves and the winds. They are not the captain, not the crew, not the barque. Well, this barque and this crew and this captain are used to these tempests and have seen more ugly seas than this."

Needless to say, Pope John did not share this view. In June, 1962, he told a group of reporters that he wanted to keep "public opinion suitably informed" about the coming Council. "It is in fact, our great wish," said John, "that journalists may not be obliged, because of a lack of sufficient information, to make guesses which are more or less true and to publish ideas, opinions and hopes which later may prove unfounded or erroneous."

Later in the summer, John took a personal interest in our own *Time* and *Life* preparation of the pre-Council numbers. He sat for the highly regarded Florentine portrait artist Pietro Annigoni, whose sketch of John was on *Time's* cover for October 5. He personally authorized the photographing of Vatican art treasures by *Life* photographer Dmitri Kessel. And one day in August at

Castel Gandolfo he popped into the office of his secretary, Monsignor Loris Capovilla, where Robert Elson, Time's London bureau chief on special assignment for Life, and I were chatting with Capovilla, and favoured us with some fifteen minutes of conversation in order to help both of us with our stories.

The Pope's favourable attitude towards our work was shared by Monsignor Capovilla, by the Secretary of State, Cardinal Amleto Cicognani, and the latter's protocol chief, Monsignor Igino Cardinale. Other Vatican figures, however, took a different tack. When I asked the Pope's maestro di camera how many persons the Pope had received in audience in 1961, he said those records were secret. (In the wrong hands, a piece of information like that could lead to disaster.) When I asked Archbishop Enrico Dante, the papal master of ceremonies, about a point in the order of the October 11 opening, he told me to call the official Vatican press office. When I called, the Vatican press office, in the person of its chief, Monsignor Vallainc, said Osservatore Romano had already published that information and why not look for it there? When I called Vallainc the next day for another scrap of information, he said, "Oh, that hasn't been published [in Osservatore Romano] yet."

Vallainc's office had not been much more help to other pressmen. Some reporters from the United States never received application blanks for accreditation to the Council. Others who did receive applications (and were able to read Italian) found instructions directing them to have "an entirely correct attitude regarding the Holy See" and demanding the application be endorsed by a clergyman. They also stipulated that newsmen would not be allowed entrance to Vatican offices and would be "equally forbidden" to talk with residents, employees or visitors to Vatican City—unless they had prior special permission from the proper authorities. Not that it would have done much good. Before the Council, a Canadian journalist went to one office for some information on the remodelling of the basilica. It was flatly refused, and when he complained he was told, "Look, there are thousands of journalists but only one Church." In Washington, D.C., Monsignor John E. Kelly, director of the Bureau of Information for the United States bishops, translated the instruction sheet and sent it to religion writers and editors around the United States as a warning. Said Kelly, "We did not want to be in a position of encouraging United States reporters to go to Rome to cover the Council with the idea that there will be adequate information service according to United States standards."

The official press office had already demonstrated its inadequacy during the seven week-long meetings of the Central Preparatory Commission. Archbishop Felici permitted Vallainc to attend the meetings, and Vallainc produced only one scrap of anything that looked like news (he announced that one commission meeting in May 1962 discussed the possibilities of going along with an old United Nations proposal for a new thirteen-month, fixed calendar), and, as already mentioned, one horrendous bit of misinformation about the Church's attitude towards the ecumenical movement.

II

"This is the damnedest mess you ever saw," raged Rome's United Press International bureau chief, Bill Sunderland, as the Council opened. "You can't find out the time of day at the Council press office."

Sunderland exaggerated. But only a little. You could find out the time by consulting a beautiful clock there, and it was generally correct. In fact, the official press office under the direction of Monsignor Vallainc had good technical equipment—a few dozen new typewriters (with European keyboards, however, which, as Bernard Daly, Canadian CCC correspondent, kept pointing out, was inconvenient for at least 25 percent of the reporters), the free use of a bank of telephone booths, wire facilities and a file of the world's major newspaper and news magazines.

But the press office was little help otherwise. When the first flood of some 900 correspondents poured into Rome, the place was in turmoil. In the accreditation office, there was no one who could speak English. When Douglas Woodruff, editor of The Tablet of London, arrived, he discovered that his application had been lost. Those whose applications were in order ended up with worthless little pieces of blue cardboard on which were printed something in Italian to the effect that the bearer could be admitted "to the Office of the Press Services, established at the General Secretariat of the Central Preparatory Commission of the Second Vatican Ecumenical Council." Anyone could and did walk into the press office on Via della Conciliazione with or without a blue *tessera*. But not even with a *tessera* could a reporter enter St Peter's Square which was railed off and guarded by squads of uniformed and plain-clothed police. On the eve of the Council, many reporters panicked when they discovered their *tessera* would not admit them to St Peter's for the opening ceremony. For that, they needed special tickets, and there were only 400 of those available. Still, I heard of no reporter who did not get in some way, if he wanted to, even though he may have ended in some remote corner of the basilica. Some men just threw up their hands and covered the event by means of television— which was beamed directly via Eurovision to Austria, Belgium, Denmark, Finland, France, Germany, England, Luxembourg, Monaco, Norway, the Netherlands, Portugal, Spain, Sweden and Switzerland.

Altogether, there were thirty radio stations and twenty television stations represented in Rome. They all found that by working with the people at Vatican Radio and with the Italian government-operated radio and television network, they got their job done. The Vatican's workmen had ripped up the marble floors of St Peter's and installed fifty kilometres of telephone lines, four and a half kilometres of television cables, three and a half kilometres of microphone cable and eleven kilometres of coaxial cable to handle the load on opening day.

The curialist mind found no difficulty co-operating in a visual presentation of Roman triumph (the "excessive pomp" of which a South American archbishop later scored as "intolerable in an age of television"). But the curialist temperament was incapable of reporting more than what the Pope would describe as "external and secondary aspects." The first day's communiqué on October 9 gave a few announcements of coming events. Its only "news" was the curt report that Monsignor Jan Willebrands had indeed gone to Moscow in late September to talk to members of the Holy Synod about the possibility of their sending observers to the Council, but that was not really news. Many Italian papers and the *New York Herald Tribune* had carried the story that morning. And when the Russian observers arrived, the press office communiqué confirming the fact came more than twenty hours after the wire services had the news.

Monsignor Vallainc's office was augmented in the week before the Council by seven priest-assistants. Their job: to translate each day's skimpy releases into German, French, Spanish, English, Polish and Portuguese. They were strictly ordered to do no more than that. Monsignor James Tucek, a laconic Texan, head of the NCWC News Service in Rome for the past seven years, was drafted into service and necessarily reduced to typing out stencils of the English-language releases, and handing out tickets to ceremonies and curious bits of official documentation "issued by the Press Office of the Second Vatican Ecumenical Council," which was supposed to give needed background to theologically uninformed reporters.

One of the papers, entitled "The Preparation of the Second Vatican Ecumenical Council," was a perfect example of the generally atrocious style and triumphal tone that would be used by official Rome. It began with the dubious statement that the first announcement of the Council "resounded far and wide throughout all the world and was welcomed as a message harbinging [*sic*] truth and peace." It also embellished Pope John's desires for Christian unity with the impossible statement that unity could come about only "if our separated brothers wish . . . to *return* to the Church."

Another paper described the preparatory stage of the Council in wonderfully vague but glowing terms. "There was no risk of the Holy Father being presented with draft Constitutions and Decrees which did not reflect really urgent and universal interests"—like the *schema* on ecclesiastical benefices, for instance. It called the Preparatory Theological Commission "the backbone of the other commissions," but it turned out to be rather a millstone: later on, the Fathers would effectively reject all six of that commission's projects and ask for revision of every one. The Commission for the Lay Apostolate "was required to lay certain foundations for developments necessary in modern life and which the Church awaits, above all, for the return to the fold of masses of dechristianized people."

But the *pièce de résistance* was a 50-page item entitled "A Few Themes Discussed in the Central Commission of the Second Vatican Council." Of this, *The Tablet* of London observed that it often read "like a hasty precis of a poor seminary manual written forty years ago. . . . It is almost too painful to reflect that it has been made available to every journalist in Rome . . . written in English so peculiarly outrageous that one hardly knows whether to laugh or cry." *The Tablet* cited passages from a discussion on the deposit of faith and the moral order. One of them:

> The field then is immense, as one can readily see; above all is that field in which swarm the pet and diverse errors of various situations in today's modern world: its technical progress, styles of life, increased means of advertising and propaganda.

"On the whole," said *The Tablet*, "one does not laugh. The men who have read this, the best of them at least, are sensitive to language; words are their trade, and they use them with some skill. Many of them are non-Catholics, but few are naturally unsympathetic. Their sympathies are ingeniously alienated from the start by this lengthy travesty of their mother tongue." The author of *The Tablet* article observed in the document an "odd juxtaposition of topics: a sketchy dozen lines on the natural and supernatural orders are followed by thirty lines of fulmination on, of all things, Spiritualism and Reincarnation, which 'was condemned by the Holy Office in 1919.'" The document used the word condemn at least fifteen times in its first chapter. Commented *The Tablet*, "The best that can be said of its anathemas is that they are aimed largely at corpses: Deism is annihilated at one point."

The man ultimately responsible for all this, Archbishop Pericle Felici, the Council's Secretary-General, actually told those present at the Council's first journalists' Mass: "Thanks to the documentation you have been given, you can be rich in every word and knowledge." *The Tablet* demurred: "We shall be in no position to complain if newspapers fail to do the Council justice."

III

As a matter of record, however, reporters for the secular press were not content with the official handouts and scrounged around the Eternal City for all the news that was fit to print. They did a fine job of avoiding the trivial and not obscuring the real truth of the Council. *America*, the United States Jesuit weekly, judged that the press "demonstrated admirable skill in handling an unusually complicated story with intelligence, taste and a laudable sense of discretion." Before the Council some members of the Catholic press in the United States wondered out loud if anything good could come from the "secular" press. But by the end of the first session Catholic editors were envious of the job the secular press had done. One of them wrote me and asked if, in the light of Council coverage, there was any more need of the Catholic press. The *Davenport Catholic Messenger* editorialized, "We owe a debt of thanks to the press—particularly the secular press—for all it has done to bring the story of the Council to the world. And we might say that those Catholics who have derided the public press are looking more and more foolish as the Council unfolds."

After the session, Bishop Gerard Huyghe of Arras, France, noted that "formerly only theologians were interested in conciliar texts. Today bishops are faced with a public opinion which looks avidly to the texts coming out of the Council." It does so, said Bishop Huyghe, because of the public press.

Pope John himself met a group of reporters in Rome on January 27, and he told us that he was quite pleased with the general coverage of the Council—that we had "understood the event of the Council itself" and had not "obscured the truth" by concentrating on incidental details.

But some disagreed with this assessment. Monsignor Rudolph Bandas, of St Paul, Minnesota, a former member of the Curia, said publicly that "the possible good effects of the Council are slowly being sabotaged by the misinformation about this great gathering released by some sections of the secular as well as the Catholic press." Bandas, a Council *peritus*, said that reports of the Council in *Time, Newsweek* and *The New Yorker* left him bewildered and saddened. The only authentic report, said Bandas, was the official communiqué which he called "surprisingly detailed and complete."

The Monsignor is entitled to his view. Many a Council Father, however, thought the official communiqué specialized in "incidental detail," pretended to say something and said nothing, and thereby did not speak the truth to a world which was waiting to hear it. This was done because the truth of the Council was too much for the Curialists, and the Curialists ran the official press office. The perverted official report is ample (but not the sole) evidence for that. Only towards the very end of the session, when some of the language assistants like Monsignor Tucek, Père François Bernard, and Monsignor Gerhard Fittkau joined the meetings and insisted on greater objectivity, did the release bear any resemblance to the whole truth.

I realized this early when a bishop met me and asked me, "What did the official release say today?" When I told him, he looked at his companion, another bishop, and said, "Well, I guess that's so," then laughed and added, "but it's misleading."

At the first (and only) meeting where the reporters were asked how they were getting along, I asked the chair if the official communiqués were written by an eyewitness. "No," said Monsignor Tucek. But then someone translated the question for Monsignor Vallainc. "Yes," answered the good Monsignor. Thus the several hundred journalists who heard that exchange in the crowded hall were poised between acceptance of the communiqué as more or less true. Many other reporters quickly grasped the general official policy, which amounted to playing down all the really important things that happened inside and concentrating instead on filling up space with reporting daily, for example, and without fail, who it was who commenced proceedings by enthroning the book of the Gospels on the altar and other newsy items like this one of October 30: "Before the commencement of discussion, His Excellency Monsignor Felici, Secretary-General, announced that

I.C.—7

the Pontifical Commission for the Vatican City would distribute to each Father an envelope containing a card indicating postal and telegraph rates to all the nations of the world and also two series of stamps issued on the occasion of the Council's inauguration, one already cancelled, the other new."

On November 9, in reporting discussion on the Divine Office, the communiqué, either reporting what was said on the floor, or, more likely, adding a fillip of its own, said that the Divine Office is "the principal work of the priest." This enraged some of the Fathers so much (one European cardinal said it was an insult to the Council), that the next communiqué was corrected to read, "the Divine Office is the principal means of the priest's sanctification, *after* the Mass and the sacraments."

Some Spanish and French journalists at the Council had proof that parts of the original communiqué were written hours ahead of time, sometimes a full day ahead. I reported this to New York, it appeared in *Time*, and I received a private denial from Monsignor Vallainc. "We don't write it ahead of time," he protested, then added reproachfully, "but now because of your report, it will have to come out an hour later." It had to come later, because now he would have to start writing the communiqué after the Council session, not before.

On November 5, the communiqué was typically jejune. It described, on almost a full page, the Mass of the morning, celebrated in the Antiochian Maronite Rite, listed on a half page the names of all those Fathers who spoke on the second chapter of the liturgical *schema*, then presented a fourteen-sentence résumé of the twenty-four speeches given—which averaged out to little more than a half sentence for each Father. It began with the startling information that "some of the speakers treated the Sacrifice of the Mass in general and others suggested changes in one or the other parts of the Mass. The need was again stressed of using caution in revising the words, gestures and prayers which have acquired great nobility in the passing of the centuries without losing anything of their original significance. It is considered therefore that the order of the Mass be retained in its substance, while admitting partial changes for the purpose of making the active participation of the faithful in the individual rites easier." One newsman, "eager for the slightest crumb of news," wondered excitedly if this meant the Council had come to some decision on "the Mass of the future." "No," one sympathetic Council theologian pointed out. "The writer of the communiqué was only trying to present a point of view expressed on the Council floor. No vote was taken."

The communiqué continued: "The innovations, it was said, must take into account through a careful and deep study the origins of every prayer and ceremony, the historical evolutions which they have undergone, and the significance which they retain more or less today. It was insisted that the Canon of the Mass especially should remain intact because of its solemnity, and for literary, liturgical, historical and juridical reasons known to all. In this respect the words of the Council of Trent were recalled." What reasons? What words? This is the kind of guessing game that reporters were expected to play at the Council. The man who read the communiqué each day in English, Monsignor Tucek, was not authorized to give any hints—and he did not. "Other Fathers [the communiqué went on] stressed the innovations which had already been made by the popes and by the Congregation of Rites from the time of St Pius X onwards. They urged that one proceed along this road with the wisdom and balance of the past, bearing in mind the changed conditions and demands of the times. Innovations were suggested in the following matters. . . ." "Aha!" cried the reporters. Here was some news. There certainly was—and I quote the version written by NCWC's competent staff.

"Among the innovations in the Mass suggested by the Fathers, the Council press bulletin reported, were:

— Reducing prayers at the foot of the altar.

— Changes concerning the sermon and the participation of the congregation in the action and prayers of the Offertory.

— Insertion of the name of St Joseph in the Canon of the Mass together with that of Our Lady.

— Greater cohesion between the two parts of the Mass.

— Reading the prayers and lessons of the first part of the Mass from the pulpit and reciting those of the second part at the altar.

— Ending the Mass with the last blessing and the *Ite missa est*."

The communiqué mentioned that the matter of "concelebration" (undefined) and "communion under two species" were discussed, and quickly said "the first" should be "reserved to monasteries" while the second raised "difficulties of a practical and hygienic order." It stated in summary that "a twofold preoccupation ran through all the speeches of the Fathers; first, to render the celebration of the Mass more solemn and as holy as possible; the second, to favour the understanding and participation of the faithful in the sacrifice of Christ through the action of the priest and their own voluntary oblation." It then ended with this typically incomprehensible statement: "It is evident that the Council has arrived at a point of thorough discussion, in which the separate speeches have the value of proposals which the assembly of the Fathers must weigh, according to the single goal of formulating the project on the liturgy in a manner which truly corresponds to the needs of souls and the welfare of the Church and of society."

No wonder many of the Fathers resented the communiqué. It was false precisely because it pretended to be a report of the session. But it was apparent that the session could not have been that dull. That very afternoon, a few hundred yards from the basilica, a Father told a press conference what he had proposed in the Council that day. Bishop William Duschak, Vicar Apostolic of Calapan in the Philippines, proposed an entirely new kind of "Ecumenical Mass" to be written by liturgical scholars of all faiths as much as possible from the words of Christ at the Last Supper in order to provide a basis of common worship by all Christians. This was news, just a proposal certainly, but an important sign of the kind of creative thinking going on inside St Peter's. Duschak's story was carried by every news service in the world and made page one of *The New York Times* on November 6.

From the beginning, the Italian papers published very informed articles on the Council. Rome's *Il Messaggero* report of the first general congregation sounded as if it came from a team of correspondents within St Peter's. Their reporters were obviously given information by their sources inside—by bishops or secretarial types who did not worry about the "secrecy of the Council."

Il Messaggero (and many other Italian papers) were generally better informed than most conciliar Fathers. Twelve hours before the Fathers knew whom they elected to the conciliar commissions, *Il Messaggero* carried the complete list. "When I came to Rome," cried one missionary archbishop, "I thought I'd be pursued by reporters seeking information. Now I find that I'm pursuing the reporters to try to find out what the devil is going on." As any fool could have predicted before the Council, the Fathers would have a hard time following what was said on the Council floor— much less what went on behind the scenes. Inevitably, this admission came from Rome itself. The Secretary-General's office told the FIS news service in late January that it was besieged with episcopal requests for a complete transcript of the proceedings, because the Fathers said they understood "only generally and in an incomplete fashion" the 800-odd speeches given.

Still, the French daily, *La Croix*, presented consistent, exhaustive reports, usually full of actual quotes from the Council floor. *Le Monde's* reporter, Henri Fesquet, turned in three or four stories a week full of insight and penetration. It was obvious that many of the Fathers and theologians were using *La Croix* and *Le Monde* to get the word. I noted many bishops using *La Croix* as a sort of *Congressional Record* to keep themselves informed. On the other hand, most English-language papers and the NCWC News Service adhered to the most scrupulous norms and would not print a thing unless it appeared in the official communiqué.

For the English-speaking press, however, the United States press panel office was a lifesaver. When they arrived at the Council, most American bishops were content to let the official office handle the press. But it soon became apparent that more was needed. The United States bishops met at the North American College, discussed the matter, and finally decided to form a panel of theologians who would meet reporters every day an hour after the Council adjourned and try to give them whatever background and clarifications they could on the subject matter of the day's official communiqué. Sometimes the communiqué was so bad that the panel was reduced to silence, and sometimes the classes (George Dugan of *The New York Times* called it a school of theology for newsmen) became vapid and irritating when they, too, got bogged down in peripheral matters. However, day by day, the panel furnished material that was carried all over the world by many of United Press International's 9,000 newspaper, radio and television clients in 111 countries; and by much of the Associated Press's estimated world readership of fifty million persons; and by Reuters' clients in every major country; and by hundreds of Catholic diocesan papers in every part of the English-speaking world; and by United States secular dailies like *The New York Times, New York Herald Tribune, Baltimore Sun, Detroit News, Detroit Free Press, Chicago Daily News, Cleveland Plain Dealer, The Washington Star, The Boston Globe*—all of whom had special correspondents assigned to the Council.

There were other centres of information. Dutch Catholics had a joint press and television office in the Olympic Hotel a few blocks from St Peter's. The French had a centre in Old Rome. The German bishops held once or twice weekly press conferences for the German-speaking press. A Spanish centre presented bishops and theologians in weekly conferences. All the centres proceeded on the always unexpressed assumption that Council secrecy did not really mean secrecy but, perhaps, "discretion." As a matter of fact, the bishops took no oath of any kind to keep anything secret. Secrecy was merely one of the Council rules, which were made, as it turned out, to be broken whenever it was expedient. The British, Irish, South Africans, Australians and Americans, however, generally took an Anglo-Saxon view of the rules and remained extremely discreet.

One single man probably contributed more than any other to "getting the story out to the world," as he put it with great enthusiasm. He was Father Ralph Wiltgen, a wiry Divine Word Missionary from Chicago who happened to be assigned in Rome doing publicity work for his order. "I want the world to learn what's happening here at the Council," Wiltgen would say.

"This is the greatest thing that's ever happened in the Church and the world ought to know about it." Wiltgen's pre-existent news service proved to be an early outlet for his own order's bishops at the Council. One of them used it to take exception to a story by the *Herald Tribune*'s Sanche De Gramont. (De Gramont had said the Germans put no Italians on their voting list, and the Divine Word Missionary said they did.) As it turned out, De Gramont was right when he wrote his story; the Divine Word bishop was right when he denied it: the Germans had a change of heart and put seven Italians on their list. But the exchange was a healthy one since it meant that two-way communication between the bishops and the world had at least begun.

Wiltgen went on to arrange press conferences, first for his bishops (there were twenty-five of them staying at the Divine Word College in Rome), then for other bishops as well. By the end of the session he had set up eighteen separate press conferences, arranged for their immediate translation into Italian or English or both, and distributed summaries of them in six languages. Time after time, when by all journalistic standards there was no news in the communiqué, a Wiltgen conference would save the day.

For his indefatigable hours on the phone, hopping buses around Rome to interview the bishops, and mailing his releases out to 300 papers, mostly in mission lands, Press Agent Wiltgen was admonished by Monsignor Vallainc for "handing out your unofficial notices in the official press office" and for "creating confusion at the Council." But Wiltgen's superior backed him up and gave him only a gentle warning not to stir up the official office unnecessarily by passing out notices under the eyes of Monsignor Vallainc.

Vallainc himself set up several press conferences with Roman theologians and, during the last week of the Council, with Cardinal Suenens of Brussels. Suenens' talk made Vallainc nervous, but was one of the highlights of the whole press situation, since it was there that Suenens himself told reporters what *he* had said inside the Council. Each Sunday during the Council, too, the official office set up a journalists' Mass, celebrated by a famous conciliar Father who would also preach. When the turn came for a South American, the office chose Brazilian Archbishop Helder Pessôa Câmara, Auxiliary Archbishop of Rio de Janeiro—and was soon sorry it did. As requested, Câmara turned in his sermon for translation into six other languages and distribution at the official office. By Saturday night, it was translated and a copy of it went "upstairs." When Archbishop Felici saw it, he blanched, ordered all copies of it destroyed, and asked Câmara not to give the sermon he had planned. However, Monsignor Tucek, still working in his capacity as NCWC press chief, got a beat on other reporters and sent the list of Câmara's remarks to NCWC in Washington.

Câmara toned down his remarks at the Mass, but his criticism of Council progress ran in many United States and mission Catholic papers the next week. According to Monsignor Tucek's story, Câmara felt the Council had failed "unforgivably" to tackle the great world issues of the day and could hardly be proud of its balance sheet. He said he resented the long and sometimes repetitious discussions but added, "I would gladly bear still longer discussions if this could definitely eliminate the impression that the Pope thinks, decides and speaks for all of us as a sovereign or a dictator in the Catholic Church."

Which was pretty strong stuff for the likes of curialist Felici.

IV

During the Church's first nineteen general councils, secrecy was no real problem. There were no newspapers, no mass media of any kind, and very few of the peoples of the world even knew about councils—or cared. The issue arose for the first time at Vatican I when much of Europe assumed that the Council was a power grab.

One news report had Queen Victoria ringing for Disraeli and asking if she should dispatch battleships to Italy. The New York Herald called the Council "a big farce, a grand archeological show, a revival of Middle Age sentiment." Harper's Weekly printed one cartoon of the Pope sailing in a creaky tub called "Ecumenical

Council." *The New York Times* called him "a degrading influence." Barricading the Church against such a press may have been reasonable in the anti-clerical atmosphere of the world in 1870.

Possibly the anti-clericalism was only a rather direct result of clericalism. Since the Reformation, since Trent, the curial mind had developed some strange mental quirks that could best be called totalitarian obscurantist, closed. They are now largely unconscious in the average curial mind, but they are nonetheless real.

Pope Leo XIII tried to change this mind-set. He threw open the Vatican Library to the scholars of the world, for instance, but the effect of this grand gesture was blunted by the Vatican officials who demonstrated their miserable little fears that the scholars would prove everything a hoax. The Protestant biblical scholar Samuel P. Tregelles received permission to enter the library to work on Codex B. But that turned out to be a little ridiculous. After passing through half a hundred guards, he was deposited in a dim room where two attendants stood over the precious document. He read it standing between them. They turned the pages for him. He leaned closer to examine a particular word. They turned the pages. . . .

Not knowing, obviously, was better than knowing. But it certainly did not have much relationship with the Church's divine mandate to teach. In his 1962 Lenten pastoral, Cardinal Montini told his people that the Council would not be "a magic and immediate remedy. The responsible efforts of the faithful, given of their own free will, will be necessary to put into effect the teachings of the Council." The bishops of India issued a joint pastoral saying the same thing—that the Council would be successful only insofar as its decisions are translated into the life of the whole Church.

But was it not unrealistic to hope that the faithful would freely make the Council teachings their own if they did not participate in the daily growth that even the Fathers themselves needed in order to understand what the Holy Spirit was trying to accomplish through the Council? Father Gregory Baum pointed out in

The Commonweal that the conciliar decrees would be a source of life in the Church "only if they represent an evolution among the people, a people living with the Church and following the progress of the Council. Should the conciliar decrees be seen merely as the imposition of a set of new obligations, they will add a new burden to Catholic life and fail to generate the renewal at which they are directed. Yet this could happen if the clergy and laity are poorly prepared to accept and understand them."

The problem of information on the Council, therefore, was and is one of knowledge and action. Either the people understand and act, or they do not understand and they do not act. Yet many in the Church gave the impression that a vigorous but mindless public relations campaign could somehow make up for lack of information. Father Denis Read, O.C.D., editor of a Wisconsin Catholic monthly, told a public relations seminar in Chicago, "There is a need for this [Council] secrecy, but the journalist doesn't see it. We have to help him see that it is necessary because of the intricacy and the implications of the issues involved." According to a report in the *Davenport Catholic Messenger*, Father Read "called for a vigorous campaign by the bureau of information in each diocese to publicize the Council, explain the issues involved [without information, Father Denis?], and thus *smooth the way* for acceptance of decisions to come from the Council."

The curialist mind (which sometimes finds even unwitting resonances as far away as Hubertus, Wisconsin) insisted on secrecy at the Council for only one reason: to preserve the "freedom" of the Fathers to discuss whatever they felt necessary without any outside influences bearing on them. Many of the Council Fathers, some of them considerably progressive in tendency, repeated this argument to me throughout the Council. I was not impressed with it.

One wonders why there should be no "outside influence" on a Council Father. Isn't he at the Council representing his flock, *in persona gregis*, as St Thomas himself put it? This, I think, hits at one of the core problems this Council (or subsequent Councils) will have to solve. It is the problem of authority in the Church. Is its authority that of a totalitarian government which decides every-

thing in some sort of Star-Chamber process and then imposes its
decisions from above? "No," comes the answer. "The Church
isn't that. But it is certainly not a democracy. It gets its authority
not from the will of the people, but directly from Christ. Its
authority is divine." But what does that imply? That the Church
must hurl down its commands and anathemas like some sort of
Vulcan? Or that it must exert something analogous to the meek-
ness and mildness of Christ who said, "Learn of me"? Is the
authority of the Church meant to dominate or serve? If it is to
dominate, then there is no need for the bearers of that authority
to listen. But if it is to serve, then those bearers of authority have
to be attentive to the expressed needs of the world.

A father asks his crying child why she is crying. There is need
here for a little dialogue. How much more need should there be
when the service is one delegated by Christ himself, the Good
Shepherd who once said, "I know mine, and mine know me"?
Between Christ (or his Vicars) and his flock there has to be an
interchange.

Since the barque of Peter has been anchored in its insular haven,
it has not tended to be terribly concerned about the overriding
problems of the humanity it has been called to serve. Or at least,
it has not been obviously concerned. Every action of the curalist
mind illustrated in the concrete what the Holy Office's Archbishop Pietro Parente once told a visiting bishop: "We are the
Church. You belong to it."

One of the real problems confronting the conciliar Fathers
during the interim between sessions of the Council was this: how
could the Council steer the barque out onto the sea of the world
with its limited knowledge of those seas? In considering the problems of war and peace, the Bomb, population pressures, underdeveloped nations, modern science, the Council obviously had to
have the facts. They had to consult experts—non-bishops, possibly
even non-Catholics—scientists, statesmen, demographers, economists. They were even under the obligation of continuing to act
in persona gregis, representing their flocks, some of whom were
very possibly full of the charismatic influence of the Holy Spirit
and would, therefore, have something important to add.

But how could the institutional Church give ear to the charismatic? Could it call on certain specified persons who, on their past performance, could be expected to shed some light on the question? Yes, it could do that. But that would not be enough. Does the institutional Church know who represents the charismatic? The Spirit breathes where it wills. I maintain, therefore, that the only way the institutional can inform (or be informed by) the charismatic is to inform everybody. The only way to do that today, I submit, is through the instrumentality of the modern press. In some future age, there may be better ways of communication. Psychologists might discover the secrets of mental telepathy. But until they do, the international press is the best way, the only practical way, to inform everyone, and, incidentally, one of the means the bearers of authority can use to assess world reaction to its ideas. As Pius XII put it, the role of the press is "to enlighten and reflect public opinion." Again, authority in dialogue with the governed whom it attempts to serve.

The press holds no divine mandate for such a role. It only happens to fit the needs of the world today. It is only a means, a channel, here and now, of communication that must always flow back and forth between the members of any society, whether it be human (the family or the State), divine (the Trinity), or human-divine (the Church),

Only a failure to meditate on the Church as the society of the faithful, or on the world in which that society lives and loves and (yes) thinks together, can lead to a policy of secrecy and suppression of facts.

The curial mind lives in past history. If it would look at the world as it is today, it would discover that its folk are waking to the realization that they somehow share responsibility in this world for both the things of Caesar and the things of God. To assume this responsibility, they need to be informed.

The anomaly of this Council's first session was that the delegate-observers officially attending the Council and the communities to whom they reported, knew what the Council issues were and the tentative answers offered. But the Catholic peoples of the world —their parish priests included—could only guess. If the second session goes as the first, the separated brethren will understand when the Council's answers are handed down in solemn brevity. But the Catholics will not. Maybe they do not mind being treated like the elder brother of the prodigal son. But I think they would like a whiff of the feast that is being prepared, or at least a tiny peep through the keyhole.

Chapter Ten

THE BARQUE OF PETER

I

FOLLOWING the brief discussion on the mass communications media ("We didn't come here to a General Council to discuss television," said one of the Fathers), the Council moved quickly to a *schema* considering the problems of unity with Eastern, that is, Orthodox, Churches. Here again, the Fathers found the scope too narrow. "How," one of them asked, "can we consider only this aspect of Christian unity?" They knew that Cardinal Bea's Secretariat for Promoting Christian Unity had formulated four other projects all dealing with the ecumenical problem. They were apparently conscious of the incomplete view of authority in the Church that was created when the First Vatican Council defined papal infallibility apart from the larger infallibility of the Church itself. At any rate, they voted almost unanimously to send this project on unity back to a joint commission of Fathers from Bea's Secretariat and from the Commission on the Eastern Churches. Hopefully, that joint commission will work out a synthesis for the next session—possibly a blueprint for further dialogue between the Churches.

During a discussion on this unity project, on November 28, Cardinal Ottaviani came to the Council floor to make a proposal on the next order of business. He asked that the Fathers not go on to the *schema*, *De Ecclesia*, on the Church, as the presidency had already decided to do. Ottaviani maintained that the *schema* was too long for the Fathers to study carefully during the few days remaining before the December 8 adjournment. He directed their attention instead to another *schema* tucked behind *De Ecclesia*, a dogmatic constitution "On the Blessed Virgin Mary, the Mother of God and the Mother of Men." Perhaps, he suggested, the Fathers could consider this instead and give it to the world as the first fruits of the first session of the Council.

Ottaviani was patently using the *schema* on Mary to distract the Fathers from the surgery he was sure they would perform on his *capolavoro, De Ecclesia*. But his plan did not work.

The Pope himself, whose devotion to the Virgin certainly needed no defence, observed to a friend that he did not consider devotion to the Virgin one of the pressing problems of the day. Many bishops received, shortly thereafter, a mimeographed document in Latin which praised the *schema* on the one hand and scuttled it on the other. It was "sober, well-ordered, and steered a fine course between the maximalistic tendencies of 'Marianism' and the minimalistic tendencies of those who make devotion to Mary a peripheral thing." But the document wondered whether this complete synthesis on Mary and an omission of similar syntheses on the Trinity, for instance, or the Word Incarnate (neither of which a Council has ever produced) would be very wise. The document further pointed out that this accent "would necessarily give our non-Catholic Christian brothers the impression that, no matter how many times the *schema* might talk about Jesus Christ as the unique Saviour, the Council would, in fact, seem to prefer Mariology to Christology."

This kind of reasoning fitted the Pope's line of thought: "emphasize that which unites and put aside that which divides." He had said it so often it had become a Roncalli cliché. But no matter how many times they heard it at the Council, the retrogressives reacted against it instinctively. One Italian bishop sputtered: "They say we should not speak of tradition or the Virgin because of the Protestants, or of primacy because of the Eastern Christians, or of atheism because of politics, or of morality because of modern man"—and the Fathers laughed.

No one was surprised when Ottaviani's suggestion was not taken seriously. The Fathers finished the Eastern Church Commission *schema* on unity and cleared the decks for the opening salvoes of what almost everyone conceded was the main task of this Council—the project *De Ecclesia*.

II

Ninety-two years before, the First Vatican Council finally produced what was to almost all Protestants and Orthodox—and even to many Catholics—a highly unnecessary declaration of the Pope's personal infallibility. If technically correct or at least free from error, it was actually meant, in part, to be an assertion of the Pope's kingly power in the face of the onmarching forces of the Italian Risorgimento. (Bishop Bernard McQuaid of Rochester, New York, observed in that Council that a definition was unnecessary since papal authority was accepted universally except in the new kingdom of Italy.) It was in fact a heedlessly divisive act, and a demonstration of the futility of formalism in the face of the nineteenth-century revolt against authority. Much of that authority had failed to commend itself to the world. It had done a brilliantly good job of establishing itself in both the civil and ecclesiastical spheres as an excuse for absolutism.

In Vatican Council II the decisive voices mounted an offensive against the purely juridical and authoritarian notion of the Church. Their weapons—the liturgy, Scripture and its early applications by the Fathers of the Church—were precisely the tools needed to hack away at the accretions of centuries and reveal the Church not as a collection of dioceses but as the people of God nourished in its daily liturgy by the actual presence of the Trinity. Their numbers, judging from the various votes up to that time, were great. And the only man who could beat them back happened to be a pope who did not insist on the monarchical authority which his court so jealously cherished.

Pope John never sat easily on the "throne" of Peter and went to extraordinary lengths not to insist on papal formalities. He called a General Council when the Church's absolutists would have told him he could do what he wished with a stroke of his pen. But he had the realism to recognize that the gift of papal infallibility did not necessarily make him a sage; it only kept him from making irrefutable mistakes in defining matters of faith or morals. It was, strictly speaking, a negative thing. But, as Archbishop

Lorenz Jaeger of Paderborn has pointed out, infallibility does not mean that the Pope will "necessarily hit upon the best possible formulation of a doctrine, or that he will institute the best possible reform." In order to deal with such profound matters, a pope may have to call a Council. Past Councils may or may not have done great things, but, humanly speaking, many heads are better than one. Theoretically at least, pope and bishops together are better than the pope alone. The First Vatican Council itself declared as much in the constitution *Dei Filius*: in a Council "the sacred dogmas of religion are defined with the greatest depth, expressed with the greatest breadth, Church discipline restored and more firmly established. . . ."

But in the ninety years between that affirmation and John's calling of Vatican II, the actual pattern of Church government itself helped to establish the general view that Councils were passé, that the Roman congregations were adequate for all purposes, that bishops were, in the words of a famed European theologian, "mere mouthpieces of Roman authority," and that laymen were God only knows where or what.

During the intellectual preparations for the Council, John maintained a magnificent impartiality. When the Council opened, he acted and spoke "like one of the bishops." Pope John did not act like a man who possessed power. Rather, power possessed him.

And even more, he did not feel that truth possessed him as an individual, but was entrusted to the Church as a sacred heritage. For this reason, John could call on all to look upon the Council as an invitation to other Christians to join in seeking the unity which Christ was preparing. If the Church were in possession of the truth in the oversimplified and commonly held sense of "the whole truth," all it would have to do would be to wait benevolently for the heretics to return. This was patently unrealistic. No, thought Pope John, the Roman Church would have to bear witness before the world to the fact that it too was still seeking truth. Only then could it begin an ecumenical dialogue with the deep sense of humility and charity that could make it possible.

III

On December 1, Cardinal Ottaviani stood before the Fathers to present, at the insistence of Pope and presidency, the project *De Ecclesia*, a formidable ninety-page document of eleven chapters. The Fathers knew they could not carry such a massive project through to a conclusion, but they did know they could use the last week of the first session of the Council to set the norms for specific and substantial changes in the *schema*. To Ottaviani, of course, this was another battle lost. But he had grown used to this new phenomenon by now and went ahead bravely.

"This *schema* was prepared with care," he told the 2,112 assembled Fathers, "by seventy members and consultors of the Preparatory Theological Commission. Then it was examined seriously by the Central Preparatory Commission, then it was reviwed by the Commission on Amendments, finally by the Pope who decided to give it to the conciliar assembly for discussion. Now, I know what you will say about it. You will say it is negative, scholastic, not pastoral, not ecumenical. I say it has been written in a pastoral and biblical sense, and in language that is able to be understood." Ottaviani paused, looked far down the nave of St Peter's at the Fathers, shrugged his shoulders and for the first and last time in the session demonstrated a bit of the old Roman. "*Sed ubi non est auditus, ibi non est loquendus*," he sighed. "*Dixi.*" "Where one is not listened to, there he should not speak. I have finished." He sat down amid the mighty applause of the Fathers who knew a good loser when they saw one.

A French bishop observed that Ottaviani was not a bad prophet. Though the assembly found many good things in the *schema*, a majority proceeded, in the next six meetings, to blast away at the explicit evidence in it of the very mentality that prevented the Church from making its witness effective in the world.

Cardinal Liénart, the senior member of the College of Cardinals, led off as usual. He said the *schema* reduced the mystery of the Church to a set of laws, that it made a strict equation between the Roman Catholic Church and the Mystical Body of Christ.

Cardinal Koenig observed that the *schema* should do more than talk about the "rights of the Church," that it should also consider its duties, its mission to humanity.

Cardinal Alfrink found a chapter on the universal teaching office of the bishops "too negative."

Cardinal Ritter said the Church should accept the work of its ecclesiological scholars and proclaim the human right of liberty of conscience.

Cardinal Spellman regretted that the role of the layman in the Church was not made more explicit.

Cardinal Doepfner said the *schema*, lacking sufficient references to the Scriptures, insisted almost exclusively on the juridical nature of the Church and hardly at all on the Church's mystical presence in the world. It made little of the collegiality of the bishops, which was quite as important as the infallibility of the Pope.

Cardinal Léger said the Council had found the way to a genuine renewal: with hard work on the part of the commissions during the interim period the Church could definitely take the first steps on that path.

Cardinal Suenens called for a document that would give the Church a new missionary spirit.

Cardinal Frings called the Ottaviani attempt too partial and too abstract, devoid of any inspiration from the East, or any appreciation for the Church's eschatology.

Cardinal Bea said the *schema* considered papal primacy out of its larger context in the infallibility of the Church, that it leaned too heavily on the traditions of a Counter Reformation theology. In effect, it did not conform to the real goals of the Council.

Cardinal Montini broke his long silence at the Council to pick up the same theme, that the *schema* should be re-organized according to the goals set by John XXIII. It should concentrate on the episcopal college and the power of the bishop in the sacramentality of the episcopate.

Cardinal Lercaro suggested the inclusion of a theology of poverty, a sign of the Church's divinity (as it was a sign of Christ's), the reassertion of which would help the Church find a way of preaching the Gospel to the masses. This, he said, it has not been doing.

The Patriarch Maximos IV scored the *schema*'s treatment of the primacy in isolation and condemned such work as contributory to the exaggerated literature on the papacy which one could find in any Italian bookshop. He read a typical passage from an Italian book for the edification of the Fathers: "The Pope is God on earth. Jesus has placed him above the Prophets, above St John the precursor, above the angels, on the level of God himself." Maximos called for the Church to purify itself from such "profane accretions."

In effect, most of the Fathers echoed the conclusions of a growing body of literature on the nature of the Church as seen in the Acts of the Apostles, the Pauline Epistles and the early Church Fathers, and they added their own reflections on the needs of the Church in the modern world. It seemed clear to them that the present state of the Church did not commend Christ's teachings to the peoples of the world and that it did call for an *aggiornamento* involving drastic change.

Bishop Elchinger of Strasbourg pointed out to the Fathers that new perspectives must dictate new directions in the Church. "Yesterday," said Elchinger, "one considered the Church above all as an institution, today as a communion. Yesterday, one looked at the Pope, today one is in the presence of the bishops united to the Pope. Yesterday one considered the bishop alone, today the bishops together. Yesterday one affirmed the strength of the hierarchy, today one discovers the people of God. Yesterday one emphasized whatever separated, today what unites. Yesterday the theology of the Church considered all its internal life, today it sees the Church turned outwards."

There were those in the Council who did not see things as Elchinger did. Bishop Luigi Carli of Segni, Italy, could not understand why the Church had to consider itself in the light of anything outside itself. "Ecumenism is not the goal of the Council," he said flatly.

For many bishops of Italy and Spain, talk of ecumenism, of love for the separated brethren, of freedom of conscience could mean the ruin of their flocks—and, given the cultural and social conditions of Italy and Spain, perhaps they had a point. Cardinal Siri, for one, felt constrained to warn his people in a pastoral letter that the Council would certainly not make the practice of their faith any easier.

But no ecumenist ever said that the faith, lived as it should be, would be easy. As a matter of fact, the ecumenically-minded have asserted just the opposite in and out of the Council. Cardinal Doepfner spoke very movingly in the Council about the Church's continual re-living of the Passion of Christ in its members—a Pauline idea certainly not easy to understand, much less live. St Paul himself spoke hard words on the kind of stumbling-block Christ was to the Jews and to the Greeks and Romans of his day. However, many believe it has been the latter-day Romans who have eliminated all the mystery, reduced life to a set of legal codes and theology to a set of barren condemnations, and established themselves in their baroque palaces at the centre of Christendom to make the laws and draft the condemnations.

Many of the bishops had long felt these things in their hearts, but they were first shocked, then delighted to hear them spoken in the nave of St Peter's by Bishop Emile Josef Marie De Smedt. He detected the reek of Romanism in the *schema De Ecclesia* and subdivided that Romanism into three diverting categories which he called "Triumphalism, Clericalism, and Juridicism." De Smedt said the *schema* "indulges too much in that pompous, romantic style we're used to reading in *Osservatore Romano* and other Roman documents. The life of the Church is presented as if it were a succession of triumphs for the Church militant. This medieval conception hardly fits the facts, hardly accords with the real condition of a people whom Our Lord called his 'little flock.' " On the week-end before the Council opening, for instance, the *Osservatore della Domenica* had cried, "The Council, like all the great events of the Church, is a battle between the City of God and the City of Satan."

As for clericalism, said De Smedt, "the traditional picture prevails in this project. You know the usual pyramid: pope, bishops, priests at the top, who, because of the power they have received, teach, sanctify and govern, while the Christian people receive it all passively and seem to occupy some sort of second place. We should not forget that hierarchical power is really transitory. In the next life, the people of God remain while the ministry of the hierarchy passes away. We all participate in the same priesthood of the people of God. The pope is one of the faithful—bishops, priests, laity, religious—we are all the faithful. We all go to the same sacraments, we all need the same God. Through the mercy of God and with the help of the Holy Spirit, we are all heading for the same Fatherland. All power in the Church is given to minister, to serve: the ministry of the word, the ministry of grace, the ministry of governing. We did not come to be served but to serve. In speaking about the Church, therefore, we ought to avoid this 'hierarchism.' We ought to avoid any trace of clericalism, of bishop-worship or pope-worship."

Time and again throughout the Council, the Fathers had heard arguments from Canon Law brought forward by the Curia. De Smedt did not have to give any examples of what he was talking about when he exposed the Church's juridicism.

From recent historical and theological studies, we learn that the motherhood of the Church was at the core of primitive Christian ecclesiology. All the baptized are sons and daughters of the Church. Through valid baptism all Christians are generated by Mother Church. In whatever way and in whatever Christian gathering they live, they are rightly sons and daughters of the Church and will remain so. They are really brothers and sisters even when they are separated. And they never lose the love of Mother Church whether they are near or far away.

But when we read about these matters in this *schema*, we see how far we can stray when we consider the Church in a purely juridical way or an aprioristic way. When the *schema* talks about members of the Church, it works out an aprioristic syllogism. It says, "He only is a member of the Church who . . . *atqui . . . ergo*. The rest are not said to be members of the Church." To speak this way is not good theology and it is not the kind of speech worthy of the Church if it is really a mother. What mother ever talked about her son this way—even if for some sad reason he did not live under the paternal roof with his brothers? What mother ever could say, "He is no longer a member of my family"? It is not fitting for Mother Church to speak this way either. This exercise in minor logic is unworthy of Mother Church.

For this exercise in rhetoric the Fathers gave De Smedt their loudest, most sustained applause of the Council's first session. The speech symbolized, in a way, the revisionist temper of the Council. Not even Pius XII's encyclical *Humani Generis* could have survived this new climate. To this Council, *Humani Generis* would have been too juridical, too scholastic, too authoritarian, too negative, too narrow, too pessimistic, destructive of theological progress, not ecumenical, not biblical, not patristic.

IV

The debate was, in effect, becoming a discussion of the most challenging internal issue of the Church—the question of authority. Is the Church a monarchy? Or a democracy? Or something analogous to both? Or neither? Monsignor André Pailler, Auxiliary Bishop of Rouen, told a symposium on authority at Notre Dame du Bec in April 1961 that any discussion of authority would have to begin with the idea of the "mystery of the Church." Said Pailler:

All our ideas, necessarily human and derived from our human experience as they are, require purification and a kind of "catharsis" before they can be applied to any supernatural reality. This is the principal law—and the cross—in all theology. It would be naïve to shut one's eyes to the fact that it is commonly forgotten.

This law must be all the more imperative when we are attempting to think about the Church, and especially about the Church from the point of view of authority, her hierarchy and her power. We are in the presence of a reality which seems well known, in close touch with human experience, all ready to fit into the usual categories. And the familiar categories in question are those of the law; these are the most rigid, the most "clear and distinct" in the Cartesian sense.

The theologian who undertakes to discourse on the Trinity has to remind himself and his hearers that though God is "person" and "nature," He is not so in the same way as a man. And man is the only object of which we have immediate experience. How much more then must the theologian, the pastor and the ordinary Christian as a member of the Church, remember that though the Church is a "hierarchical society," *it is so in a different way from the various societies of which we have actual experience in our daily lives.* The various ways in which authority is explained, exercised, submitted to and lived in the Church today quite clearly indicates, so it seems to me, that this requirement is not always complied with. . . . Any statement about it will have to be of an essentially analogical type. God is the Lord, but not in the same sense as the lords of this world. . . . And the Church's derivative "lordship" is unlike the "lordships" of earthly kingdoms. . . .

In searching the mystery of the Church, and its authority, the Fathers used different analogies. De Smedt had singled out the idea of the *motherhood* of the Church, and in this he found an image in Matthew 23:37—"as the hen doth gather her chickens under her wings." Another bishop, Emile Guerry of Cambrai, France, concentrated in his intervention of December 4, on the idea of the bishop as the *imago patris*, "the image of the father," an idea so basic and so forgotten in these latter days that even the Pope was startled to hear it in the Council. That very evening he sent a letter to Archbishop Guerry together with three volumes of his works on St Charles Borromeo and a precise indication of a long passage in one of them on "the bishop as father."

Some of the Fathers, to be sure, opposed such notions with a reaffirmation of the need for juridical precision. Bishop Biagio Musto of Aquino cried out against those who dared to speak in St Peter's itself against the essential principles of an institutional, hierarchical Church. He cited II Timothy 4 in which St Paul recommends his disciple to be firm in his doctrine against false teachers seeking novelty, and suggested the Fathers could profit from a reading of this passage. At this, the Fathers began to murmur. Some tapped their breviaries on their seats. Others cried, "Inadmissible!" "Inadmissible!" The presiding Cardinal (Ruffini) quickly cut Musto off. Many applauded. (As Pope John later said, "We were not friars singing in a choir.")

Before the Council, Archbishop Guerry had underlined the disastrous effects of the overinstitutionalized Church.

A purely or essentially juridical conception of the Church, with its deviations in practice, is, unfortunately, much more widespread than one would think among the Christian people, with the exception of a magnificent minority of the faithful. The bishop is reputed to be a sort of prefect, priests functionaries, sacraments residues of magic rites, religion a group of laws (Sunday Mass, abstinence, etc.) to which one submits because of a feeling of exterior discipline, and from which one escapes without understanding their true value, as happens with the laws of the State. How much these persons need to learn, from the doctrine of the Mystical Body, that in the Church—Mystical Body and visible society—it is a matter of the communication of a life, of the very life of Christ, of the life of the Holy Spirit for the health of the world. . . . In the hour in which, in the Catholic Church, increasingly more concern is demonstrated for the unity of Christians, a definition of the Church as the visible body of Christ would certainly provoke an immense echo.

At the Council, many Fathers also saw the possible impact of their revisionist notion on separated Christians and on the world at large.

Bishop Gerard Huyghe of Arras underlined the need to look at the Church as an instrument of Christ's service, this being a necessary step towards Christian unity. "Many of our contemporaries ignore the Church or battle against it. One even meets men who know and love Christ but do not recognize the Church. Moreover, it even happens that the Church, far from bringing men closer to Christ, drives them away. . . . The world is asking one question of this assembly as it sits here: "What sayest thou of thyself?" (John 1:22). The Church will be judged in the centuries to come by the answer it gives here now." According to Bishop Huyghe, the Council would have to establish the collegiality of the bishops, a missionary spirit, an authority that would not dominate but serve. "The ministers of whom St Paul speaks must serve the common good. The Church isn't divided into two classes, one that commands and one that obeys. Everyone has to serve. And the Sovereign Pontiff is called the servant of the servants of God."

Those attacking the Ottaviani *schema* were not attempting to diminish the authority of the Church. But they were saying that the Church's authority was a special thing because it was divine and that the juridical, absolutist view of authority that prevailed in the *schema* was all too neglectful of that fact. As Bishop Pailler put it, "Authority in the Church at every level, while fully preserving its genuine character as a sacred authority, will always aim to elicit a religious and not a purely human type of obedience. And this implies that the religious reasons for any given direction should be completely explained."

V

During and after the session, some Curialists attempted to defend Roman centralism against the consistent attacks of the outlanders. "We're not closed to new ideas," protested one of the secretaries from the Holy Office during the Council. Cardinal Ottaviani complained to a friendly French weekly that "public opinion is not well informed. It confuses the Holy Office with the Inquisition." But Ottaviani did not explain the differences. When I asked one high Vatican official what they were, he said, jokingly, "I don't think the Holy Office burns people any more."

Actually the Supreme Sacred Congregation of the Holy Office of the Inquisition dropped the "Inquisition" part in 1908 to shield itself from the odium inspired by that name. It normally uses another shield these days, the name of the Pope himself.

Anyone who has ever discussed the Holy Office with Ottaviani or his aides is quickly reminded that the congregation's prefect is the Pontiff himself. "The Roman Curia," explains Ottaviani, "is the organ the Pope uses to *govern* the Church. The Curia carries out what the Pope decides." This is true but only in theory. All too often, as Archbishop Eugene D'Souza of Nagpur, India, told the Council, a bishop will spend months finding the solution to a problem, then find it quashed by an obscure clerk who can find no precedent for it in any of his dusty books.

Ottaviani, Pietro Parente, and their tight little office pursue a vigorous campaign of thought control around the world. They order books and theses squelched, forbid lines of special research, hold secret trials, serve as witness, judge and executioner without giving their victims a chance to know they are being tried—much less offer any defence. One of the conciliar Fathers who knows from personal experience how the modern Inquisition works has asked the Council for "a holy inquiry into the most holy Inquisition" because, he says, "its present application of secrecy supposes a one-way street for vehicles carrying weapons for the blasting of reputations. There is, in practice, 'no entry' for vehicles carrying weapons of defence. Attempted defence involving exposure of false charges or mistakes is a new crime."

The Holy Office (with its power over every other Roman congregation) has an uneviable record—even, perhaps especially, in the last thirty years, dating roughly from the signing in 1929 of the Lateran Treaty with Mussolini. (One theologian from the provinces claims that the Holy Office's top men received their mind-set under Fascism.) It abuses secrecy to "preserve the faith," block theological progress, and ruin careers. In certain cases the Holy Office will condemn a man's work, forbid him to publish it, and then forbid him even to say he has been forbidden.

Sometimes the Holy Office will speak semi-officially through *Osservatore Romano*—as it did before the Council in the case of Jesuit Riccardo Lombardi's book—and thereby put a man's whole career in shadow. Sometimes it will not speak at all and achieve its censorious results just as easily. In the spring of 1962 it ordered a 1960 pastoral letter of the Dutch bishops removed from circulation in Italy and forced the Dutch bishops to explain that they themselves had done so because of "errors in translation." Sometimes it will speak through the Pope himself, as it did when he signed the Apostolic Constitution *Veterum Sapientia* which prescribed an increased use of Latin in seminaries in an attempt to settle "the Latin question" before the Council even began.

The Holy Office speaks through some of its members teaching in Roman seminaries. One of them, Monsignor Antonio Piolanti, Rector Magnificus of the Lateran University, gave his students running commentaries on the Council during the first session. "There are rationalist theologians going about Rome seducing innocent foreign bishops," said he. Another time, "The pillars of orthodoxy are Siri, Ruffini and Ottaviani." And one day just out of the blue, apropos of nothing: "Remember, the Pope can be deposed if he falls into heresy." (We reported these little gems in *Time* and Monsignor Rudolph Bandas, rector of the diocesan seminary in St Paul, Minnesota, took *Time* to task in the United States diocesan press. He quoted Piolanti as saying, "The statement is so queer and ridiculous that it is hardly worthy of an answer. Anyone who has the least intelligence will be able to evaluate these gratuitous assertions." Which is not really a denial, is it? Piolanti would be hard pressed to deny what was heard and noted down by several hundred of his students.)

The Holy Office also speaks through some members of the Vatican diplomatic corps. One of the best known of them is Archbishop Egidio Vagnozzi, Apostolic Delegate in the United States, who seems to consider himself the right arm of the Inquisition in the United States. Vagnozzi has put pressure on bishops to silence professors who do not teach according to the Ottaviani line, and he has gone to the front lines to attack the biblical movement or the liturgical movement or whatever other movement among American Catholics that does not happen to suit him at the moment.

It is not always Cardinal Ottaviani who initiates these moves. Sometimes his assistants take over. One of them is Archbishop Pietro Parente who got his post as "assessor" (which is the modern

title of the chief inquisitor) by having his name "announced" to
fill the vacancy at the very instant that Pope John was sounding
out someone else for the job. Pope John either had to accept
Parente or humiliate Ottaviani. He accepted Parente.

The Pope's *coppiere* is a victim of the general hatred of the Holy
Office because it thinks he is "soft on Communism." Under
Ottaviani, the Holy Office has had a strong anti-Communist
bias. It supports a Roman version of the John Birch Society called
the Pius V Institute which, until 1962, gave large cash prizes for
strong anti-Communist action, but has recently preferred to.
funnel its funds into more secret projects around the world.

Cardinal Bea, too, draws the wrath of the Holy Office. Bea,
under the direction of the Pope, had prepared a *schema* for this
Council on the Jews, which attempted to break down the puta-
tive theological basis for anti-Semitism that has flourished among
Catholics for centuries. It is, in fact, the oldest tension. If the Pope
could break this tension (in addition to many others), it would
certainly fit into his general plan to commend Christ in a new
world aborning. As soon as the Holy Office heard about the proposed *schema* on the Jews, however, it went into action and alerted
various Arab nations. Their diplomats to the Holy See raised such
a fuss and threatened such reprisals against Catholics that Bea had
to withdraw the *schema* before he was to present it to the Central
Preparatory Commission in June 1962.

"I wouldn't have believed all this if I hadn't seen it," said one
United States bishop in bewilderment.

An American member of the Curia laughed at the bishop's
naïveté. "What do these bishops think this is? A Boy Scout jam-
boree?"

VI

In his September 11 radio message the Pope had affirmed,
"The world indeed has need of Christ and it is the Church which
must bring Christ to the world." This message was, says Cardinal Bea, the result of John's meditation on the *schemata* fashioned
by the preparatory commissions which hardly considered any-

thing but the internal matters of bell, book, and candle. He then listed the principal problems of this world in crisis: the family; their daily bread; poverty; social justice; underdeveloped nations, religious liberty; and the greatest problem of all: peace.

For a time it seemed to John that his Council would never get around to these real problems. Providentially, however, the liturgical and scriptural *schemata* would certainly prepare the Fathers (and, ultimately, the Christian people) to approach world problems with evangelical empathy. In a liturgical reform, the people would become involved in the saving action of Christ in the world. In a scriptural renewal, they would dig even deeper into the inspired word itself. But he hoped that this would only be the preparation for their involving Christ in the world as he had never been involved before. This was the Christ of St Paul's letter to the Colossians: "in him all created things took their being, heavenly and earthly, visible and invisible." This could perhaps be the cosmic Christ of a Teilhard de Chardin, redeeming even the planets and the distant stars.

Many of the Fathers, seeing this need themselves and rejoicing in the fact that the Pope saw it too, chafed at the intramural discussions that droned on and on. Not even in the discussion of the *schema* on the Church did they see how the Council could reach the point of considering the larger problems of humanity.

One of the problems was that not even the Church's scholars had made up their minds about the relationship between the Church and the world. In 1962 Jesuit theologian Gustave Weigel told the Council of Religion and International Affairs, "There are two dimensions to the one world we live in. One dimension is the sacral and the other is the secular. . . . The Churches, quite sincerely and quite consistently with their own commitments, do not believe that they have any˘commission to bring about the Kingdom of God before the eschatological era. . . . The Churches do not feel, nor should they, the mission of making the secular world a faithful copy of Paradise. In some paradoxical but true sense, the Churches are in enmity with the world."

This sounds suspiciously like the old mentality of the Two Cities. It could be compared with the vision of Pope John and

an advance guard at the Council who saw no inherent contradiction between Christ's Mystical Body and the world it is supposed to redeem. Looking at the Church as a juridical entity, of
course, or looking only at the institutional Church, one approaches
the problem abstractly and inevitably winds up with an opposition between the two abstractions, Church and State. But the
people of God are not abstractions. They happen to be the citizens
of the U.S.A. or the U.S.S.R. or the U.A.R. or the U.K., and all
of them are charged by Christ to become other Christs wherever
they are.

Unless the institutional Church, the teaching Church, wants
to let Christians attempt this difficult task alone, without any
guidance, then it cannot, as Father Weigel suggests, "be in enmity
with the secular world," or fail to bring its substantial wisdom
to bear on the problems that anguish humanity that is yet far
from Christ. For the first time in history, perhaps, the entire
population of the world is faced with the possibility of a dilemma
that has been termed "Belsen or Hiroshima plus." Half of that
same population is starving. Two-thirds of it lives in desperate
poverty (while the other third spends billions for "defence").
Perhaps, as Father Weigel says, "it seems a little sanguine to think
that the Churches can do now what they have not been able to do
in the past . . . that the Churches could even achieve as much as
they did in former crises." Still the human race has never seen a
crisis like this before, and crisis can be the beginning of conversion
—not only for the world, but for the institutional Church as well.
The institutional Church has never been challenged like this
before, never been asked by a preponderant part of world opinion
to offer answers that make some sense. In looking to itself, the
institutional Church, the Council, actually, began to realize that
its old answers were not the real answers, in the sense that they
had no validity for the world.

When Cardinal Suenens rose to address the Council on December 4, it became apparent that the questions for which answers
must be found would be asked. The Belgian cardinal was an
impressive figure, tall, lean, greying at the temples, his eyes flash-
ing out of deep eye sockets. Though one of the youngest and

newest cardinals, he already had a reputation as a towering intellectual, and the Fathers listened intently.

Said Suenens: "This Council should aim at making the Church the real light of the nations." He then proposed that the Church in Council not only consider itself but also engage in a dialogue with other Christians and with the whole world. To do this, he said, the Council would have to move into the broader, more engrossing problems of life and death that face the world today. "We must say something about the very life of the human person, the inviolability of that life, its procreation, its extension in what is called the population explosion. The Church must speak on social justice. The moralists have written volume after volume on the Sixth Commandment but they have been practically silent when it comes to determining the social responsibility of private ownership. What is the theological and practical duty of rich nations towards the *Tiers-Monde* or the nations who suffer from hunger? The Church must speak about bringing the Gospel to the poor and some of the conditions the Church must meet to make that Gospel revelant to them. The Church must speak about international peace and war in a way that can help enlighten the world."

Many were stirred by his words.

In his private apartment, John XXIII sat watching on closed-circuit television, and he too, was stirred. "At last, the Fathers are beginning to understand what this Council is for," he said.

VII

But not all of the Fathers understood. A few days before, Archbishop Dino Staffa had met with the conciliar Commission on Education and given them a demonstration of Romanism at its worst. Staffa is consultor of the Supreme Sacred Congregation of the Holy Office, of the Sacred Consistorial Congregation, of the Sacred Congregation for the Oriental Church, of the Sacred Congregation of the Council, of the Sacred Congregation of Religious, juridical consultant to the Secretariat of State of His Holiness, consultor of the Pontifical Commission for the Authentic Interpretation of the Code of Canon Law, a member of the Pontifical Commission for the Ecclesiastical Archives of Italy, of the Pontifical Commission for Motion Pictures, Radio and Television, of the Pontifical Commission for Latin America, and secretary of the Sacred Congregation of Seminaries and Universities. When he addressed the conciliar Commission on Seminaries, Studies and Catholic Education (to which he had been appointed by the Pope himself), he could have been expected to be reasonably attuned to the thought of John XXIII. Instead he made it clear to the other twenty-five members of the commission just how he would perform his varied functions on the poop of the barque of Peter. "During recess, they say our commission is supposed to rewrite our *schemata* according to the mind of the Council. Well, what *is* the mind of the Council? Here today and gone tomorrow."

Inevitably Staffa's words drifted back to the Pope. Though John was then fighting off a serious anaemia caused by internal haemorrhaging from what doctors thought was a stomach ulcer, he exercised one of the few sharply independent acts of his pontificate. He was, after all, the president of the Council and he knew from the voting, moreover, that a majority of the Fathers agreed with him. He promptly drafted six definite norms that spelled out "the mind of the Council" for anyone who had not yet understood it. The draft was nothing if not a charter for change.

Furthermore, said John, he would not leave the revision of the *schemata* up to the very men in Rome who had botched them in the first place. He called for a mixed commission of bishops to carry on the work of *aggiornamento* and established a new coordinating committee of middle-roading and liberal cardinals to make sure that the forces in Rome which opposed his *aggiornamento* would not undo the achievement of the first session.

He added further that he would expect the bishops of the world to consider themselves still "in Council" and engage in a sort of Council-by-mail-order by studying the re-elaborated *schemata* and posting their observations back to Rome. During the preparatory phase of the Council, an individual bishop's observations may not have been heeded. It was too easy for the Curialists to log the observations and then forget them. Now, in the interim period of his Council, Pope John would avoid that possibility. "Where expedient," said he, "let the suggestions of the Fathers be conveyed to Rome through the presidents of the episcopal conferences." This represented a definite shift of power away from the Curia and out into the hands of the *periferisti*. In the past, the Curia could ignore one bishop. It would now have more difficulty ignoring the possibly unanimous requests of 159 French bishops or of 241 United States bishops or even of the sixty-eight bishops from Germany. Up to this time, the papal delegate or nuncio was the mediator between pope and bishop. Now, even before the subject came up for discussion at the Council, John had elevated the episcopal conferences to that intermediate role.

The curial reaction to this was predictable—but nonetheless shocking. Official translations from the Latin of the Pope's six norms omitted great blocks of the Pope's thought and, most important, any references at all to the new role of episcopal conferences. If the Curia ignored this order, perhaps it would be forgotten. The Fathers, of course, had all received copies of the original Latin document on December 6. But it is likely that many of them were content to read the "official" translation. (The American bishops, to mention one group, appeared not to have read the original: they made no plans for a general meeting during the interim and no plans to collate their observations to the new *schemata*.) The public had to be content with the bowdlerized version until various reviews (including the Jesuit weekly, *America*) discovered the discrepancy in March of 1963.

VIII

The seventh day of December 1962 was not the most momentous day of the first session of the Council known as Vatican II. But it was the last day of the Council's general meetings and is one of the most vivid in my memory. Those twenty-four hours symbolized for me the spirit of the Council.

I A.M. I said good-bye to the last of some fifty supper guests.

8 A.M. I left my home for the five-minute drive to St Peter's.

8-15 A.M. I joined the last remnants of the Council press corp outside the press office on the Via della Conciliazione to queue up and be led inside St Peter's for a glimpse of the conciliar Mass.

8-30 A.M. We were escorted into St Peter's Square, around the side of the basilica and into St Peter's itself. We emerged on a little reviewing stand behind the Bernini *baldacchino*. The Council Fathers were filling their green airliner seats on both sides of the nave—which looked like nothing so much as a football stadium. We were given end-zone seats and watched the Council Fathers chatting before the start of Mass.

9 A.M. We heard Mass said in the original language of the Last Supper by Monsignor Gabriel Ganni, Coadjutor Bishop of Beirut, Lebanon.

10-15 A.M. Archbishop Pericle Felici pronounced the Latin words *exeant omnes*—everybody out—and we filed out, leaving the Council Fathers to cast their decisive votes on liturgical reform. Each of the Fathers took his special magnetic pen and marked an X on his punch card. Seminarian-ushers picked up the cards and fed them into the Council's computer and then the Fathers proceeded to get their last thoughts on *De Ecclesia* into the record. Cardinal Koenig led off with what had become a recurring theme in the Council: that the Church ought to become less Roman and more Catholic, ought to subordinate its ecclesiastical mentality to evangelical goals and purge itself of everything that dims that witness. And that brought the Fathers back to where they had started when they announced their intentions in their "Statement to all Humanity" on October 20.

10-20 A.M. With my senior editor from New York, William Forbis, who had flown to Rome to talk to me about *Time*'s choice of Pope John as Man of the Year, I cut through the red tape at the Vatican's bronze doors and we were finally admitted to the offices of the Secretary of State.

10-30 A.M. We began a chat with protocol chief, Monsignor Igino Cardinale (when he is made cardinal, he will be called Cardinal Cardinale) about Pope John's health, his role in world peace, his hopes for the Council. The Monsignor was interrupted by various crises: one phone call from the Mwami of Burundi who was worried about arrangements for his December 16 visit to Pope John, and finally a summons from Archbishop Dell'Acqua who was upset because the Pope had just expressed a wish to drop in on the Council Fathers. I asked permission to follow the Pope into the Council session. Cardinale said no as diplomatically as he could.

11-30 A.M. We left Cardinale's office.

11-32 A.M. Cardinale caught us on the way to the elevator and said, "Wait a minute."

11-40 A.M. Cardinale rushed out of Archbishop Dell'Acqua's office with permission for us to follow the Pope into St Peter's and phoned the gendarmes to tell them we were on our way.

11-42 A.M. Archbishop Felici announced the results of voting on the liturgical *schema's* preface and first chapter. Although dozens of Fathers had spoken against this reform in the debates, and although subsequent amendments had only served to strengthen the progressive character of the proposal, final tabulation showed only eleven Fathers against it. To the Council's progressives, euphoric over other battles fought and won, this was a sweet message. True, they would have to vote on other chapters. But they would be mere formalities. "Within the preface and first chapter," a member of the Liturgical Commission told me, "are the seeds of all the other reforms." It was true also that the Pope would have to ratify the action. But no one thought he would attempt to veto what the Council had spent so long achieving.

11-45 A.M. Forbis and I were running around the back of St Peter's from the Cortile San Damasco. A Vatican gendarme shunted us up a higher road to the Vatican gardens where we puffingly discovered we had been detoured so that the Pope's black Mercedes would not find us in its path. We hustled down past shouting gendarmes to get a glimpse of John being driven by.

11-50 A.M. We were admitted to the Santa Marta entrance of St Peter's, directly behind the Pope, and landed in a box about fifty feet from the Bernini altar. This was John's first visit to a general meeting and an open demonstration to the Fathers that he was regaining his health after a week of serious illness. He was pale, very pale, but obviously happy and smiling. He told the Fathers how pleased he was with the progress of the Council. His talk (in Latin) was unusually brief. But his message was clear: you have done a fine job here. Let us patch up our differences and go on with more good work. Then he walked out without ceremony.

12-05 P.M. Cardinals, patriarchs, archbishops, bishops, superiors of religious orders followed suit, chatting as they departed, most of them obviously pleased over the Church's new directions and the Pope's apparent vigour. Cardinals Bea, Suenens and Léger, possibly the most inspired trio of the Council, walked by, deep in conversation. Cardinal Ritter waved. Forbis and I walked up the length of St Peter's and out the front door. The sun was shining brightly and the air was wonderfully warm. For once, I was a part of that cascade of colour that poured out of St Peter's and down the *scala regia* each day at noon. I met Hans Küng on the steps, told him with a laugh that a Roman paper had reported his conference at the United States press panel of two days before and called him a Protestant minister. He too laughed. How could any progressive do otherwise on a day like this? Whatever pessimism Küng may have had before the Council now had disappeared. "Inspiration has gripped the Council," he said.

12-40 P.M. Met a Council theologian who could not make my supper the night before, so I talked him into having lunch at Alfredo's. There, over the best pasta Rome had to offer (which is saying quite a bit), he gave Forbis and me his views on the last two months' battles. He said that many might try to scoff at the first session as a do-nothing affair, but that the Church had in a few weeks overcome centuries of stagnation. He insisted that the first session marked the end of the Counter Reformation.

3-05 P.M. Forbis departed for London. The theologian and I drove back to the Via della Conciliazione and we traded bits of information.

3-30 P.M. We dropped into the press panel of the United States bishops were eight theologians and four bishops gave their impressions of the first session. All of them said, in one way or another, that the Church was headed in a new direction.

4-30 P.M. Drove to the penthouse of Signora Grassellini, a famed designer of Vatican stamps, to see if her almost completed portrait of Pope John could possibly serve as our Man of the Year cover portrait.

5-10 P.M. Arrived at the Pensione Sitea where the editor of a United States Catholic paper interviewed me on my experiences covering the Council.

6-10 P.M. Checked into my office, read the mail, typed my notes.

8-30 P.M Arrived home only slightly late for a quiet dinner party with three theologians from the Council.

9-50 P.M. Got a telephone call intimating that the joint Ottaviani-Bea commission meeting that had just ended in riot and confusion.

10-30 P.M. Closed my eyes to rest them for a minute.

12-30 A.M. Woke up with some embarrassment but discovered my guests had not missed me a bit.

1-00 A.M. Said good-bye to my guests.

IX

Those twenty-four hours I have recorded seemed charged with promise for the future. The overwhelming number of bishops and theologians at the Council were ready to begin moving the barque of Peter out onto the sea of the world. But that night the sinister turn of events at the mixed commission meeting indicated that some on the barque intended to drag anchor.

For a week the mixed theological commission had been meeting in an attempt to get the scriptural *schema* into a form acceptable to the Council Fathers. They had divided up into subcommissions and had rewritten most of the sections word for word, and had then come back together and approved most of the draft. Cardinal Ottaviani was unaccountably absent from all the meetings. On this Friday night, however, Ottaviani appeared with Assessor Parente, bearing an important-looking sheaf of papers which he distributed to the Fathers and theologians present.

Ottaviani and Parente settled down in their seats. Roman-born, little-travelled Cardinal Alfredo Ottaviani, seventy-two, secretary of the supreme Sacred Congregation of the Holy Office, and the brilliant, calculating career man, Archbishop Pietro Parente, also seventy-two. They made quite a team. The stolid, purposeful character of Ottaviani wedded to the subtle manoeuvrability of Parente. Around them orbited all the other figures of the Roman dicasteries like dependent moons. Between them they ran the interlocking directorate that cemented the Roman Curia.

The physiognomy of each man complemented the other. Ottaviani's permanently furrowed forehead raftering the low compact skull curving back abruptly like the refusal to a direct question, the pentagonal chin, the neckline hidden beneath the bulging jowl, an overall look of doubting sphinx-like immobility. Parente's substantially smaller countenance, narrow forehead, prominent nose, mobile mouth, an overall impression of restlessness, of one who knows the corridors and ways inside the temple, who possesses the keys to arsenal and treasury alike, the hieratic functionary who explains the Enigma and relies on the immovable truth of the Sphinx. *Semper Idem.* Ottaviani's eyes: one half closed, the effect of an ailment, lulled one with the half-formed idea of myopia and at the same time pulled one up with a jerking impression of a wary eye peering through barred shutters; the other eye wide open and staring in downright challenge, in silent reproof. Parente's eyes: twin caravels dancing upon the sea of events, travelling swiftly, knowingly across the waves of human faces, confident that he kenned the balance of bureaucratic power and its decisiveness in any crisis.

Ottaviani incarnated the old order, its obstinacy, its refusal to change, its admitted strength, an antique cast in ancient bronze, silently unmalleable, quietly unreceptive. Parente was the voluble echo of the old order's insistence, its stored-up stratagems, its sharp resourcefulness, the cold liquid distillation of a former age, still in a state of precipitation, still repellent of any foreign admixture.

But both men had a shock coming. The commission members scanned the documents distributed by the pair and decided quickly that they were a blatant attempt to steamroller the commission with "special instructions" from the Pope himself. Page one was a note from Ottaviani to the mixed commission. In it, the Cardinal said that he had received this document from the Secretary of State and that, "since the transmission was made by order of the Supreme Pontiff, it can therefore be legitimately deduced that the mixed commission ought to give the ideas the weight they deserve." Page two was a noncommittal letter from Cardinal Cicognani saying the document had come to the Pope and that he [Cicognani] was passing it on to the commission without comment. Five pages followed, a document laying down six stern directives about the course of biblical studies and citing four examples (out of context) that purportedly "denied the historicity of important Old and New Testament narratives." It was signed by nineteen cardinals: Bacci, Traglia, Antoniutti, Ruffini, Siri and Urbani of Italy; Agagianian, the Armenian Rite prefect of the Propaganda Congregation; De Barros Câmara of Brazil; Santos of the Philippines; Godfrey of Great Britain; McIntyre of the United States; Gonçalves Cerejeira of Portugal; Heard of Scotland and the Roman Curia; Caggiano of Argentina; Wyszynsky of Poland; Quiroga y Palacios and De Arriba y Castro of Spain; Concha of Colombia; and Quintero of Venezuela.*

Bishop De Smedt quickly asked if the Pope had seen the document at all. Parente leaped to his feet. "Whatever comes from any of the Roman dicasteries automatically comes in the name of the Pope. The Pope therefore has spoken. That is the important thing."

That did it. Everyone began to talk at once. This was precisely what was wrong with Roman centralism. The Roman dicasteries *were* the Pope and would continue to act independently of the Pope, even contrary to his expressed wishes, and attempt to pass off their action as coming "from the Supreme Pontiff himself." Bishop De Smedt, his voice heavy with emotion called someone a *mascalzone*, a scroundrel. But the word was not strong enough to draw anything more than a laugh from Cardinal Ottaviani.

---

* Various reviews have stated that five cardinals later withdrew their names from this document, but some discrepancies make it difficult to ascertain exactly which ones. At any rate, these nineteen names were the ones on the document presented on December 7.

As for the rewritten *schema*, Ottaviani would have none of it. "After all," he said, "I am one of the co-presidents, and I was not present when these chapters were approved."

On the next day, December 8, the Pope showed that he had no illusions about the Council's accomplishments. True, in the last week of the session, the Fathers had enlarged their scope to something worldwide. And, roughly and tentatively, they had re-examined the role of the Pope and now saw his authority as something meant to serve rather than dominate. They had examined the place of the bishops and saw them not as mere representatives of the Pope, nor their territories simply as organizational units, but as successors of the Apostles in local Churches. They had examined the role of the Roman Curia and saw it not as a buffer between bishops and the Pope but only as an administrative service. They had examined the role of laymen and saw that the latter were not apostles because of a shortage of priests but because they were members of the Church and sharers in a royal priesthood. The Fathers became aware of the necessity for dialogue in this human-divine society, and they had tried to find ways in which this society might again become incarnate in the world.

But all of this was merely introductory. On December 8, the last day of the session, the Pope presided over the Mass of the Virgin in St Peter's (purists said it was the first strictly "liturgical" ceremony ever presided over by a modern pope) and pronounced his judgment of the first session. "The Council is an act of faith in God," said John, "of obedience to his laws and a sincere effort to correspond to the plan of redemption. The first session has been an introduction, slow and solemn, to the great work of the Council. . . . In so great a context, it is understandable that some time was needed to reach an understanding on what was cause for comprehensible and anxious divergences. Even this had demonstrated to the world the holy freedom of the sons of God in the Church."

The first session was over. John's Council would move into a second phase, a period of study and reflection and a gathering of strength for their decisive moving of the barque of Peter.

I.C.—8*

Chapter Eleven

UNDER WAY

I

A T the end of the first session, I took a long walk with Cardinal Joseph Ritter of St Louis. We started on the Janiculum Hill at the North American College shortly after lunch, made our rambling way down to the Piazza di Spagna, watched the people of Rome build a monument of flowers for the Virgin on her feast of the Immaculate Conception, then turned back into the shadow of the Janiculum. We talked at length, and most of our conversation concerned the events of the session's final week and their meaning. The Cardinal was very free, not a bit worried that I might twist his talk into heresy. I know that I am not twisting it when I report that he spoke in a metaphor of movement (much as John F. Kennedy did during the 1960 presidential campaign). "The Council was called to give direction," said Ritter. "To change direction. It's really worked out that way. To change direction from narrowness and restrictions. This means great things for the future. Now the bishops are looking out to the world. Now the Church can serve the world. Now we're in a process of transition. We're moving. And the Holy Spirit will not allow us to turn back." In his ruminative, profoundly simple way, Ritter was speaking, for at me least, the final lines of that great drama—the first session of Vatican II.

The Cardinal helped me realize that Pope John had, in his peculiarly pragmatic way, unchained the Body that is the Church and let it prove to itself that there was no calcification in its joints. In the last week of the session, the Fathers had shown their realization that Christ was still incarnate in the Church and that, therefore, the Church was still growing and alive in the world. The Cardinal saw the ideas of the final week as the expression of a development of doctrine, the kind that must come in a living body. It may have been, we agreed, that this development got a strong boost during the prophetic period when Cardinal Emmanuel Suhard was Bishop of post-war Paris.

Suhard's description of the Church may have marked the turning point in its modern history: "The Church," Suhard wrote in *Growth or Decline*, "remained frozen in feudal forms which worked in times past. In our time, instead of being fused with society . . . the Church is absent from the City. She hovers over humanity instead of being incarnate in its flesh and blood." But whether or not that turning point came with Suhard, we agreed that at last the Church had changed direction—and changed decisively, so that nothing could really pull it back from its new course.

Bishop Thomas Gorman of Dallas–Forth Worth (who, I thought, had come to the Council as something of a sceptic) told the United States press panel, "As the work of the Council developed, I think the impression grew in all of us that this was something that wasn't dealing with the past but a forward-looking Council. We've exchanged ideas, we've grown in our knowledge of problems Christians face today. We look forward with great confidence to the days that lie ahead."

Gorman hit it exactly. The first session was a period of radical revisionist thinking, rather than one of great concrete accomplishment. It was a time when the bishops were able to work out a whole new way of looking at reality, to form a new epistemology and a new language.

Father Thurston N. Davis, editor of the Jesuit weekly review, *America*, could judge that "Vatican II has . . . created a new atmosphere of amity and urgency with respect to the unity of all Christians. It has opened windows locked for centuries. It has provided an immense showcase for a display of the democratic side of the Church's life. It has ventilated questions long shut away unanswered. And it has done this in a setting of overwhelming evidence of the faith, devotion, zeal, general competence and amazing catholicity of the bishops of the whole earth."

What Cardinal Ritter, Bishop Gorman and Father Davis implied was that the Council was moving the Church into the service of a world in transition. Some few would disagree. Bishop Russell Joseph McVinney of Providence, Rhode Island, for instance, could not see that the transition would be too drastic. "I don't foresee too many changes. . . . Why change? We have had a flourishing institution for 2,000 years and, as the saying goes, 'Why break up a winning team?' " But Bishop Anthony John King Mussio of Steubenville, Ohio, summed up the Council's spirit as one "moving away from the old way of doing things, from old forms, from confusing terminology, from customs and habits which have long since become anachronisms."

From outside the Church, too, the change seemed evident. Said *The Christian Century*: "It is already evident that the Council may prove to be the most important religious event of our time. . . . Even without the present Pope, forces long pent-up in the Roman Catholic Church and loosed by him through the Council would surely continue to make their influence felt." Dr Martin Niemöller, a German Lutheran, remarked that "perhaps we are nearer to the one Christian Church than we thought even a short while ago." He said he was cheered by "the great change within the Catholic Church under Pope John which none of us had dared to believe in." Willem Visser 't Hooft, general secretary of the World Council of Churches, said the Council proved that the Church had "a greater capacity for renewal than most non-Roman Christians and, in fact, many Roman Catholics considered possible."

Dr George H. Williams of Harvard University believed the Council's new climate touched on the miraculous. "I am a student of history," said Williams, "and I have found an atmosphere such as this only at this moment of history, at this Council of the twentieth century. I don't think that any major problem is in any sense solved. Nevertheless, the whole atmosphere is so different that, as Cardinal Bea says, it is a 'real miracle.' "

In his talks at the Harvard Colloquium in March 1963, Cardinal Bea singled out three major results of the Council's first session: (1) the establishment of his Secretariat for Promoting Christian Unity as a permanent and official body set up to deal "not only with Reformed but Eastern Churches as well," (2) a clearly ecumenical outlook fostered by the presence inside the Council of other Christian observers, and (3) "the new realization that all Christians of any and every denomination belong to each other."

Many did not overlook a result that was almost too obvious: the Council Fathers' realization of their own unique character. Jesuit Father Robert Graham, who covered the Council for *America*, described it as "an awareness of their collective existence." Wrote Graham before the session was half over: "Many came to Rome with the expectation of finding out here what the mind of the Church is. Now, somewhat to their fright, they realize that they are the architects of the mind of the Church; they are the Council itself. With and under the Pope, the 'Fathers' are the supreme legislative body of the Church. In this conviction, the bishops are preparing to assert their authority as teachers. The theologians, for all their learning, and the papal administrators, for all their experience, are noticeably taking a back seat."

And at the end of the session, Bishop Clarence G. Issenmann of Columbus, Ohio, reported that "individual bishops are leaving Rome with a more clearly defined sense of belonging to the Church" and would return "with a new group consciousness." Bishop John P. Treacy of La Crosse, Wisconsin, used more technical language: the world's bishops, he said, found "a renewed sense of their collegiality as successors of the Apostles."

In February 1963, Archbishop Emile Guerry of Cambrai devoted a good part of a pastoral letter to the first session's manifestation of the episcopal collegiality. He gave the best definition so far of collegiality: "the solid responsibility which all the bishops of the world carry, under the authority of the Pope, for the evangelization of the world and for moving the Church into the world."

II

With their new-found collegiality, the bishops discovered a way to commend the authority of Christ in the twentieth century. They did so not by attempting to dominate but to serve, to adapt to the world in a reasoned and reasoning manner. Reasoned and reasoning: this was the characteristic tenor of the first session.

"The use of power is an issue vital to every generation," Archbishop T. D. Roberts had told me during the Council. "It has never been more urgent than today, in a world all but reduced to ruins by totalitarian abuse of authority." In their major work of the first session, the Fathers attempted to correct the old, but partly justified, impression that the Church was indeed totalitarian. By refusing to take any overt leadership in the Council, by letting it bog down of its own weight, Pope John literally forced the bishops to find their collegiality. He forced them to turn back the clock to Vatican I and, as Archbishop Guerry explained, "to dissipate the impression that the Church had made a substantial modification in its make-up by reinforcing the authority of the Pope and centralizing everything in Rome." This alone would have its impact on other Christians. The Fathers got into the spirit of things and took to heart the Pope's opening Council statement about "re-formulating the old doctrine." They proceeded to begin a reasoned inquiry into (1) the Church's forms of worship and its hitherto unreasoning regulation from central Roman offices, and (2) the Church's policy towards the science of Sacred Scripture. As French Jesuit theologian Jean Daniélou put it, "The task of the Council . . . [was] to express the permanent truth in its present applications. Otherwise, Christian faith and morals would appear as strangers to the problems of men, and not because of their content but because of their faulty presentation. Then the Church would be responsible for jealously protecting riches which it ought to dispense generously."

To do this, of course, the Fathers would have to think, would have to revise many old, half-formed ideas that had been hatched in the incubus of sheltered seminaries and siege mentalities. Since their seminary days, many of the Fathers had learned to come to grips with the world in almost every respect but one—theologically. But in the atmosphere of the Council, in a freedom from diocesan cares they would never have had at home, in close contact with European bishops and theologians who had been working on a theology of encounter, the bishops proved they could come to grips with a reasoned theology as well. Few of the bishops were disturbed by the new ideas, and discovered instead that it was precisely the new ideas which would help them move their Church into the world as it is, and talk to men as they are. Editorialized the French review *Informations Catholiques Internationales*: "All the bishops look to the new traits of the man of today: *technicisé, socialisé, deraciné.* . . . Perhaps they see this man as one who must be *informé.*"

Some retrogressives who projected their own disturbance over new ideas to the "simple faithful" claimed there was an essential opposition between theological truth and the piety of the masses, and that theological truth must as a rule yield to pastoral considerations. To this, the Jesuit biblical scholar John L. McKenzie replied in *America:* "If it is now legitimately assumed that the faithful will be better Catholics if they are ignorant, then we have a theological novelty more novel than any thesis of modern theology. . . . A traditional function of the pastoral office is teaching. One who conceals the truth may know what he is doing, but he is not teaching."

But the majority of Fathers were not willing to gloss over anything in the interests of not rocking the boat. They rejected any implications that the Church was monolithic or absolutist, and proceeded to carry on a dialogue, a reasoning process—a sign of health in any community of humans. To the delegate-observers, this was an impressive thing. To them, the liberty of the Council discussion was the most impressive fact of the first session. It demonstrated, said one |of |the observers, "the extraordinary vitality of the Church." And it opened up possibilities of change within the Council, of change back home, of greater changes in the second Council session. The spirit of freedom had been turned loose and, with that, there was no predicting where the creativity would end.

During the first session many Fathers openly admitted how much they were learning (or at least hearing articulated for the first time). "We heard men dare to say things we'd privately been thinking for a long time ourselves," said one American bishop. And Cardinal Spellman told a group of United States servicemen one morning, "Well, I've got to be going to school now. This *is* a school we're attending, you know."

Liberty at the Council had its effect at home. As one theologian remarked in Rome, "The bishops can't talk this freely here and then go back home and try to keep their own priests quiet." He was right: the Council spirit of freedom and openness was exportable. Perhaps the most compelling lesson was learned in the United States itself when the Catholic University of America kept four progressive theologians from participating in a student lecture series. The outcry against this policy, ostensibly formed by the rector of Catholic University, William J. McDonald, came with most force neither from the vocal laity nor from a group of liberal priests, but from the United States hierarchy itself. And the most remarkable thing was, as Monsignor John Tracy Ellis charged, such suppression had been going on at Catholic University for almost a decade without protest. Now in the spirit of the Council, that policy of suppression was given a sharp blow.

III

Throughout Scripture and throughout the liturgy, the Church is described as the bride of Christ. In its efforts to make the bride of Christ "black but beautiful" to the millions not impressed with white skin, in its efforts to "adapt" its worship and its message, the Council Fathers were only using common sense, only attempting to commend Christ to millions who otherwise would never see him as the Way or the Truth or the Life. At last, a Council would look at the Church not in terms of itself, but in terms of the world. This did not necessarily mean that the Council was attempting to make Christianity "comfortable" in the Atomic Age. Christianity could never be true to itself and be a "comfortable" thing. In a sense, Christ would always have his Judas and his Pontius Pilate. As Father John Courtney Murray once said, "The big thing is to be hated for the right reason."

But many were wondering, during the interim period between

sessions, where the new spirit of accommodation and openness would lead. Some pessimists said it meant "the end of the Roman Catholic Church." Some optimists said it meant "the unity and peace of the whole family of peoples." The only thing certain was that John and his bishops would be sailing on uncharted waters in an attempt to bring Christ to the world.

But how would they do it? By drafting seventeen *schemata*, seventeen documents, seventeen recondite formulations on the nature of Scripture, of the liturgy, of the Church? On seminary training, or the Virgin, or religious orders?

Would these seventeen *schemata* really do the job? Would they move the Church into the modern world? Perhaps, as the editors of *The Commonweal* suggested, "it is unfair that the Council should bear the weight of answering this question. . . . Nevertheless, what the Council does is bound to be taken as the fullest contemporary expression of the Church's self-understanding. . . . Pope John XXIII himself has led and encouraged the Church to set its sights very high at the Council. He has asked for nothing less than a magnificent display of the Church's contemporary witness to Christ's saving Word."

Well, the lesson of the first session (during which the Council Fathers did not finish one single *schema*) moved the Church ahead approximately three centuries—from the sixteenth to the nineteenth. The Fathers were not merely bandying words. They were attempting to make an intelligent witness to a common faith. They did seem to be acting in *persona gregis*, representing their flocks. Jean Guitton, the French layman and theologian whose friendship with John XXIII secured him the honour of being the only Catholic layman who observed the Council from inside, reported that "John XXIII was amazed to see that his simple words, 'I want to call a Council, I hope for the union of Christians, I want there to be a dialogue' would have such a profound reaction among Catholics and non-Catholics." Many of the bishops were also amazed at the interest of peoples everywhere in the Council. Newspapers and magazines reflected that interest and this, said one member of Cardinal Bea's Secretariat, had a profound influence on the Fathers. It was, in fact, one of the factors that helped the Fathers find their collegiality, their sense of universal responsibility for moving the barque of Peter.

Many of the Fathers still had rather narrow views of what that world was or what it demanded of the Council. French Dominican Yves Congar has described that world as one in which "one man out of every four is Chinese, two men out of three are starving, one man out of every three lives under Communism, and one Christian out of every two is not Catholic." In such a world, no thinking Council Fathers could hope to commend Christ by presenting the Church as a narrow, sectarian body. They would have to make the Church, to use the divine language borrowed by Pope John, an attractive young girl, "without spot or wrinkle." But in the first session, the Fathers made a beginning. They began to abandon the defensive ghetto-mindedness of the Counter Reformation and began to acquire a growing consciousness of the Church not as a clerical or sectarian thing but as a potentially living extension of the whole Christ in the world.

Once on that path, it would seem unlikely that the Council Fathers could return for a second session to engage in discussion of minor matters. No, they would have to look at the world as it was and address themselves to the problems of Christian and human unity, of religious and political liberty, even to questions of life and death: of war and peace, of the Bomb, of poverty, population and disease.

Said an Irish theologian in Rome: "It is slowly sinking into the minds of the bishops that a great wind has blown through the city and the world. The Church is looking out through opened windows over the wall of the Iron Curtain to the whole world. The bishops who come back next September will never know how much they've changed in the meantime. Only in a hundred years will historians see how pentecostal this first session was."

But no one believed that the Fathers did not have a long, long way to go. As the Church presented itself in the year of Our Lord 1963, the majority of men (the one out of four who was Chinese, the one out of three who was living under Communism, the two out of three who were starving) could hardly give a damn about the triumph of the Church or its ability to withstand any siege, even the assaults of all the devils in hell. Not even the nominal Catholics in Rome itself seemed to care much about this kind of Church.

No, the Church of the future would have to be relevant to men, would have to take the steps necessary to make itself somehow meaningful to the five thousand million human beings that would be inhabiting the planet in the year 2,000.

Why all this concern for relevance on the worldly plane? Neither Christ nor his Apostles preached against the evil institutions of their day, not against slavery or prostitution, or war, or hunger, or disease. True, but many Christians, obviously acting under inspiration, had, through the passing centuries, evolved a social consciousness that was a direct application of the Master's teachings. This *prise de conscience* would aim at changing the very structures of society. As Maryknoll Father Albert Nevins put it, "The Church is the totality of its members acting in unity to transform the world. The prime mission of this Church is not to the individual as such but to mankind as a whole. It is a mission that activates love in the world, a part of that same love that led God to the act of creation." Or, as Jesuit political scientist Donald Wolf put it, "The mission of the Church is not to save souls but to save men. And that means man in all the complexity of his spiritual and temporal, individual and social nature."

For some years, now, through most of the nineteen-year pontificate of Pius XII, this theory has been evolved by many thinkers in the Church: "The Church is the leaven placed by the Lord in the whole mass of humanity. Its duty is to serve as a ferment, that is to say, it must Christianize the whole of humanity."

But the theory has not noticeably taken hold. Was there anything wrong with the theory? Why did it not seem to catch hold? Partially because it was imposed from the top; it was just one more dreary directive from Rome. Partially because it was a trifle clerical; the Church would act as a leaven through the laymen—because, as Pius XII said, there were not enough priests to do the job. And through it all was the underlying thought, hardly ever expressed, that somehow the world was bad and not really worth leavening; or that it was impossible to leaven. Jesuit theologian Karl Rahner told me as much in his room one morning at the German College. "You can't confuse the secular and the sacral," he said. "If you do, you end up with another—and worse—form of clericalism."

Rahner called the idea of the *consecratio mundi*—the consecration of the world—"an American idea." Perhaps it is. If so, good. Perhaps this is the contribution which socially conscious Americans (of all nationalities) can make to the Council. The idea that Christians must be a sign to their generation as their Master was a sign to his is undeniably strong in United States Catholicism today. The Incarnation makes the human more human. The follower of Christ sees the Trinity in all things and all things in the Trinity. There was a time when he gave a cup of cold water in the name of Christ. But in the twentieth century, he wants to give more because he sees he can give more. "If scientists and engineers put their talents to work," asked Holy Cross Father Theodore M. Hesburgh, president of the University of Notre Dame, "do you believe that there would be 900 million illiterates in the world, with all the riches of human culture closed to them? With modern communications, one master can teach millions—but it isn't being done, except in a few isolated places where it has begun without our help."

Hesburgh was talking to a group of scientists at the California Institute of Technology, but he could just as well have been talking to any group of Christians. According to the Jesuit palaeontologist and philosopher, Pierre Teilhard de Chardin, the mission of modern Catholics is the *christification* of the universe, the full Incarnation of Christ in time—the Christ of St Paul's letter to the Colossians: ". . . in him all created things took their being, heavenly and earthly, visible and invisible; . . . He too is that head whose body is the Church."

Such a conception, of course, implies much more than a clericalized Church. It implies a Church in which all men and women see their role in the christification of the world. Without that, any conciliar statements on war and peace or the responsibility of the rich nations to the poor nations would be barren.

A conciliar statement on the problems of humanity, such as the one Cardinal Suenens called for on December 4, would carry the Church beyond the social encyclicals precisely because it would be something elaborated and discussed and made their own by all the bishops, the teachers of their flocks. But it would still have its dangers. It might be looked upon as merely one more high-sounding bit of moralizing. Cardinal Suenens, the cardinal charged with getting this project before the Fathers, does not want it to turn out this way. When he made the proposal, he said it must be a "dialogue with the world," not a new set of unrealistic norms to be imposed on Catholics or ignored with subconscious feelings of guilt. It would have to be a statement of principles and an offer, an offer to the world of assistance: how can we help? As it was put by Monsignor George Higgins, a Council theologian and a director of the NCWC's Social Action Department, "Maybe the best thing the Council could do would be to say to the world, 'We don't have the answers to the population problem or to the problems of war and peace.' Maybe the best thing the Council could do would be to tell the theologians and the scholars and the scientists to get to work."

Archbishop Karl Alter of Cincinnati admitted that the Council should indeed address itself to the greater problems of humanity. "Too often," he told me, "we think of getting down our creed, our position, our moral code and be done with it. We haven't really thought hard enough about what the Incarnation means. For too long we've held the world at arm's length." But Alter did not see how the Council could take the necessary step. The bishops do not have the facts at their command to be able to make intelligent decisions or give intelligent guidance in, for example, the question of nuclear disarmament. "Any concrete proposals we might make may not be mediation but merely meddling," said Alter.

Cardinal Suenens had an answer for that. "What the Council really needs," said he, "is lay experts, the world's greatest scientists, demographers, economists, doctors—lay experts. Then the Council would have the facts." The goal in all this, said Suenens, would not be "to put the Church into politics," but it would be to direct all Christians into a world that needed the leavening influence of Christ very badly.

The eternal logic in human events, the world's vocalized needs, seem to dictate such a course. The Council cannot help but turn to the world's problems.

Said Jean Daniélou: "Men today are seeking an equilibrium in a world of change. Ethics are upset. But ethics are still needed. . . . Men of today, even if they are not Christians, expect the Church to show them their responsibilities in the world they live in. In the world of nuclear energy and planetary exploration, in psychoanalysis and biology, television and films. Charity, poverty and chastity always remain as the essence of the Christian ideal. But their way of being lived must be expressed at the concrete levels of human existence."

IV

In order to work out a charter for modern man, however, the Council will have to realize that no simple document hatched by a Roman Catholic assembly working alone could commend itself. The world will not accept the Message unless and until Christians are one. This is the lesson of Christ's prayer for unity in John 17. "That they all may be one, . . . that the world may believe that thou hast sent me." In other words the ultimate Christian witness will not come to the world until the world sees some kind of Christian unity. In light of the Council what are the possibilities for that? In general, they are good.

The ecumenical movement has come further in the past four years than it had come in the previous forty. New attitudes have been struck. For quite some time Catholics in the United States have wanted to work with Protestants on a variety of projects. The interracial question (as far as interdenominational co-operation was concerned) had gone begging for a solution for decades until Protestants, Catholics and Jews met in Chicago a month after the first Council session was over. It was the first time in history they had come together for a national meeting. An American theologian explained, "The bishops were holding back from these kinds of meetings out of fear—fear of Rome. Now, Pope John has given the Church a freedom from fear."

Since the first session of the Council, American Catholics have noticed the change. Hardly a week goes by in any diocese without the Ordinary or his representative engaging in some kind of dialogical encounter with Protestant or Jew. A friend who was trying to keep track of these meetings by clipping various diocesan papers finally gave up. The stories became too common. It was like collecting Lincoln-head pennies.

Even the evangelist Billy Graham felt the balmy winds of change. At one time bishops thundered against him in their pulpits. But after the first session he flew into the Catholic metropolis of São Paolo, Brazil, for one of his crusades and discovered the bishop there at the airport to welcome him.

Attitudes are important; perhaps most important of all. Openness and friendliness go a long way, and the Council Fathers demonstrated ample stores of it. Sergio Méndez Arceo, Bishop of Cuernavaca, went so far as to ask the Council to reconsider Catholic attitudes towards Jews and Masons, both of which, he said, need drastic revision. To Hans Küng the signs of the future were unmistakable. "The Church has at last addressed itself to an energetic and active encounter with our separated brethren."

But would those attitudes change any of the latter-day Catholic dogmas which might prevent Protestants and Orthodox from meeting Catholics at some future crossroads? That depends on what one means by change. As Cardinal Bea told the Harvard Colloquium, "Compromise on points of faith which have already been defined is impossible. It would be quite unfair to our non-Catholic brethren to stir up false hopes of this nature. Nor is there a possibility that the Church—even in its zeal for eventual union—will ever be content with a recognition of 'essential dogmas,' or that she will reverse or withdraw the dogmatic decrees drawn up at Trent. Again it would be simply dishonest to suggest that there is any likelihood that the dogmas of the primacy and the infallibility of the Pope will be revised."

I wonder if all Catholics would agree with these words (which Bea had first checked with the Holy Office). Bea himself pro-

ceeded in that very same talk to Harvard to explain how the
Church could change its teachings on, for example, the nature of
the Church, Church authority, the apostolic succession, the
Petrine office, and the authoritative teaching mission of the Church.
Said he: "The traditional formulas which express the points of
doctrine of interest to non-Catholic Christians have often been
misunderstood. The Council, therefore, can re-state them in a
manner more intelligible to the modern mind. As the Pope explicitly stated in his inaugural speech, 'the substance of the ancient
teaching of the deposit of faith is one thing, the manner in which
it is expressed is another.' It is therefore not only possible but
necessary to clothe this teaching in forms which are accessible and
attractive to the way men think today."

One wonders whether this is not just a tricky way of saying the
doctrine will not change and change at the same time? Isn't it a fact
that when a theologian attempts to express an ancient teaching in
"forms accessible and attractive to the way men think today," that
he is making a real change? The thought and the word are closely,
inseparably intertwined. In his day, Cardinal Newman came close
to being identified as a heretic for his theories on the development
of doctrine, but his ideas make even more sense today. Doctrine
does develop. The insights of each generation add something to
the doctrine, and give it a new life and relevance. Those who look
upon the deposit of faith as a sack of pearls fear such change. Those
who rely more on the inspiration of the Spirit and his guidance
through history do not fear it but welcome it with high hopes.

Bea himself has written in this vein more than once, hailing
the role of scholarship in the ecumenical dialogue and recognizing
that even Catholic propositions "due to a historical evolution in
our own theological formulations . . . do not always express the
full depth and richness of revealed doctrine." Within the world
community of scholars, there is already an increasing common
ground. As Dr George Lindbeck, professor at Yale University
and Lutheran delegate-observer to the Council, avows, "Parallel
and convergent progress in biblical scholarship will be hastened
along by this Council. Historical scholarship is the gift of God to
our era."

Good scholarship, of course, takes time. In this case, scholars—Protestant, Roman, Orthodox—will need time to evolve new and newer formulations. But with goodwill and good scholarship, there is no inherent obstacle to their discovering mutually reconcilable aspects to truth, which is, after all, one.

In many ways, Pope John pointed out the *unum necessarium*: great cordiality of heart and the optimism that can allow everyone to emphasize what unites and overlook what seems to divide. For the theologian, this means, in the words of Hans Küng, "a theology of mutual encounter in which the truth is illuminated by understanding love instead of a state-of-siege theology with love subordinated to so-called truth, a theology which is, in fact, a preparation for union." For the men and women in the street, this means co-operative Christian action. Father Gustave Weigel says, "Pope John wanted to see Christianity leaven this new world and he likewise saw that a divided Christianity can't do it. But even now we can work together and maybe in working together we will come together in other ways. . . ." Said a delegate-observer: "For the first time in history, the Church sees partners in those who don't belong to her." Such an approach may not appeal to a formal logician, but it is the spark that could bridge polarities and produce a current to charge the world with Christ.

Epilogue

As he lay dying on the last day of May 1963, Angelo Giuseppe Roncalli, the 262nd Pope of Rome, received his Roman cardinals. He told each of them he was "on the point of leaving." It was as if he were going on a journey and would not see his friends and associates for a while. Having fulfilled his role as *Pastor et nauta*, the fisher of men, having set the barque of Peter out onto the sea of the world, he could now himself set forth on the sea of eternity, almost alone. He called for Viaticum (The last Holy Communion means Christ "with you on the way"—*a via tecum*) and soon he was off.

But not before he told many he was offering his life "for a good outcome of the Ecumenical Council and for peace among men," which was, in effect, his dying wish. To the last he was quietly insistent on his basic vision. Intuitive, not always well expressed, perverted sometimes by those around him, it came across nevertheless in the Second Vatican Ecumenical Council and in the hopeful love for all men of good will that was expressed in *Pacem in Terris*. With no ambiguity now at the end, with the lucidity of a dying man, he repeated and repeated his wish, "that the great work will be crowned with success."

Pope John XXIII was a gentle revolutionary. Far from being the caretaker that the Church expected, John created an atmosphere in which, said Jesuit theologian John Courtney Murray, "a lot of things came unstuck—old patterns of thought, behaviour, feeling. They were not challenged or refuted, but just sort of dropped."

In place of the dogmatic answer, John asked questions, and encouraged others to join him in finding out whether old forms were still right forms, customary methods were effective methods. Said Father Murray in *America*: "He raised some questions himself—notably the great, sprawling, ecumenical question—to which he returned no definitive answers. He encouraged the raising of other questions, both old and new, both theological and pastoral—and even political. The symbol of him might well be the question-mark—surely a unique symbol for a pope."

And, of course, merely asking questions was enough to indicate how tinny and irrelevant conventional responses of the past were now. Should the Church shun the secular world, clinging to the City of God in fear of contamination from the city of man? Pope

Pius XII, as his encyclicals and allocutions made clear, firmly answered no. But Pius remained a prisoner of the Church's past. It was left to John XXIII—neither intellectual nor theologian—to challenge the Church to understand a world in turmoil.

Thanks to his charismatic warmth and pliancy, the Roman Catholic Church seemed to change from wariness of new trends in the secular world to acceptance of them. It is not odd, considering the scope and influence of a pope, that one man seemed to be responsible for it all. What is extraordinary is that the change was visible in the space of one year: 1962. Before that John had been a puzzling pope.

One event swept doubts away and put John's true intentions clearly in focus: the Second Vatican Ecumenical Council. To a man such as Vittorino Veronese, who as president of the Banco di Roma, former president of Italian Catholic Action, and former Director-General of UNESCO, understands the Roman Catholic Church and the world it lives in as few men do, Pope John moved the Church to the brink of a new future. "He has put the Church in rapport with itself and the world," Veronese told me. "For the first time, the Church is attempting to understand the world and make a bridge between itself and the world. Now we can see that the Church and the world have the same frontiers."

Human unity—he sometimes referred to it under the more familiar but elusive term, peace—was one of Pope John's haunting concepts. To achieve it, he believed that all Christians should appear as a witness for Christ to the whole world. Without displacing the Church's traditional ideological objections to Communism, he began exploring the possibility of lessening tensions with the East. It was a *politique* based more on love than anything else. When he was editing *Pacem in Terris* and came to a passage that noted how both sides in the cold war had entered the nuclear arms race for defensive purposes, John added, "and there is no reason to disbelieve them." Did he mean that? Answered a man who helped him write the encyclical: "This was a strategic statement of the Holy Father. He said, 'Who really knows? And anyway, I cannot posit bad faith on the part of either party. If I did, the dialogue would be over and the doors would be closed.' "

Pacem in Terris was a declaration of interdependence. In it, John laid down that men of this century needed to keep peace, avert nuclear war, and co-operate for the achievement of economic, social, cultural and political ends which are "honourable and useful."

For centuries, the Church had taken an unrealistic posture and in its own dogmatic way been readier to judge and condemn the world rather than to help save it. *Pacem in Terris* represented the most compelling call that any pope ever made to all men of good will to collaborate in areas of common interest. In it, Pope John implied, the time had come for the Church to take a share in the mysterious providential movements of men towards human unity. He wanted to help the entire body of Christians to go along with these movements, to take a share in the modern world, to co-operate with men of every race and religion and contribute "to the building up of a community of peoples based on truth, justice, love and freedom," to lead the way and become "a spark of light, a centre of love" among men.

Not all Catholics, not even all of the Church's cardinals appreciated John's problematic. Some in the Roman Curia thought his exploration of Christian unity was a danger to the faith, and openly regarded a free, unmanaged Council as a threat to their authority. "They are men of zeal, I am sure," John told a friend a short time before he died. "But they are not running the Church. I am in charge, and I won't have anyone else trying to stop the momentum of the Council's first session." Other Catholics on both sides of the Atlantic rejected the spirit that led to his social encyclicals and his "opening to the East." Right-wing Italian Catholics dubbed John "The Red Pope" and sneered that his failing health was a sign of divine displeasure.

What Pope John was really up to was this: he was commending goodness to the world, preparing the way, he thought, for commending Christ. Even at his death, on June 3, 1963, it was obvious that he had already made a fine start. Cables of condolence poured into the Vatican Secretary of State from Protestants, Orthodox, Jews, Moslems, Buddhists and even atheists. Press, radio and television throughout the world gave evidence of deepest affection. Affection was the keynote of every comment in Britain. In the United States the press generally gave his death more space than they had given to the deaths of past Presidents. The Communist press hailed John as the "Pope of Peace," Nikita Khrushchev, the president of Russia's Council of Ministers, cabled his admiration for John and sent official representatives of the Moscow Patriarchate to Rome for the Requiem— the first time that kind of gesture had been made for almost a thousand years.

Almost no one believes that the Church can fail to continue commending Christ in much the same way. As Pope John's private secretary, Monsignor Loris Capovilla, told me one day not long ago, "The Holy Father is only planting a seed, you know. He knows that somebody else will reap the harvest." Somebody will indeed: the Church and the world John loved.

ROME,
June 12, 1963

INDEX OF PERSONS

Adzhubei, Alexei, 44
Adrian VI, Pope, 2, 3, 4, 8, 40
Agagianian, Cardinal Gregory Peter, 226
Alexei, Orthodox Patriarch of Moscow, 95
Alfrink, Cardinal Bernard Jan, Abp of
  Utrecht, 71, 105, 135, 148, 159, 205
Alivisatos, Hamilcar, 17
Alter, Karl J., Abp of Cincinnati, 59, 239
Anfinoguenov, Nicolai, 99
Annigoni, Pietro, 180
Antoniutti, Cardinal Ildebrando, 226
Athenagoras, Patriarch of Constantinople,
  17, 37, 93–95

Bacci, Cardinal Antonio, 156, 226
Bandas, Mgr Rudolph, 186–187, 214
Batista, Fulgencio, 13
Baum, Gregory (O.S.A.), 39, 70, 137,
  174, 195–196
Bea, Cardinal Augustin (S.J.), 33–42, 43,
  46, 65, 68–69, 71, 77, 90, 94, 95, 97–100,
  105, 136, 146, 150, 156, 159, 160, 175,
  176–177, 200, 205, 215, 223, 224, 230,
  241–242
Bekkers, Willem, Bp of 's-Hertogen-
  bosch, 124
Benedict XV, Pope, 3
Beran, Josef, Abp of Prague, 44
Bernard, Père François, 187
Boegner, Marc, 17
Borovi, Archpriest Vitali, 91
Buckley, William F., 46–47
Bueno y Monreal, Cardinal José Maria,
  Abp of Seville, 27, 47, 135
Bugnini, Fr Annibale, 61
Burundi, Mwami of, 222
Busimba, Joseph, Bp of Goma, 75–76
Butler, Dom Christopher, 161
Butler, Dom Cuthbert, 141

Cabana, Georges, Abp of Sherbrooke, 170
Caggiano, Cardinal Antonio, Abp of
  Buenos Aires, 71, 78, 226
Câmara, see de Barros Câmara and
  Pessôa Câmara
Canali, Cardinal Nicola, 8
Capovilla, Mgr Loris, 14, 43, 181, 246
Cardinale, Mgr Igino, 43, 181, 221–222
Carli, Luigi, Bp of Segni, 170, 206
Carraro, Giuseppe, Bp of Verona, 110,
  136
Cecchetti, Mgr Paolo Igino, 150

Cerejeira, Cardinal Manuel Conçalves,
  Patriarch of Lisbon, 226
Charue, André M., Bp of Namur, 164
Charles, Pierre (S.J.), 24
Charrière, François, Bp of Lausanne,
  Geneva and Fribourg, 38, 161
Cheng, Paul, Aux. Bp of Taipeh, 157
Chenu, M. D. (O.P.), 30, 59, 118, 139
Chichester, Abp Aston (S.J.), 76
Chrysostomos, Orthodox Abp of Athens,
  92
Cicognani, Cardinal Amleto, 71, 109, 176,
  181, 226
Concha, Cardinal Luis, Abp of Bogota,
  226
Confalonieri, Cardinal Carlo, 62, 71
Congar, Yves (O.P.), 60–61, 89, 112, 118,
  139, 163, 236
Conway, Mgr John D., 55–56
Cordeiro, Joseph, Abp of Karachi, 16
Costantini, Vittorio M. (O.F.M.Cap.),
  Bp of Sessa Aurunca, 170
Cullmann, Dr Oscar, 100, 177
Cushing, Cardinal Richard, Abp of
  Boston, 9, 59, 137

Dahlberg, Edwin T., 17
Daly, Bernard, 182
Daniélou, Jean (S.J.), 112, 232, 240
Dante, Abp Enrico, 79, 126, 181
Davis, Thurston N. (S.J.), 229
de Arriba y Castro, Cardinal Benjamin,
  Abp of Tarragona, 226
de Barros Câmara, Cardinal Jaime, Abp
  of Rio de Janeiro, 226
de Gaulle, General Charles, 13, 120
De Gramont, Sanche, 193
Dell' Acqua, Abp Angelo, 43, 222
de Lubac, Henri (S.J.), 89, 112, 139, 163
de Proença Sigaud, Geraldo, Abp of
  Diamantina, 170
De Smedt, Emile Josef Marie, Bp of
  Bruges, 38, 99, 166–9, 207–9, 210, 226
de Vito, Albert C., Bp of Lucknow, 136
Devoto, Alberto, Bp of Goya, 136
Doepfner, Cardinal Julius, Abp of Munich,
  57, 67, 71, 105, 106, 115, 164, 205, 207
D'Souza, Eugene, Abp of Nagpur, 105,
  123, 136, 213
Dugan, George, 192
Dumont, Christopher (O.P.), 39, 91
Duschak, William (S.V.D.), V. A. of
  Calapan, P.I., 190

Echeverria Ruiz, Bernardino (O.F.M.), Bp of Ambato, 170
Elchinger, Arthur, Coadj. Bp of Strasbourg, 156, 206
Ellis, Mgr John Tracy, 234
Elson, Robert, 181
Etoga, Paul, Bp of Mbalmayo, 75

Fanfani, Premier Amintore, 93
Felici, Abp Pericle, 20, 55, 62, 65, 67, 106–107, 113, 137, 140, 141, 157, 170, 171, 172, 180, 182, 185, 187, 194, 221, 222
Fenton, Mgr Joseph Clifford, 152
Fernandez, Aniceto (O.P.), 136
Ferrero di Cavallerleone, Abp Carlo, 136
Fesquet, Henri, 191
Fisher, Geoffrey, former Abp of Canterbury (now Lord Fisher), 19, 36, 41
Fittgau, Mgr Gerhard, 187
Florit, Ermenegildo, Abp of Florence, 161–162
Forbis, William, 221–223
Franco, Generalissimo Francisco, 47
Frings, Cardinal Josef, Abp of Cologne, 57, 66, 71, 104–105, 106, 158, 205

Ganni, Gabriel, Chaldean Coadj. Bp of Beirut, 221
Garcia de Sierra y Mendez, Segundo, Coadj. Abp of Oviedo, 136, 170
Gargitter, Giuseppe, Bp of Bressanone, 110
Garofalo, Mgr Salvatore, 158
Gilroy, Cardinal Norman, Abp of Sydney, 71, 164
Gilson, Etienne, 48–49
Godfrey, Cardinal William, Abp of Westminster, 135, 226
Gorman, Thomas K., Bp of Dallas-Fort Worth, 103, 229
Gracias, Cardinal Valerian, Abp of Bombay, 58, 67, 70, 135, 165–166
Graham, Billy (evangelist), 241
Graham, Robert (S.J.), 175, 231
Grassellini, Signora, 224
Gronchi, President Giovanni, 44–45
Guano, Emilio, Bp of Livorno, 110
Guerry, Emile, Abp of Cambrai, 57, 162–163, 210, 211, 231, 232
Guitton, Jean, 235

Hakim, George, Melchite Bp of Akka, 164
Halifax, Lord, 31
Hallinan, Paul, Abp of Atlanta, Georgia, 124–125, 126
Hamer, Jerome (O.P.), 39, 91
Häring, Bernard (C.SS.R.), 149
Heard, Cardinal William, 226

Heenan, John Carmel, Abp of Liverpool, 38, 140
Henry, Harold, Bp of Kwang Ju, 75
Hesburg, Theodore M. (C.S.C.), 238
Higgins, Mgr George, 239
Hitler, Adolf, 24, 32
Hoffman, Paul, 103
Holland, Thomas, Coadj. Bp of Portsmouth, 38
Hollis, Christopher, 70
Hurley, Denis, Abp of Durban, 119, 135
Huyghe, Gerard, Bp of Arras, 186, 211

Innocent III, Pope, 22, 43, 89
Isnard, Clemente José Carlos, Bp of Nova Friburgo, 124
Issenmann, Clarence G., Bp of Columbus, Ohio, 231

Jackson, Dr Joseph, 97, 99–100
Jaeger, Lorenz, Abp of Paderborn, 16, 38, 203
Jenny, Henri, Aux. Bp of Cambrai, 124
John XXIII, Pope, passim 2–20, 28–38, 41–56, 60–90, 93–122, 130–133, 138–145, 156–175, 178–181, 184–186, 201–205, 210–211, 215–235, 242–246
Johnson, Lyndon B., 48
Joseph, St, 134, 136, 142, 148, 189
Jungmann, Josef (S.J.), 112, 123

Kelly, Mgr John E., 181–182
Kémérer, Jorge (S.V.D.), Bp of Posadas, 136
Kessel, Dmitri, 180
Khruschchev, Nikita, 44, 45, 46, 50, 246
Klepacz, Michal, Bp of Lodz, 170
Kobayashi, Peter, Bp of Sendai, 136
Koenig, Cardinal Franziskus, Abp of Vienna, 53, 66, 67, 70, 105, 106, 139, 159, 205, 221
Kotliarov, Archimandrite Vladimir, 91–92
Küng, Fr Hans, 56, 66, 89, 139, 223, 241, 243

Lagrange, Marie-Joseph (O.P.), 26, 145
La Ravoire Morrow, Louis, Bp of Krishnagar, 124
Ledochowski, Vladimir (S.J.), 24
Léger, Cardinal Paul Emile, Abp of Montreal, 53, 58, 69, 159, 205, 223
Leo XIII, Pope, 3, 195
Lercaro, Cardinal Giacomo, Abp of Bologna, 110, 205–206
Lichtenberger, Arthur, Presiding Bp, Episcopal Church, U.S.A., 36
Liénart, Cardinal Achille, Abp of Lille, 66, 67, 71, 105, 106, 150, 158, 204
Lindbeck, Dr George, 242

Lombardi, Riccardo (S.J.), 66, 213
Lyonnet, Fr Stanislaus (S.J.), 153

McCauley, Vincent (C.S.C.), Bp of Fort Portal, 105
McDonald, Mgr William J., 234
McGrath, Mark, Aux. Bp of Panama, 136
McIntyre, Dr Carl, President of International Council of Christian Churches, 92–93, 100
McIntyre, Cardinal James F., Abp of Los Angeles, 161, 226
McKenzie, John L. (S.J.), 152, 233
McManus, Fr Frederick, 125
McQuaid, Bernard, Bp of Rochester, N.Y. (1868–1909), 202
McVinney, Russell Joseph, Bp of Providence, R.I., 230
Malachy, St, 3
Manek, Gabriel (S.V.D.), Abp of Endeh, 160
Martimort, Aimé, 121–122
Martin, Joseph M., Abp of Rouen, 38
Marty, François, Abp of Rheims, 136
Mary, The Blessed Virgin, 21, 119, 134, 148, 189, 200–201
Mathieu, Cardinal, 141
Maximos, see Saigh
Mazelis, Bp Petras, Ap. Ad. of Telsiai, 78
Medeiros Delgado, José, Abp of Maranhão, 136
Melas, Giuseppe, Bp of Nuoro, 136
Mèndez Arceo, Sergio, Bp of Cuernavaca, 241
Meouchi, Paul Pierre, Maronite Patriarch of Antioch, 36, 76
Mercier, Cardinal, 31
Meyer, Cardinal Albert, Abp of Chicago, 71, 166
Mindszenty, Cardinal Jozsef, 44
Montini, Cardinal Giovanni Battista, Abp of Milan, 71, 110, 114, 131, 140, 157, 195, 205
Moorman, John, Anglican Bp of Ripon, 97, 101, 102
Morcillo Gonzalez, Casimiro, Abp of Zaragoza, 160
Muckermann, Friedrich (S.J.), 24
Muldoon, Thomas W., Aux. Bp of Sydney, 136
Murray, John Courtney (S.J.), 60, 61, 234, 244
Mussio, Anthony John King, Bp of Steubenville, Ohio, 230
Mussolini, Benito, 24, 25, 213
Musto, Biagio, Bp of Aquino, 210–211

Nabaa, Philippe, Melchite Abp of Beirut, 130
Nenni, Pietro, 46

Nevins, Albert (M.M.), 237
Newman, Cardinal, 242
Nicodim, Abp (Moscow), 92–93, 94, 95
Nicomedo, Enrico, Abp of Bari, 170
Niemöller, Dr Martin, 230
Nierman, Pieter Antoon, Bp of Groningen, 38
Nikolayev, Andrian (cosmonaut), 48

O'Connor, Abp Martin, 65, 67
O'Donovan, Patrick, 103
Oesterreicher, John, 39
Olaechea Loizaga, Marcelino, Abp of Valencia, 136
Ottaviani, Cardinal Alfredo, 21, 41–42, 44–45, 60–61, 62, 65, 66, 67, 68, 74, 76, 82, 93, 112, 132, 135–136, 139, 143, 154, 156, 157, 160, 163–164, 165, 172, 173, 175, 176, 177, 200–201, 204, 212–213, 214, 215, 224–227
Our Lady, see Mary, The Blessed Virgin

Pailler, André, Aux. Bp of Rouen, 209–210, 212
Parente, Abp Pietro, 74, 164–165, 197, 213, 214–215, 224–225, 226
Pawley, Canon Bernard C., 91, 99
Pessôa Câmara, Helder, Aux. Abp of Rio de Janeiro, 194
Pius IX, Pope, 25, 70, 87, 114, 194
Pius X, Pope St, 3, 122, 189
Pius XI, Pope, 3, 31, 45, 109, 146
Pius XII, Pope, 3, 24, 36, 37, 38, 41–42, 60, 74, 78, 88, 109, 122, 123n., 144, 146, 147, 150, 154, 156, 166, 198, 209, 237, 245
Pildáin y Zapiáin, Antonio, Bp of Canary Isles, 136
"Pinay, Maurice", 177
Piolanti, Mgr Antonio, 150, 154, 214
Pitra, Cardinal Jean-Baptiste, 18
Pizzardo, Cardinal Giuseppe, 55, 150, 154
Pla y Deniel, Cardinal Enrique, Abp of Toledo, 71
Popovich, Pavel (cosmonaut), 48

Quarracino, Antonio, Bp of Nueve de Julio, 170
Quintero, Cardinal José, Abp of Caracas, 226
Quiroga y Palacios, Cardinal Fernando, Abp of Santiago de Compostela, 158, 226

Rahner, Karl (S.J.), 28, 60, 71, 89, 112, 139, 140, 156, 163, 238
Ratzinger, Fr Joseph, 139, 156
Rau, Enrique, Bp of Mar del Plata, 124
Rauscher, Cardinal, 63, 141
Read, Denis (O.C.D.), 196

Reinhardt, G. Frederick, 86
Ritter, Cardinal Joseph, Abp of St Louis, 159, 205, 223, 228–229
Roberts, Abp Thomas D. (S.J.), 58, 67, 75, 232
Rolim de Moura, Zacarias, Bp of Cajazeiras, 136
Romeo, Mgr Antonino, 150, 154
Roncalli, Saverio, 108
Rouquette, Robert (S.J.), 134
Ruffini, Cardinal Ernesto, Abp of Palermo, 62, 71, 126, 154, 156, 158, 159, 170, 171, 172, 211, 214, 226
Rugambwa, Cardinal Laurean, Bp of Bukoba, 166
Ryan, John J., 115
Rynne, Xavier, 155

Saboia Bandeira y de Mello, Carlos (O.F.M.), Bp of Palmas, 136
Saigh, Maximos IV, Melchite Patriarch of Antioch, 36, 76, 80, 119, 125, 126, 159–160, 206
Santos, Cardinal Rufino, Abp of Manila, 226
Satoshi Nagae, Lawrence, Bp of Urawa, 123
Schillebeeckx, Edward, 139, 163
Schlink, Dr Edmund, 98–99
Schmidt, Stefan (S.J.), 38
Schneirla, Rev. William S., 151
Schoiswohl, Joseph, Bp of Seckau, 136
Schuster, Dr Zacharias, 100
Schutz, Prior Roger, of Taizé, 17, 97
Schwarzenberg, Cardinal, 141
Segni, President Antonio, 79
Sheen, Fulton, Aux. Bp of New York, 111
Sheerin, James (Paulist), 105
Simon, Fr Richard, 145
Siri, Cardinal Giuseppe, Abp of Genoa, 71, 85, 109, 158, 207, 214, 226
Skydsgaard, Dr Kristen E., 101–102
Slipyi, Josyf, Ukrainian Abp of Lwow, 44, 176
Soegijapranata, Albert, Abp of Semarang, 160
Spadafora, Mgr Francesco, 140, 152–154
Spellman, Cardinal Francis, Abp of New York, 71, 126, 205, 235–236
Staffa, Abp Dino, 130 131, 218–219
Stanley, David Michael (S.J.), 147
Stockwood, Dr Mervyn, Anglican Bp of Southwark, 118
Strossmayer, Bishop Josip Georg, 99
Suenens, Cardinal Léon Joseph, Abp of Malines-Brussels, 71, 105, 112, 159, 193, 205, 217–218, 223, 239

Suhard, Cardinal Emmanuel, 229
Sunderland, Bill, 182

Tappouni, Cardinal Ignazio, Patriarch of Antioch, 71, 141
Tardini, Cardinal Domenico, 12, 13, 14, 20–21, 60, 173
Tavard, George (A.A.), 39
Tedeschi, Mario, 78, 93
Teilhard de Chardin, Pierre (S.J.), 26, 174, 216, 238
Thiandoum, Hyacinth, Abp of Dakar, 136
Thurian, Max, of Taizé, 97
Tisserant, Cardinal Eugène, 71, 80, 106, 157, 158
Traglia, Cardinal Luigi, 226
Treacy, John P., Bp of La Crosse, 231
Tregelles, Samuel P., 195
Tromp, Sebastiano (S.J.), 40, 175
Tucek, Mgr James, 64, 69, 184, 187, 189, 194

Urbani, Cardinal Giovanni, Patriarch of Venice, 109, 226

Vagnozzi, Abp Egidio, Ap. Del. to U.S.A 66–67, 126, 130, 150–152, 214
Vallainc, Mgr Fausto, 67–68, 179–182, 184, 187, 188, 193
van Bekkum, Willem, Bp of Ruteng, 123–124, 126
van Velsen, Gerard, Bp of Kroonstad, 39
Veronese, Vittorino, 245
Veuillot, Louis, 180
Vielmo, Cesare (S.M.), V. A. of Aysén, 136
Villepelet, Jean Joseph, Bp of Nantes, 160
Visser 't Hooft, Willem, 17, 39, 68, 230

Weber, Charles, Bp of Ichow, 136
Weigel, Gustave (S.J.), 39, 91, 216, 217, 243
Willebrands, Mgr Jan, 32, 39, 41, 74, 91, 92, 94, 175, 183–184
Williams, Dr George H., 102, 230
Wiltgen, Ralph (S.V.D.), 192–193
Wolf, Donald (S.J.), 237
Woodruff, Douglas, 138, 182
Work, Martin, 56
Wright, John J., Abp of Pittsburgh, 53, 56, 113
Wyszynski, Cardinal Stefan, Abp of Gnienzo and Warsaw, 47, 78, 119, 226

Zerwick, Maximilian (S.J.), 153
Zoa, Jean Baptiste, Abp of Yaoundé, 164–165